MORRIS AUTOMATED INFORMATION NETWORK

P9-DGX-273

FEB 3 2006

Chester
Library

DISCARD

250 West Main Street
Chester, NJ 07930

THE CALIPH'S HOUSE

ALSO BY TAHIR SHAH

House of the Tiger King

In Search of King Solomon's Mines

Trail of Feathers

Sorcerer's Apprentice

Beyond the Devil's Teeth

THE CALIPH'S HOUSE

Tahir Shah

BANTAM BOOKS

THE CALIPH'S HOUSE
A Bantam Book / February 2006

Published by
Bantam Dell
A Division of Random House, Inc.
New York, New York

All rights reserved.
Copyright © 2006 by Tahir Shah
Illustrations by Laura Hartman Maestro

Book design by Glen Edelstein

Bantam Books is a registered trademark of Random House, Inc., and the colophon is
a trademark of Random House, Inc.

Library of Congress Cataloging-in-Publication Data
Shah, Tahir.
The Caliph's house / Tahir Shah.
p.   cm.
ISBN-10: 0-553-80399-9
ISBN-13: 978-0-553-80399-0
1. Shah, Tahir. 2. Morocco—Description and travel. 3. Travel writers—
Morocco—Biography. I. Title.
DT310.2.S527 2006
964'.38053—dc22   2005053656

Printed in the United States of America
Published simultaneously in Canada

www.bantamdell.com

This book is for Ariane and Timur,
and for their lives at the Caliph's House

ACKNOWLEDGMENTS

I could not submit this book without thanking three women:
Elisabeth, your generosity was greater than you can know.
Emma, the sound of my voice hinted at my gratitude.
Rachana, with much love and thanks for staring severe
uncertainty in the face.

Tahir Shah
Dar Khalifa, Casablanca

Look into the eyes of a Jinn, and
Stare into the depths of your own soul.

—MOROCCAN PROVERB

THE CALIPH'S HOUSE

ONE

Two reeds drink from the same stream.
One is hollow, the other is sugarcane.
——MOROCCAN PROVERB

THERE WAS A SADNESS IN THE stillness of dusk. The café was packed with long-faced men in robes sipping black coffee, smoking dark tobacco. A waiter weaved between the tables, tray balanced on upturned fingertips, glass balanced on tray. In that moment, day became night. The sitters drew deep on their cigarettes, coughed, and stared out at the street. Some were worrying, others dreaming, or just sitting in silence. The same ritual is played out each evening across Morocco, the desert kingdom in Africa's northwest, nudged up against the Atlantic shore. As the last strains of sunlight dissipated, the chatter began again, the hum of calm voices breaking gently over the traffic.

The backstreet café in Casablanca was for me a place of mystery, a place with a soul, a place with danger. There was a sense that the safety nets had been cut away, that each citizen walked upon the high wire of this, the real world. I longed not merely to travel through it, but to live in such a city.

My wife, Rachana, who was pregnant, had reservations from the start. These were fueled all the more when I ranted on about the need for uncertainty and for danger. She said that our little daughter required a secure home, that her childhood could do without an exotic backdrop. I raised the stakes, promising a cook, a maid, an army of nannies, and sunshine—unending, glorious sunshine. Since moving from India eight years before, Rachana had hardly ever glimpsed the sun in the drab London sky. She had almost forgotten how it looked. I reminded her of what we were missing—the dazzle of yellow morning light breaking through bedroom curtains, the drone of bumblebees in honeysuckle, rich aromas wafting through narrow streets, where market stalls are a blaze of color, heaped with spices—paprika and turmeric, cinnamon, cumin and fenugreek. All this in a land where the family is still the core of life, where traditions die hard, and where children can grow up knowing the meaning of honor, pride, and respect.

I was tired of our meager existence and the paltry size of our apartment, where the warring couple next door plagued us through paper-thin walls. I wanted to escape to a house of serious dimensions, a fantasy inspired by the pages of *The Arabian Nights,* with arches and colonnades, towering doors fashioned from aromatic cedar, courtyards with gardens hidden inside, stables and fountains, orchards of fruit trees, and dozens and dozens of rooms.

ANYONE WHO HAS EVER tried to make a break from the damp English shores has needed a long list of reasons. I have often wondered how the pilgrims on the *Mayflower* ever managed to get away at all. Friends and family regard would-be escapees as crazed. Mine were no exception. At first they scoffed at my plan to move abroad, and when they realized I wasn't interested in the usual bolt-holes—southern France or Spain— they weighed in with fighting talk. They branded me as irresponsible, unfit to be a parent, a dreamer destined for failure.

The pressure to abandon my dream mounted. It became so great that I did almost back down. Then, one dreary winter morning, I passed a crowd of people on a central London street. An elderly man at the middle of the group was being wrestled to the ground by two police officers. He was dressed in business attire—pressed white shirt, silk tie, and three-piece suit, with a plump red carnation pinned to his lapel. In a bizarre display of eccentricity, he had taken off his trousers and was wearing his underpants on his head. The police, who were not amused, were busy cuffing the man's hands behind his back. A young woman nearby was screaming, begging the authorities to lock "the madman" up. As the man was bundled into an armored police van, he turned and shouted:

"Don't waste your life following others! Be individual! Live your dreams!"

The steel doors slammed, the vehicle sped away, and the crowd dispersed—all except for me. I stood there thinking over what I had seen, and what the supposed madman had said. He was right. Ours was a society of followers, trapped by an island mentality. I made a promise to myself right then. I would not be subdued by others' expectations. I would risk everything and leave the island, dragging my family with me. Together we would search for freedom, and for a land where we could be ourselves.

CASABLANCA'S EVENING RUSH OF traffic rivals any in its ferocity. But it has never been so wild as it was on the late spring day that I took possession of the Caliph's House. I had sat in the café all afternoon, waiting for the rendezvous with the lawyer. He had told me to come to his office at eight P.M. At seven fifty-five I pressed a coin to the tabletop, left the café, and crossed the street. I passed a glass-fronted hotel flanked by proud date palms. An empty tour bus stood outside it, a pair of donkey carts beside, each piled high with overripe fruit. A moment later I was climbing up the curved stairwell of a dilapidated Art Deco building. I rapped at an oak door on the third story. The lawyer opened it, greeted me stiffly, and led the way into his office.

There was an official-looking Arabic document on the desk. The lawyer ordered me to read it through.

"I don't know Arabic," I said.

"Then you'd better just sign it," he replied, glancing at a gold Rolex on his wrist.

He handed me a Mont Blanc. I signed the paper as instructed. The lawyer stood up and slid a hefty iron key across the desk.

"You are a very brave man," he said.

I paused for a moment to look him in the eye. He didn't flinch. I lifted the key. As I did so, I was knocked to the floor by the force of a violent explosion. The windows blew inward, shattering with spectacular energy, sending a hailstorm of glass through the office. Deafened, covered in broken glass, and confused, I struggled to my feet. My legs were shaking so badly that I had trouble standing. The impeccably dressed legal man was crouched beneath his desk, as if he had previous experience of this kind. He rose silently, dusted the glass from his shoulders, straightened his silk tie, and opened the door for me to leave.

Out on the street, people were screaming, running in all directions, fire alarms shrieking, police sirens wailing. There was blood, too. Lots of it, strewn across faces and over slashed clothing. I was too shaken to be of any use to the injured, who were now streaming from the glass-fronted hotel. As I observed them in slow motion, a small red taxi pulled up fast. The driver was calling desperately from the passenger window:

"Étranger! Monsieur étranger!" he yelled. "Come quickly, it's dangerous for the foreigners!" I clambered in and he swung the wheel, hurling us into the slipstream of traffic.

"It's bombers, suicide bombers," he said, "they're going off across Casablanca!"

The red Peugeot slalomed westward, out of the center of town. But my mind was not on the traffic, the bombs, or the blood. Rather, it was on my wife, at home in London. I could see the news flash tearing over the TV screen, and her clutching our toddler to her very pregnant belly. I felt sure she would now be in no mood to embrace a new culture and a dream. She had been fearful of Morocco's Islamic society, especially in light of Al Qaeda's September 11 attacks and the second Gulf conflict, which had toppled Saddam Hussein only days before. But it was too late to turn back. The money had been paid, the documents signed, stamped once, and stamped again.

In my hands was the key: a symbol of the future or, perhaps, of a deranged purchase. I stared down at it, taking in the ancient iron notches, cursing myself for having courted danger so openly. At that moment, the driver slammed on the brakes.

"We have arrived!" he exclaimed.

MY REASONS FOR MOROCCO were many. They were endless, and began a long time ago. Throughout my own childhood, my father, who was an Afghan, had wanted to take us to his homeland. But the nation's enduring wars prevented us from ever venturing to the lofty mountain strongholds of Afghanistan. So, from the time we could walk, my sisters and I were frequently bustled into the family station wagon, vinyl cases laden high on the roof. Our gardener would drive us from the dull, serene lanes of the English countryside, through France and Spain, and up into Morocco's High Atlas Mountains.

For my father it was a chance to reveal to his children fragments of his own homeland. We found a tapestry of mountain passes and steep-sided valleys, of deserts and oases and imperial fortress cities, a culture bound by the tribal codes of honor and respect. For my mother, it was an opportunity to snap up all manner of bargains, from caftans to candlesticks, and to order the delirious heaps of hippies home to their own mothers far away.

We would spend weeks at a time trundling through the mountains, and driving down to the soaring dunes of the Sahara, where the "blue men" traipsed in from the desert, their dark skin dyed by indigo robes. There would be regular breaks to throw up in the bushes, to gorge ourselves on cactus fruit, and to trade our pocket money for chips of amethyst at the quarries in the hills.

My earliest memories are of the great walled city of Fès. Cobbled lanes no wider than a barrel's length, dimly lit and bewitching, where street-side stalls sold anything you could ever wish to buy. There were mountains of spices and fresh-cut herbs—saffron, aniseed, paprika—pickled lemons and mounds of gleaming olives; small cedar boxes inset with camel bone; fragrant leather sandals and terracotta pots; rough Berber rugs, golden caftans, amulets and talismans.

By far my favorite corner of the *souq* was where the black magicians would go to buy ingredients for their spells. The walls of those shops were hung with cages. In them were live chameleons, cobras, salamanders, and forlorn-looking eagles. There were cabinets, too, made from battered Burma teak, their drawers brimming with dried whale skin, the hair of dead men, and other such things, so my father said.

Morocco had brought color to my sanitized English childhood, which was more usually cloaked in itchy gray flannel shirts and corduroy shorts, acted out beneath an overcast sky. The kingdom had always been a place of escape, a place of astonishing intensity, but, beyond all else, a place with a soul. With a young family of my own, I regarded it as my duty, my responsibility, to pass on the same gift to my children—a gift of cultural color. It would have been far easier to have given in and not to have made the great escape from the island's shores. But something deep inside me goaded me on: a sense that if I did not seize the moment, I would regret it for the rest of my life.

There was another strong reason for Morocco—my father's father. He spent the last years of his life in a small villa near the seafront in Tangier. When his beloved wife died at just fifty-nine, he was broken. Unable to bear the memories, he moved to Morocco because they had never traveled there together. One morning while walking the usual route down the hill, from Café France back to his home, he was struck by a reversing Coca-Cola truck. Unconscious and bleeding, he was rushed to the hospital, where he died hours later. I was too small then to even remember him, but I felt a sadness all the same.

WE SEARCHED MOROCCO FOR months, desperate to find a house where my delusions of grandeur could run wild. Our starting point was Fès, undoubtedly Morocco's greatest jewel. It is the only medieval Arab city that remains entirely intact. Walking through the labyrinth of streets that make up the vast medina is like stepping into *The Thousand and One Nights*. The smells, sights, and sounds bombard the senses. A stroll of a few feet can be an overwhelming experience. For centuries, Fès was a place of impressive wealth, a center of scholarship and trade. Its houses reflect a confidence in Arab architecture almost never seen elsewhere, their decor profiting from a line of apprentices unbroken for a thousand years. We found the alleyways of the old city teeming with workshops where the traditional skills of metalwork and leather tanning, of mosaic design, weaving, ceramics, and marquetry, were still transferred from father to son.

By chance we were taken to a large merchant's house on the northern edge of the old city. It had been constructed in the grand Fasi style and dated back at least four hundred years. Six cavernous salons were clustered around a central courtyard, each one adorned with mosaic friezes, the floors laid with slabs of marble hewn from the Middle Atlas Mountains. Around the courtyard, columns towered up to the sky, and at its center stood a lotus-shaped fountain crafted from the finest alabaster. High on an adjacent wall was a modest glassless window, veiled by a wooden filigree screen, a lookout point from what once would have been the harem.

The man showing off the building was a kebab seller with contacts. He said it had been empty for just a handful of years. I balked at the remark—the place was in need of desperate repair. It looked to me as if it had been abandoned for at least half a century.

"In Morocco," said the kebab seller with a smile, "an empty house invites the wicked."

"You mean thieves?"

The man shook his head violently.

"Not wicked people," he said, "wicked forces."

At the time, I had no idea what the agent meant. Brushing his comment aside, I began at once negotiating for the house. The problem was that it was owned by seven brothers, each one more avaricious than the last. Unlike the West, where a property is either for sale or it is not, in Morocco, it can be in the twilight zone of realty—possibly for sale, possibly not. Before even getting to the price, you must first coax the owners to sell. This coaxing phase is an Oriental feature, no doubt brought to the region by the Arabs as they swept across North Africa fourteen centuries ago. As you sit over glasses of sweet mint tea, cajoling madly, the vendors look you up and down, inspecting the craftsmanship of your clothing and the stitching of your shoes. The better the quality of your attire, the higher the price is likely to be.

I must have been too well dressed on the morning of my meeting with the seven ghoulish brothers who owned the merchant's house. After four hours of coaxing, cajoling, and quaffing gallons of mint tea, they agreed in principle to a sale. Then they spat out a fantasy price and narrowed their eyes greedily. My bargaining skills were undeveloped. I should have stayed, sucked down more tea, and bargained through the afternoon and into the night. But instead I leapt up and ran out into the labyrinth, cursing. In doing so, I had broken the first rule of the Arab world—never lose your cool.

WE LEFT FÈS AND made for Marrakech, the pink desert oasis in the shadow of the Atlas Mountains. In recent years the city has seen a property boom, as well-heeled Europeans have bought up crumbling mansions, known as *riads,* in the medina, and restored them to forgotten glory. Walk down any street, with its fray of hawkers, scooters, bicycles, and donkey carts, and you pass rows of plain, silent doorways. You may think nothing of them, but behind each one is a palace.

The rapid flood of foreign money has sparked a revival of traditional crafts: among them *zelij* mosaics, terracotta tiles known as *bejmat,* and dazzling plasterwork, prepared from egg whites and marble dust, called *tadelakt.* The Europeans' eagerness to buy such wonderful buildings is matched only by the local Marrachis' willingness to dispose of them. In the medina of Marrakech, everyone has the same dream. They all long to sell their ruined ancestral home for vast profit and move to a prefab apartment block in the new town. We may yearn for rustic detail and old-world charm, but those who have it set their minds on vinyl wallpaper, fitted carpets, and all modern conveniences.

I must have dragged Rachana to more than seventy riads in Marrakech. None had the grandness of the merchant's house in Fès. But one of them did steal my heart. Its courtyard was laid out on an impressive scale, filled with orange blossom and lavender. The only problem was that it stood across the street from a busy abattoir, and the circulation of air made sure the only scent was of death.

So we packed our bags and sloped home to London, where I fell into the deepest depression I have ever known. My friends lampooned me. As they saw it, I had tried to escape the magnetic pull of the British Isles, but had been swept back to shore. Each evening I would read our little daughter, Ariane, a bedtime tale of princesses, dragons, and a forlorn merchant's house so far away.

Weeks passed. A wet winter became an even wetter spring. One gloomy day I was huddled up on the sofa, a woolen blanket wound around me, mumbling to myself like a madman with a cause. The telephone rang. I picked it up. On the other end was the mother of an old school friend. We swapped pleasantries while I wondered why she might be calling. Then she came to the point: She had heard through the grapevine that I was searching for a Moroccan house. She owned a place in Casablanca, she said, and was keen to sell it. The lady was too discreet to tell the price, and I too nervous to ask it. All she said was that it was an important property called Dar Khalifa, which means "the Caliph's House," and that it was in need of someone who would love it very much. Lowering her voice to no more than a whisper, she added: "It will need a strong man to take it on." I jumped up from the couch, unfurled the blanket like a matador tempting a bull, and scribbled down the details.

The day after the telephone conversation, I landed at the Mohammed V Airport on the southern edge of Casablanca. The guidebooks warned people to stay away from the city at all costs. They all agreed that it was the black hole of Morocco's tourist trade. I had never been there before except to change trains. In any case, I thought I knew all about it, because I had seen *Casablanca* with Bogart and Bergman.

An hour after landing, I found myself in a taxi cruising down a pleasant corniche lined with cafés and well-groomed palms. The sun was bright overhead, and the air tinged with the light scent of a salt breeze blowing in from the sea. The cab pulled away from the coast road and rolled down a palm-lined avenue. On both sides, dazzling white villas rose up like icebergs. In front of each, a large car was neatly parked, all shiny and new, a trophy of wealth.

The taxi drove a little further, crossed an invisible boundary of some kind, and entered a sprawling shantytown. There were donkey carts, chickens, cattle wandering aimlessly about, and a herd of goats blocking the way. The afternoon muezzin, the call to prayer, was raining down from a modest white-washed mosque at the side of the rutted track. A group of boys were kicking a homemade soccer ball about in the dusty alleys that ran between the low cinder-block shacks roofed in rusting tin. Three haggard men were huddled nearby in the shade, wrapped in *jelabas,* traditional hooded robes. Beside them stood a set of haphazard market stalls, and across from them, a young woman was selling a box of chicks dyed pink.

At the far end of the shantytown, the taxi halted near a plain doorway set in a filthy stone wall. Before paying the driver, I checked with him that he had the right address. I felt sure there was a mistake. But he nodded, pointed to the ground, and nodded again. I got out and rapped at the door. A moment passed. Then the door opened a crack.

"Is this Dar Khalifa, is this the Caliph's House?" I asked.

A coarse voice answered in French, the language of colonial Morocco: *"Oui, c'est ici."* Yes, this is it.

The door swung inward very slowly, as if a secret was about to be revealed. Entering, I found a fantasy worthy of a far wealthier man than I.

There were courtyards overflowing with date palms and fragrant hibiscus flowers, fountains perched in symmetrical pools, mature gardens planted with bougainvillea, cacti, and all

manner of exotic trees, an orange grove and tennis court, a swimming pool and, beyond it, stables.

The guardian welcomed me, kissed my hand, and led me down a long galleried corridor into the main building. Stepping inside for the first time was like slipping into a dream. A maze of rooms stretched out. There were arched doorways with cedarwood doors, octagonal windows glazed with fragments of colored glass, mosaic friezes and stucco moldings, secluded courtyards, and so many rooms—salons, studies, laundry rooms and kitchens, staff quarters, pantries, and at least a dozen bedrooms.

But the Caliph's House had been empty for almost a decade. Its walls were discolored with algae, its tiled floors were grimy and in need of repair. Alarming damp patches had taken hold on every surface, and a number of ceilings had caved in. Cobwebs hung across doorways like lace curtains, birds nested in the lamps, and termites had burrowed into the massive wooden doors. A burst water pipe had transformed one bedroom into a lake, and most of the shutters were hanging rotten on their hinges. As for the gardens, they had become a jungle through which savage dogs roamed.

The house had a presence, a sense of faded grandeur. Like an old society belle, it was run-down and wrinkled, but it had lived. You could imagine the history, the parties, the secrets. It must sound absurd, but I felt an energy from the first moment, almost as if it knew I was there.

THREE MONTHS AFTER FIRST setting eyes on Dar Khalifa, it was ours. My wife had secretly hoped I would give up on Morocco, but the house had won her over. She had felt its spirit, too. Like me, she regarded it as a positive force, and could imagine the children running free within its walls.

Fortunately, the English owner had needed no coaxing to

sell. She had known instinctively that the bank balance of a struggling author was pathetically dry. And she had been well aware that a Moroccan paying the market price would have ripped the building down and put up monstrous apartment blocks in its place.

SO IT WAS THAT on the evening of the multiple suicide attacks, I first crossed the threshold as the owner of the Caliph's House. Inside, the three guardians were standing at attention, saluting, awaiting orders. As if by some medieval right of sale, they came with the property. There was Mohammed, a round-shouldered brute of a man with a week's growth of stubble and a nervous twitch. The others called him the Bear. Beside him was Osman. He was younger, with a smile that never left his lips, and a cool, collected disposition. He had worked at the house since he was a child. Finally, there was Hamza, leader of the troupe. Tall and respectful, he pressed his hand into mine before placing it on his heart.

I asked urgently whether they had heard about the suicide bombers. Hamza shook his head. There were other more pressing problems, he said.

"What could be more serious than the multiple suicide attacks?"

"Jinns," came the reply.

"Jinns?"

The three guardians nodded in unison.

"Yes, the house, it's full of them."

When you buy a home abroad, you have to prepare yourself for the unexpected. I knew there would be language problems and cultural barriers to overcome. But nothing had readied me for an army of invisible spirits.

Muslims believe that when God created mankind from clay, He fashioned another species of creature, too, from fire.

They go by various names—Jinns, Genies, Jnun—and are believed by all to share the earth with us, living in animate objects. They are born, get married, bear children, and die, just like us. Most of the time they are invisible to humans, but they can take almost any form they wish, most commonly appearing in the hours after dusk, disguised as cats, dogs, or scorpions. Although there are some good Jinns, most are wicked. Nothing gives them greater pleasure than injuring humans for the discomfort they imagine we cause them.

I asked the guardians for advice on dealing with the problem. Osman spoke for the others: "Kill sheep," he said softly, "you will have to kill some sheep."

"Some? How many?"

"One in every room," explained the Bear.

I did a quick calculation.

"There must be twenty rooms, at least . . . that's an entire flock. It would be a bloodbath!"

The guardians blinked. Then they nodded again. They knew the traditions, and in Morocco, tradition is the bedrock of life. A boarded-up mansion in the West might attract squatters. But in the Arab world, as everyone was quite well aware, an empty house is a magnet for the wicked. Leave a place empty for a few weeks or more, and before you know it, it's full from the floor to rafters with an invisible legion of Jinns.

TWO

Do not stand in a place of danger trusting in miracles.

THE FIRST NIGHT WE SPENT AT the Caliph's House was a rite of passage. The guardians had pleaded with us not to stay there until the wayward Jinns had been dispatched. I protested vehemently. It seemed insane to move into a hotel when we had our own home. After much wrangling, Hamza, Osman, and the Bear saw that I would not be swayed. They ceded, so long as we followed a few guidelines. These included all of us sleeping in the same room on a single grimy mattress, around which a circle had been etched with a lump of coal. We were instructed not to open the windows, despite the suffocating press of summer heat. Nor were we permitted to sing, laugh, or speak in anything but a whisper. I asked why.

"Because it will anger the Jinns."

The guardians recapped the list of warnings: "No laughing, talking, walking around, or thinking impure thoughts."

"Is that it?" I asked.

Osman's smile vanished. "No, no," he said fearfully. "There is something far, far more important to remember."

"What?"

"Disobey, and unspeakable terror will befall you."

My wife rolled her eyes. "What is it now?"

The Bear swallowed hard. "Whatever happens," he said, stooping in dread, "do not go anywhere near the toilet in the night."

As I was quickly to learn, there is no place more satisfying for a mischievous Jinn to lurk than just beneath the surface of water. Rachana, who had given birth to our son, Timur, only three weeks before, choked.

"That's impossible," she barked.

"We will do our best," I said meekly.

We entered the house in single file as dusk became night once again. There was no electricity, and so candlelight was our guide. It threw long, spectral shadows across the walls and glistened on the backs of a thousand cockroaches darting in all directions at the sound of human intruders. Hamza led the way down the long corridor, across the great salon, and then upstairs.

As we moved through the mansion, picking cobwebs from our faces, the thought of a hotel nearby with electric lights, television, and usable toilets became all the more appealing. Once we were installed in the bedroom itself, the hotel room fantasy beckoned again. We crouched down on the mattress, my wife holding the newborn baby to her chest, and I clutching Ariane to mine. It was a miserable moment. I looked at Rachana through the flickering candlelight and whispered, "Welcome to our new life!" We were both about to laugh, but then we remembered that laughing was forbidden, as it angered the Jinns.

The square-shaped bedroom had a high ceiling, small windows, and what looked like cryptic charcoal symbols strewn across the mottled walls. Some were mathematical designs, others like cave paintings of animals sketched by primitive man.

I tucked Ariane into bed and told her a story about a brave little girl who wasn't scared, even when people tried to frighten her. There was a knock at the door, as if the tale was a cue of some kind. The three guardians were waiting. They had come, they said, to wish us luck. Osman threw a handful of salt into each of the four corners, and the Bear recited a verse from the Qur'an. Before they scurried away, Hamza warned again not to use the toilet on any account.

At first the night passed easily enough, although the chorus of donkeys from the shantytown, the mosquitoes, and the stifling heat kept us awake. I was tempted to throw the windows open, but leaving them shut seemed a small price if it would keep the guardians at ease and the spirits at bay. Eventually, we fell asleep, cuddled together like kittens on the vile old mattress. Then, at four A.M., came a voice from the darkness. It was hoarse and bellowing, and it was near. It became so loud that it managed to drown out the clamor of the donkeys and the savage dogs fighting in the shantytown. Rachana clutched me, and Ariane began to howl with terror.

"What is it?"

"I think it's the muezzin, the call to prayer."

I tried to get back to sleep, but was overcome by the desperate urge to pee. I held it in for an hour, until I could stand no more. The Jinns would have to forgive me, I thought. Very quietly I slipped into the bathroom and began to relieve myself. The pleasure was broken when a shadowy figure with a thick mustache leapt from behind the door. It was Hamza. He flipped down the lavatory cover in mid-flow.

"Get out of here!" he whispered caustically.

"You get out of here!" I shouted.

We wrestled together for a moment or two in the blackness, me struggling to lift the cover with my free hand, and he desperate to slam it shut.

"I haven't finished!"

"This is very dangerous," he replied.

"I can't help it. It's nature's call."

"You don't know what you're doing!" he yelled.

The baby was woken by our brawl. Then Rachana screamed for silence. I summoned all my strength and pushed the guardian out of the toilet. He disappeared into the garden, cursing.

Before I knew it, Ariane was peeling back my eyelids and looking in. Sunlight was streaming through the small windows. I could hear the melody of birds singing on the window ledge outside as my nostrils picked up the odor of fresh baked bread, no doubt from a stall in the shantytown. The bedroom was bathed in a blissful innocence. This is it, I thought, this is our new life.

AS FAR AS THE guardians were concerned, Dar Khalifa's proximity to a mosque was more than fortuitous. They regarded it as the single factor that had kept us safe during the first night. The imam's summoning of the devout to prayer was seen as a powerful purging force in itself—as if he were blessing us five times a day. To me, the raspy voice, amplified through an old loudspeaker, was more of an irritation than a blessing.

We had arrived in Morocco frazzled by the island culture we had left. We were paranoid, unhealthy, and overworked. In the West we are driven by an extreme form of guilt—if you are not seen to be working like a dog, you're perceived as being slothful. It was very clear that things in Morocco were quite different. A mantle of levelheaded comfort enveloped life, even

in Casablanca, one of the busiest of all North African cities. I
found people rushed about only when they needed to, and not
because they knew that others were watching them.

The first days were tranquil. We bought essentials, ate pic-
nic meals on the overgrown lawn, and set about exploring the
house. Ariane liked to lead the way, tramping through the endless rooms searching for unhatched eggs in the bird nests or
chasing mice. We worked out where each corridor led, which
room lay behind each door, and we trawled through the bric-a-
brac left by the previous owner. The idea of renovation didn't
even occur to us; it was hard enough to believe the house was
ours.

Dar Khalifa is set at the far end of a long rectangular sheet
of land. It looks out on the swimming pool, the gardens, stables, and an assortment of smaller buildings. The house itself
has been built in stages over time. On the right side is the oldest courtyard garden, dominated by an outcrop of banana trees
and towering palms. The sitting rooms, kitchens, dining room,
and entranceway form the main body of the house, along with
two further courtyards—one outside the kitchen, and another
on the left side, where it also adjoins the garages. The tennis
court stretches out behind, with a cluster of changing rooms,
a well, and servants' quarters. On the second floor there are
bedrooms and an expansive roof terrace, and along the left side
of the house is a later annex—two more bedrooms with a guest
suite above.

From the start the guardians were amiable, but they kept a
distance. It seemed as if they were uneasy that people had
moved back into the Caliph's House. They would watch us
from behind a wall or a garden hedge and duck out of sight
when we turned to face them. I found it amazing that in the
decade the mansion had been empty the guardians had kept the
stables as their hideaway. They had never opened up the house
and enjoyed its space, and had only ventured inside on rare

occasions. I supposed it had something to do with their fear of the Jinns.

We managed to get some of the lights working and cleaned the bedroom until it shone. Rachana strung up homemade curtains, and I scoured ten years of algae from the toilet. Hamza found me on my hands and knees scrubbing the bowl with a toothbrush. He screwed up his face.

"There are no Jinns in here, not now," I said.

The guardian waved a finger back and forth. "They don't like that," he quipped. "They like to be left alone."

I didn't reply, but went off to buy a set of plastic garden chairs, as there was no furniture at all. Later, when I arrived home, I went for a pee. To my surprise, the toilet was filled with what looked like the leftovers from lunch. I asked Ariane if she had thrown up.

"No, Baba," she said earnestly.

I walked out into the blazing sunshine. The guardians weren't to be seen. I called their names. No reply. So I ambled down to the stables, set in one corner at the end of the garden, shrouded by a mass of pink bougainvillea. I could make out the sound of feet running down a path and a door closing, but I couldn't see anyone. The stable doors were all tightly shut. I prised them open. Three stables were filled with broken garden tools, ladders, and knots of old wire. The door of the fourth was ajar. I pushed it wide open. Hamza was sitting inside on a paint can topped with a wad of gray asbestos. He was panting, as if he had been running. I asked him if he had any idea how the toilet came to be clogged with chicken stew. He stared up at me and adjusted the asbestos.

"The Jinns are not happy," he said, "and when they are not happy they get angry."

I was about to ask another question, but Ariane was screaming out on the lawn. I ran over to see what was going on. She was sitting under a fruit tree, hands over her eyes, bawling.

Above her, on one of the low boughs of the tree, was a string. From the string there hung a dead tabby cat. I pulled it down and called Hamza.

"What's this doing here?"

The guardian furrowed his brow. "It's bad," he said.

"I know it's bad, but who did this?"

Hamza shook his head, picked up the cat and took it away.

ON OUR THIRD DAY in Casablanca, I met a French diplomat called François through the friend of a friend. He was living in a spacious apartment with his family and had a job at the French consulate. I asked him about Morocco, expecting him to praise it—after all, he had been based in Casablanca for ten years. He looked at me across the lunch table, his sapphire eyes cool as glacial ice.

"This country's a time bomb," he said, mimicking an explosion with his hands. "It's a career cemetery, too. Work here and you'll never work again!"

I asked him about Moroccan people.

"Don't trust anyone," he snapped. "Fire the first ten people who walk into your office, and rule with an iron fist!"

"But Casablanca seems very European."

"Hah!" cracked François. "We're close to Europe, but don't make the mistake that I did."

"What mistake's that?"

"Don't think for a minute people are going to be like Europeans," he said. "They may be wearing the latest Paris fashions, but in their minds, they're Orientals." François paused to tap a fingertip to his temple. "In there," he said, "it's *The Arabian Nights*."

I told him about my experience with the toilet and the Jinns.

"Of course," said the Frenchman, "everyone believes in that

stuff . . . just like the tales of Aladdin, Sindbad, and Ali Baba. There's no question about it. Why? Because Jinns are in the Qur'an. That's why. Try to get anything done and the wall of superstition hits you head-on. Try to avoid it, pretend it's not there, and you'll trip up."

"So what's the answer?"

François lit a Gauloise and exhaled. "You have to learn to coexist," he said, "learn to appreciate the culture, and to navigate through treacherous water."

"How do I do that?"

"Shun the most obvious solution," he said.

BACK AT THE HOUSE, the guardians were clustered around the toilet bowl, calling prayers down to the Jinns. Rachana said they had barred her way and threatened to lock the door if we continued to bother them. She was very worked up when I found her, insisting she would move into a hotel unless I sorted my workers out. I led the guardians outside. They lined up in the long corridor, saluted, then stared at their feet.

"This can't go on," I said. "We need to use the bathroom. It's a matter of hygiene as much as anything else."

The Bear squinted in the afternoon sunlight. "The Jinns want blood," he said.

"Well, they're not going to get any. You can go and tell them."

"A few drops would do," said Osman.

"Absolutely not!"

"But you can prick your finger," the Bear said. "It wouldn't hurt. You could let the blood drip into the toilet. It would make the Jinns very pleased."

"Oh yes," Hamza echoed, "it would make them very pleased."

The Bear held up a pin. He just happened to be carrying it.

I wasn't about to start feeding my blood to imaginary forces of the underworld.

"Can't one of you give them your blood?"

"No, no, no," the Bear riposted. "You are the new master of the house and so only your blood will do."

We filed up to the toilet again and stared into the bowl. The thought that only my blood would suffice made me feel somehow important, indispensable—as if I was in charge. The Bear handed me the pin. I pricked my forefinger and let a large, single droplet of crimson blood splatter into the water. The guardians smiled broadly like Cheshire cats and took it in turns to shake my hand.

From then on, they seemed to regard me with a little more respect. Osman brought a pot of chicken soup for us the next night. He said his wife had made it from a recipe that had been in her family for six hundred years. One mouthful and, he claimed, we would dance like angels inside. I was touched by the thoughtfulness and rather liked the idea of dancing like an angel. The soup was flavored with fresh coriander and saffron and a hint of ginger. It was quite delicious and made a change from our stark diet of bread and triangles of processed cheese. The morning after that, Hamza crept into the bedroom and sprinkled us with pink rose petals while we slept. And, so as not to be outdone, the Bear presented us with talismans fashioned from black calfskin. There was one each, of differing sizes—ranging from large to very small. We tied them around our necks dutifully and praised their craftsmanship.

THE FIRST DAYS SLIPPED BY. Talk of Jinns died down, but I knew the subject was still very much on the agenda. Hamza would roam around the house reciting verses from the Qur'an or sketching magic squares on the whitewashed walls. He said the squares were amulets. They were formed of nine smaller squares, each with a number written inside. Add up the three numbers of any line, and you got the number fifteen. When I asked what they were for, Hamza said they would help bring *baraka,* divine blessing, back to the Caliph's House.

The focus of his prayers was the largest courtyard, in which there lay a wonderful secret garden. It looked like the oldest part of the house. At each end there stood a long salon with a colonnaded verandah. The room at the east end had fabulous cedar doors twenty feet high and a pair of giant matching windows carved with geometric designs. I planned to turn it into a library lined with bookshelves from the floor up to the ceiling.

After a week at the house, I realized that I still hadn't seen inside the room at the western end of the courtyard. I tried the handle but it was firmly locked. Hamza was crouching behind a squat palm tree, going over a magic square with a nugget of coal. I asked him to open the door. He saluted, then pretended not to understand. When I repeated the request, he seemed displeased, but ambled off to fetch the key.

As the chief guardian, nothing was more important to him than maintaining control. He controlled Osman and the Bear, anyone who came to the house, and, through skillful corralling, he managed to control us, too. The most effective method of staying in control was to lock all the doors at all times, unless one of us was in the room. Even then he quite frequently locked us inside. He kept all the keys in an old shoebox. There were hundreds of them. I would leave the kitchen for a few seconds to take a plate of food to Ariane, and when I came back, the room would be locked. The same with the bathroom— leave it for a moment and you couldn't get back in. Sometimes you would hear Hamza's worn leather-soled slippers shuffling away and the box of keys jangling.

I waited twenty-five minutes at the locked courtyard door for Hamza to return. He may have been hoping I had lost interest and had gone on to do something else. When he did finally turn up, the shoebox under one arm, his head was stooped low. He rummaged in the box for a moment and winced in declaration: "The key isn't here."

"You haven't looked very hard. Let me have a look."

The guardian covered the mouth of the box with his hands. "I'll look, I'll look!" he said, delving a second time.

Ten minutes later he was still rummaging.

"It's not here," he said with certainty.

"Doesn't anyone ever go in there?"

"No, they don't," Hamza said. "No one's been in there for years."

The secrecy made the locked room all the more intriguing. I began to speculate on what lay behind the door.

"There are other, more interesting rooms," said the guardian. "Don't bother with this one."

"Have you ever been in there?"

The guardian swished the air with his hand. "Oh yes," he said. "It's very boring."

"When did you go inside?"

Hamza thought for a moment. "Many years ago," he said.

"But it's an important part of the house," I said assertively. "Let's open it up."

I suggested we get a hammer and break the lock. At that moment, the muezzin rang out across the shantytown and Hamza hurried away with his shoebox of keys.

"I must go and pray," he said, calling back.

The question of the locked room continued to grate on my mind. When I asked Osman about it, he said Hamza was the only person who had ever been inside.

"He always goes there at night," he said.

"You mean he goes in now?"

"Of course," said Osman. "He goes in there every day."

"What's inside?" I asked.

Osman grimaced, slapped his hands to his cheeks in horror, and sank his teeth into his upper lip. He was wheezing.

"What's inside the locked room?" I repeated.

"I don't know," he said. "Really, believe me, I don't know."

DESPITE THE MATTER OF the mysterious locked door, relations with the guardians continued to improve. Then, one morning as I was going into the courtyard, I spied Hamza leaving the room. The moment he saw me making a beeline for him, he slammed the door shut. I tried the handle. It was locked fast.

"Can you please open this door, right now."

The guardian glanced away. His brow was running with sweat. "It is locked," he replied.

"I know that, but you just came out. You have the key."

"I don't," he said. "I swear to Allah that I do not have the key."

I was about to search Hamza, but something stopped me. For some reason, I felt it better to leave him alone. I'm not sure why. It was very strange. I should have pressed him to hand over the key then and there, but I didn't, almost as if something was affecting my decision.

ALTHOUGH WE HAD NOT started renovating the house, we did buy a few things to make life more comfortable—crockery, lamps, extra mattresses, and more garden furniture. But we soon found that no taxi driver was keen to venture into the shantytown. They said its jagged track was far too rough on their precious vehicles. So I decided to rent a car.

Osman was the first to catch wind of my plan. He said it was a fine idea, that he and the other guardians would assist me, as I was new to the Moroccan car rental scene. I thought this meant they would point me in the direction of a large, well-respected rental firm. But it did not. It meant something quite different. Hamza came to our bedroom that evening and said that he and the others had arranged everything.

"What do you mean by 'everything'?"

"No problem, Monsieur Tahir. We have found a nice car. It's very very nice."

He then explained that the butcher never drove his car because of his bad back, so it made perfect sense for me to take it on. What made less sense was the fact that the vehicle had been used for twenty years to ferry sheep carcasses from the slaughterhouse to the fly-smothered butcher's stall.

Sitting in it was like being strapped into a curious scientific experiment in which the passengers were the guinea pigs. The seats were encrusted with dead maggots, and the air around them alive with flies. No matter how many you killed, there were always more.

After taking one look at the vehicle, I thanked the guardians, praised the butcher's generosity, and politely refused the arrangement.

"It doesn't have enough space," I said.

"What do you mean?" said the butcher. "You can fit ten dead sheep in there." He thumbed to the rear seat. "There's plenty of room for your entire family."

"I was hoping for a four-by-four."

"This is far stronger than any four-by-four!" snarled the butcher.

"It has *baraka*," said Osman. "It will bring you good luck."

I looked at the sordid heap of blood-splattered metal, with its cracked windscreen, smashed lights, and maggot-ridden seats.

"Go on," Osman whispered, "try it. For a few days only."

"All right," I said gruffly, "for a few days."

Only later did I begin to understand the game. It was a game I didn't know I was playing, a game that everyone in

Morocco—not only foreigners—is forced into by their family and friends. Moroccans see it as their duty to help those they are close to. Not being of assistance at all times can bring dishonor and disgrace on the family. This wonderful tradition has evolved into a state in which everyone tries desperately to get you to do what they think is best for you. I knew the system well from years spent in Asia. Had I rented a car from Avis, Budget, or Hertz, the guardians and their families would never have been able to live down the shame—the shame of not getting involved.

LIKE ALMOST EVERY OTHER vehicle in Casablanca, the butcher's wretched Toyota was dented on every side and was falling to bits. I hated it, but at the same time, I valued it for the veil of authentic camouflage it provided. When out driving, no one would take me for a foreigner, or so I thought.

The moment I crept timidly into the ferocious stream of traffic, retching from the stench of rotting blood, I stood out like a pacifist on a battlefield. Moroccan traffic isn't like normal traffic. It's armed combat, a war of wills, in which only the very bravest have a chance to survive. Every driver, except for me, was an expert in swerving. You could veer sharply to the left or right without any warning and be quite certain that all the other cars would swerve out of the way.

On the first day on the road, I realized that I had to find someone who could help get things done and act as a bridge between us and everyone else. The constant swerving was fraying my nerves. I called François and asked him for advice on how best to choose an assistant.

"You have to show your teeth," he said, "It's dog-eat-dog out there. A man with no teeth is swallowed in one gulp."

"I'll be hard," I said weakly. "I'll ask tough questions. I'll bare my teeth."

"That's not enough," the Frenchman said frostily.

"What else can I do?"

"Tell each applicant to bring their family tree to the inter-view."

"What good will that do?"

François clicked his tongue at my ignorance. "Hire the person with the longest family tree," he said. "They'll have contacts. They'll be survivors."

I thanked François, but he wasn't listening.

"Tell me," he said, "did you fire the first ten people who walked into your office?"

"No, not exactly, François. You see, I don't have an office, and the only people I have working for me were inherited. I can't fire them. It would be unkind."

There was silence.

"Hello. Are you there?" I stammered.

"You're going to be eaten alive," said François.

THREE

An old cat will not learn how to dance.

A SMALL ADVERTISEMENT PLACED IN A local newspaper attracted a good crop of applicants. I went through the résumés with care, whittling them down to just two. Giving directions to the Caliph's House was so extremely difficult that I decided to hold the interviews at the nearby Café Corniche. I had begun to frequent the establishment, attracted by espresso so strong that it coursed through the intestines like crude oil surging up from the wellhead. Nothing gave me more joy than sitting at a shaded outdoor table, watching the world rage by. In Britain I used to feel at fault for whiling away more than a couple of minutes in a café. You felt you needed an excuse to be there at all. But in the Arab world, there is no pursuit more honorable for a man than sitting, hour after hour, staring out at the street, sucking down tarlike café noir.

The first candidate for the position of assistant was a prim, well-spoken girl of about nineteen. She was called Mouna. Her hair was covered neatly by the *hejab* scarf she wore, and her dress had full-length sleeves, tight at the wrist, and a hem so long that it dragged along the floor behind her. As soon as I set eyes on Mouna, I knew that someone was trying to protect her from the kind of staring men who patronized the Café Corniche.

When I asked if she had brought her genealogy, Mouna handed me a roll of thick paper. I unfurled it and glanced at the many lines of Arabic names.

"Very impressive," I said.

"My family are proud of their heritage," she replied.

I asked what jobs she had had before.

"My father doesn't like me working," she said softly. "He would kill me if he knew I was even here."

"I'm sure he wouldn't go that far," I said, laughing.

Mouna's russet eyes looked into mine very hard. She was silent for a moment.

"Oh no, you are wrong," she said solemnly. "He would."

There was an uneasy silence. Mouna sipped her orange juice.

"Sometimes my father becomes very enraged," she said. "If he found me here now, he wouldn't just kill me, he would kill you as well. You see, it's a matter of my family's honor."

I handed Mouna back her family tree and came out with a list of clumsy excuses. I imagined her father stalking me through the streets of Casablanca. For all I knew, he was already on his way.

"I'm sure you would make an excellent assistant," I said, "but I have given the job to someone else."

Mouna was disheartened for a moment. "It's always the same," she said mournfully as she left. "No one will employ me when they hear about my father."

The second applicant was a man named Adil. His résumé informed me he had lived in New Orleans for five years, where he had managed a cemetery. Despite the oppressive heat, he was wearing a thick leather jacket lined with sheepskin, with a bloodstain on the collar. He was close shaven and had a mop of greased black hair, a broken nose, and small darting eyes. During the twenty minutes we sat together, he knocked back three double espressos and smoked five cigarettes. He shook like a crack addict going cold turkey.

I asked him first how he had liked the U.S. It's a good solid question, one that tends to loosen people up.

"Lots of bitches," he said.

"You liked the girls?"

"No, the hookers."

He ran his hand up his nose, sniffing it. "I can smell 'em now," he said.

"What about work at the cemetery?"

"What about it?"

"Well, wasn't it gruesome?"

Adil pulled the bloodstained collar of his jacket tight to his neck. "The bitches loved it," he said.

I didn't know what he meant, but decided to move swiftly on. I asked for his family tree.

"That's bullshit."

"Why do you say that?"

"Because it isn't the future . . . it's the past."

After twenty minutes Adil got to his feet, lit a sixth cigarette, and said, "I'm out of here."

"Don't you want the job?"

"No way, man," he mumbled, shaking. "Got no time for jobs."

I walked back to the house, pondering why a guy would turn up for a job interview if he had no time to work, or why a girl would want to be my assistant if she knew her father would hunt us down and kill us both.

As I reached the shantytown the imam approached me. I had seen him from a distance, loitering in front of the whitewashed mosque. He was short and bearded with a severely wrinkled face, a small mouth, and a gray turban wound tight around the top of his head. He shook my hand, then rubbed his thumb and forefinger together.

"*F'lous,*" he said, grinning, "*argent,* money."

I smiled a great deal, pretended not to understand, and hurried away down the lane. The garden door opened before I knocked. I crossed the threshold through the coolness of Hamza's shadow. The guardian had been waiting for me. He saluted and said there was a problem, something that couldn't be put off for a moment. I asked for a minute to wash my face.

"It can't wait."

"Not even for a minute?"

The guardian frowned. "No, not for a second!" he said forcefully.

Hamza proceeded to lead me down the garden path. At the end stood a tall wrought-iron gate. It must have been exceptionally beautiful once, long ago, before the rust set to work crumbling the curlicues. Behind the gate was a patch of good land, about the size of a tennis court. Hamza opened the gate.

"Who owns that land back there?" I asked.

"You do, Monsieur Tahir," he replied.

"Are you sure?"

"Of course."

The land was encircled by a wall, the edges planted with trees. There was an assortment of palms, eucalyptus, juniper, and fig, and a burgeoning asparagus plant.

"Are you sure I own it?"

Hamza nodded. He led me through a haphazard crop of sunflowers, giant golden heads following the sun. At the far end of the wall, beyond an expansive slab of concrete, was another doorway. I followed the guardian through it to find a small, dilapidated outbuilding with its own walled garden.

"Who owns this?"

"You do, monsieur," said Hamza.

I could not understand why no one had told me before of the building and its secret garden. The sense of getting something entirely for free filled me with pleasure. But my joy was quickly erased when I saw what Hamza was pointing to. At his feet was another dead cat. It looked as if it had been gutted. The animal was covered in flies.

"Who did this?"

Hamza rubbed his nose. "It is a problem," he said.

"I know, but who did it?"

"Qandisha," said Hamza. "Qandisha did it."

"Who's he?"

The guardian filled his lungs full of air and sighed very deeply. Then he went back to sit in his old wicker chair in the stables. Getting answers out of him and the others was not easy. There were only three of them, but they had established their own close fraternity, bound by a code of strict silence.

Over the next few days, I asked Hamza, Osman, and the Bear again and again about Qandisha. Where did he live? What did he have to do with the house? Whenever the name was spoken, the guardians would become tense. They said they couldn't tell me, that there was nothing to tell. I begged. I pleaded. Still silence.

A WEEK PASSED. RACHANA ordered me to stop trying to find out about Qandisha and start finding an assistant again, one who could hire a nanny. I interviewed seven more people. None of them were suitable for one reason or another. Then, out of the blue, a young woman arrived at the Caliph's House. She spoke good English, and smiled a lot, as if someone had told her to do so. Her hair was long, very dark, and shiny, like newly roasted coffee beans. She announced that her name was Zohra and handed me a family tree. It stretched back seventeen generations.

"When can you start?"

She looked at her watch. "At once," she said.

"You are hired."

We made a list of things to do—find a nanny, and a maid who could double as a cook, find an architect, and a school for Ariane, buy all manner of odds and ends, explore Casablanca, and look into the paperwork of Dar Khalifa.

Zohra took precise notes whenever I spoke. It hinted at a professional training.

"I used to work in the film business," she said in a calm voice. "Hollywood shoots all its desert adventures down at Ouarzazate. I worked on *Gladiator, Troy,* and *Black Hawk Down.*"

"Did you meet any stars?"

Zohra blushed. "I fell in love with Brad Pitt," she said.

RACHANA BEGGED ZOHRA TO search for a maid and a trustworthy nanny for Ariane. We had only been in Morocco four weeks, but everyone we met lectured us on whom to choose. Some said only girls from the mountains could be trusted, others that only a desert woman would do, or one from Fès, Meknes, or Marrakech. Moroccan society is founded on a system of helpfulness. But people are so obliging that you can almost find yourself being suffocated by their kindness. Before we knew it, women—young, old, and extremely ancient—were arriving at the door. As word spread, they came from farther and farther afield, claiming to have been sent by friends of friends of friends.

One morning four women arrived from the mountains. Each one had a similar rugged, wind-chapped face with a tattooed chin and a floral scarf tied over her hair. Their hands were rough, like the hull of a ship that has been at sea for many months, and their nails were broken through honest work. I asked how they had come to hear of the vacancy.

"In Morocco," said Osman, "word spreads like a fire tearing through the depths of Hell."

The women spoke a Berber dialect, the original language of northwestern Africa. None of them knew more than a few words of Arabic, and they understood no French at all. The Bear, who was from the mountains himself, talked to them in Berber.

"They tell me they have been traveling for days," he said. "They came from a village in the High Atlas, near the Gorge of Ziz. It's taken them five days to get here."

The Berber women explained through the Bear that they were all widows and were in desperate need of work. There was no money in their village, they said, and life was very hard. They confirmed that they could cook, clean, do the laundry, and look after the children. Better still, they would work for a fraction of the going rate. All four of them would sleep in one room, and would charge the same as a single maid from Casablanca. Each one had brought a bedroll and a knapsack. They looked at me eagerly, their lined faces awaiting the instruction to begin. I asked Zohra what she thought.

"Let's give them a week," she said.

Hamza led the women to one of the empty rooms on the ground floor. They unfurled their bedrolls, lay down, and fell fast asleep.

TRAIPSE THROUGH AN ENGLISH supermarket and take a look at the fruit. It sits there staring up at you primly. It's perfect, not a blemish on any of it. Every apple, every pear, orange, and plum, is identical to the next in color, weight, and size.

Each one is shrink-wrapped with two or three others, labeled with a nation's name. The melons are from Barbados, the pineapples from Tanzania, the kiwis from Thailand, and the strawberries have been flown in from the southeast of Brazil. There's virtually nothing grown in Britain, and certainly nothing local.

The first time I went shopping for fruit and veg with Zohra, it was to a vast open market, popular for the freshness of the stock. Wherever I looked, there were great mounds of produce, with no cellophane or bar codes in sight—mountains of scarlet tomatoes, oceans of lemons and green beans, cartloads of pumpkins, strawberries, and succulent figs. At first I found myself cursing the irregularity and the imperfection. The crops were abundant, but they were different shapes and had the odd speck of brown. But I remembered my grandmother's caution that taste is more than skin-deep.

The economy of English life had trained me to buy only what I knew we would use, and not an ounce more. In Morocco we could ease into comfortable excess. On my first shopping expedition, I bought forty pounds of giant tomatoes, twenty pounds of red peppers, half a dozen cauliflowers, seven lettuces, a sack of onions, another of apples, and three hundred oranges for making juice. The huge sack of oranges cost what I would have paid for only a dozen in London.

OVER THE FOLLOWING WEEK I explored Casablanca, taking in the many quarters that made up the whole. Although she was from Rabat, Morocco's capital, Zohra was a knowledgeable guide. She took me to the port—the largest in Africa—where I hoped our furniture would soon be arriving by cargo ship, and she showed me the old medina, and the sprawling new conurbation of Maarif, where fashionable stores and restaurants teemed with the nouveau riche. By far the most interesting area was Old Casablanca.

Built by the French after they annexed Morocco in the first decade of the last century, the buildings had the sweeping lines of classic Art Deco and Art Nouveau. I spent hours strolling there, staring up, picking out the details—the floral façades and gilded domes, the orderly wrought-iron balconies, the mullion windows and stone balustrades, and the sleek, rounded walls of a robust age. Casablanca was the first city in the world to be planned from the air. Looking at it, one thing was astonishingly clear—that the French regarded it as a jewel in their imperial crown. The buildings lining Avenue Mohammed V, the main thoroughfare, were a statement of domination, an exclamation of French colonial might.

We wandered through colonnades where a chic clientele once snapped up the latest styles of the thirties and forties. Seventy years later and downtown Casablanca was a byword for danger and dereliction. The grandeur was still there, but it was hiding—under a blanket of verdigris and grime. People hurried through fast. No one bothered to look into the shop windows anymore. Most of them were boarded up anyway. Doorways were homes to the homeless, and the backstreets were running with feral dogs and oversized rats.

I asked Zohra why the old quarter had been deserted, why people had felt it necessary to build the stylish new district of Maarif when they already had one of the most beautiful city centers in the world. She thought for a long time as we walked.

"People don't realize what they have until they have lost it," she said.

ONE MORNING, OSMAN FOUND me sitting under a banana tree in the courtyard garden. He approached cautiously, as if he wanted something. I smiled. He shuffled forward, dipping his head, his hands clasped over his heart. When he got to me, he saluted.

"Monsieur Tahir," he said.

"Yes, what is it, Osman?"

"Qandisha is still not happy."

That name again. I frowned. The guardian wiped his face with his hands.

"Tell me, Osman, who exactly is Qandisha?"

He didn't reply.

"Did he used to work here?" I prompted. "Is he an angry ex-employee or something like that?"

"No, no, not like that," said Osman.

"Well, is he from the shantytown?"

"No, he is not from the shantytown," said Osman.

"Then where does he live?"

The guardian licked his lips anxiously. "In the house," he said. "Qandisha lives in Dar Khalifa."

"But I haven't seen him here. Surely I would have noticed if a man called Qandisha was living in the house."

There was a long pause. Osman rubbed his eyes.

"But he's not a man," he said.

"Oh, Qandisha's a woman?"

"No, not a woman either."

Again, Osman paused.

"Qandisha's a Jinn," he said.

THE WOMEN FROM THE mountains cleaned the house from top to bottom, and each afternoon they cooked a plate of couscous wide enough to feed a family of twenty-five. When they were not cooking or cleaning, they could be found sitting on the kitchen floor, gossiping in their Berber tongue. They tended to keep to themselves and didn't fraternize much with the guardians.

After learning the name of the resident Jinn, I brought the subject up with Zohra. She took it very seriously.

"You will have to do an exorcism," she said.

"You don't believe in it, too, do you?" I laughed.

Zohra didn't say anything at first. Then she said:

"This is Morocco, and in Morocco everyone believes in Jinns. They are written in the Qur'an."

She went down to the stables and talked to the guardians

for a long time. At the end of the discussion, she came to explain.

"Each night you must put out a large plate of food for Qandisha," she said. "There should be couscous and meat, the best food, not scraps, and you must lay it out yourself."

I could hardly believe that such a levelheaded woman would believe in such superstition but, with Osman's help, I asked the maids to prepare a special dish and leave it for me at dusk. I didn't say why I needed it. I felt stupid, that I was giving in, but thought it was worth trying once.

That night, the Berber women did as I had asked. They made a fabulous plate of couscous with pumpkin, carrots, and a tender chunk of lamb buried in the middle. It smelled delicious. I carried it out into the garden. Hamza showed me exactly where to place it—behind a low hedge. He shook my hand, bowed, then shooed me away.

Next morning I hurried down to the garden, ran across the lawn, and found the platter. It had been picked clean. There was nothing left, not a single grain of couscous. The Bear was raking the grass nearby.

"Qandisha was hungry," he said.

FOR THREE NIGHTS THE women from the Gorge of Ziz prepared ever more lavish feasts, and for three nights the platters were devoured. It was obvious the guardians were the only beneficiaries of the banquets. They were in high spirits. I wondered how long to allow their ruse to continue. Zohra said a natural break would occur, and it did.

On the morning of the fourth day, one of the maids was picking sprigs of rosemary, which grew wild in the garden. She was singing to herself. The sun was not yet high. Its syrupy yellow light streamed through the lower branches of the trees, warming the air. I was on the upper terrace reading a book of

Moroccan proverbs. The tranquillity was suddenly shattered by a high-pitched shriek. I peered down over the garden and saw the mountain woman waving her hands turbulently above her head. She had dropped the rosemary. It lay at her feet, along with a dead black cat.

Fifteen minutes later, Hamza called me to come downstairs. The Berber women had tied up their bedrolls, packed their knapsacks, and were waiting to be paid.

"Where are they going?"

"Back to the mountains," said Osman.

"Is the dead cat scaring them away?"

"Not the cat," said Hamza, "but the Jinns."

WE HAD NOT BEEN living at Dar Khalifa very long when a stout elderly man in tweed tapped on the door. His face was craggy and coffee brown like a bar of nut chocolate. On his head was a frayed cloth cap, and on his chin a swirl of white hair. He looked at the ground when I greeted him, and asked in good French if I had any postage stamps to spare.

"I will pay you," he said, "a few dirhams for each."

Until then the postman had brought nothing in the way of mail. I suspected he was having trouble finding the house. I apologized.

"Can you come back next week?"

The man blinked twice. "Will you forget?" he said.

I promised not to and, with that, my friendship with Hicham Harass began.

ZOHRA PROVED HERSELF TO be efficient and kind. She put up with the glaring gaps in my knowledge of Moroccan culture and helped to fill them in. The formality of the first days eased away, and we found ourselves chatting about our lives and our dreams. One afternoon, as we swerved through the traffic in the butcher's car, Zohra confessed her secret. There was something she had to tell me, she exclaimed, something that I had to know about her if we were to be friends.

"What is it?" I asked.

"You will think badly of me," she said.

"Tell me, tell me what it is."

"I am engaged to be married," she said without looking at me.

"Oh, who's the lucky man?"

"His name is Yusuf. He's an Arab. He lives in New Jersey. We met on the Internet."

"That's great news. When is the wedding?"

Zohra dabbed the tip of a finger to her eye. "There's no date yet," she said.

"The distance must be very difficult—with you here and him over there in the U.S."

"Oh yes, yes, it is," said Zohra earnestly. "It's a terrible strain. But we communicate every day. We are deeply in love, and when you are in love," she went on, her voice rising in tempo, "when you are in love, distance doesn't matter."

I changed the subject and asked Zohra if she had found an architect. I was eager to start work on renovating the house, and we needed someone who could plan the building work. We were still living in one room, while the rest of the house lay empty. Zohra dabbed her eyes again and said she had indeed made contact with an architect. He was young, dynamic, had studied in France, and had won praise for his innovative designs. She had set up a rendezvous for the following afternoon.

NEXT DAY AT FOUR P.M. we rumbled up to the architect's office, located on a swish side street in Maarif. At first I thought we ought to have taken a taxi, but the blood-soaked butcher's car suggested a lack of excess funds. The architect's office had tall glass doors open to the street, an array of potted palms, and elevator music piped in from miniature speakers hidden in the ceiling. There weren't the clouds of cigarette smoke or the mass of papers and blueprints more usually found in architectural offices. Instead, the walls were hung with oil paintings of traditional Moroccan scenes—a tribal wedding, a shepherd carrying a wounded sheep, a landscape of Marrakech with the snow-capped mountains rising up behind.

A secretary ushered Zohra and me to soft imported chairs at one end of a walnut-veneered desk. She served espresso with a twist of lemon, and squares of dark Swiss chocolate. I praised the paintings.

"They are for sale," the secretary said, handing me a catalogue.

After ten minutes of waiting, a broad-shouldered man with slick black hair and manicured nails swept through the glass doors. He was clothed in a handmade gabardine suit with monogrammed buttons. On his feet were snakeskin shoes, and around his waist was a slim sharkskin belt. A stream of cigar smoke swirled behind him like a vapor trail. Apologizing profusely for being late, he cursed the Prime Minister for keeping him waiting so long.

I told him about the Caliph's House, and said once, and then again, that my budget for renovation was small. The architect, Mohammed, laughed, lit a fresh Cuban cigar, and inhaled.

"What is money?" he said grandly in a high voice before leaning back in his chair. "It's just expensive paper."

I repeated for a third time that my budget was limited, and explained I was an impoverished writer waiting for a big break. The architect was about to say something, but his cellular phone began to ring. Excusing himself, he answered it and spoke fast in French to an infuriated woman at the other end. The lady was beside herself with anger. When he hung up, the architect blushed.

"Women are very special," he said uneasily, "*n'est-ce pas?*"

We arranged for him to visit Dar Khalifa the next afternoon and left the gallery office. On the way home I asked Zohra how she had come to meet Mohammed the architect.

"Through the dental community," she said.

NEXT MORNING I SENT Zohra to the Land Registry to look through the archives for Dar Khalifa's file. I wanted to get an idea of the building's history and to find out who had lived there before us. During our first weeks in Casablanca, I asked dozens of people about the Caliph's House. Most of them had something to tell. Some said it was formerly the summer residence of the Caliph of Casablanca, whoever he had been; others that it was once owned by an important magistrate, a confidant of the king. One old man, who was selling used copies of French magazines on the street, declared the house had been a high-class brothel back in the fifties. He squinted with delight at the memory.

"The girls who worked there were angels," he said, pressing the fingertips of his right hand to his lips in a kiss. "But, alas, they were reserved for French officers."

Someone else told me the building was used by high-level American diplomats during the Anfa Summit back in January 1943. I had read that President Roosevelt and Winston Churchill chose Casablanca to discuss wartime strategy and had planned their attack on Japan at the summit. Their talks were held nearby in the district of Anfa, making it plausible that their staff had made use of the Caliph's House.

At the Land Registry, Zohra hadn't found any mention of the Anfa Summit or any clues whether the house had been a brothel. She couldn't even say when exactly the house was built.

"What was in the file, then?"

Zohra looked down at the ground, unsure of how to break bad news.

"There isn't a file for Dar Khalifa," she said.

Every large building in Casablanca had a file bound in red cloth lodged at the Land Registry. But there was a gap of exactly four inches on the shelf where our dossier was supposed to be. The clerk had told Zohra that someone had taken it and not put it back.

"I begged him for more information," she said, "and it was then he told me something very bad."

"What?"

"That someone paid a bribe of twenty thousand dollars to lose the papers."

"Who would have done such a thing?"

"Your neighbor," she said.

I didn't understand. Our neighbors were a respectable family from Fès. They came from one of the old clans. Their ancestors had built themselves the famous Palais Jamai, now run as a magnificent hotel. We had only met a few times, but they had lavished us with welcoming gifts, and had always been ready to explain the intricacies of Moroccan life. We valued them as real friends.

Zohra read my mind. "Not the Jamais," she said softly, "they are good people."

"Then who?"

"Your other neighbors. Come with me. I'll show you."

Zohra led me up the guardians' homemade ladder onto the roof. Shading my eyes in the dazzling afternoon light, I gazed out at the warren of cinder-block homes and the gilded waves of the Atlantic in the distance.

"These are all your neighbors," said Zohra.

"I'm sure none of them have twenty thousand dollars to spare as a bribe."

Zohra wiped the moisture from her chin.

"That one does," she said, motioning over the jumbled shanties.

She was pointing to a large whitewashed home with over-sized windows and a green tiled roof. It stood at the far end of the shantytown, and was encircled by date palms and a wall topped with razor wire. The house was so far from our own that I hardly regarded its occupants as neighbors at all.

"They're miles away," I said. Until that moment, I had had nothing to do with them. One thing was certain—they were despised by the residents of the shantytown. This was evident because each morning, as the husband drove his Mercedes four-by-four at high speed down the slum's track, a gang of boys would line up and hurl stones at it. I knew, too, that his wife was in her late thirties, that she dyed her hair plum purple, wore a great deal of gold, and dressed like a Russian nightclub singer.

"Should I go and confront him?" I whispered feebly.

Zohra's face froze in a mask of fear. "Absolutely not!" she snapped. "Do you have any idea who he is?"

I shook my head.

"He's Casablanca's Godfather," she said. "Challenge him and he could snatch the children. Before you know it you'll be getting fingers through the mail."

NEXT AFTERNOON, MOHAMMED THE architect arrived in a very fine black Range Rover. His initials were painted on all four doors, and there was an open box of Montecristo No. 5s on the leather upholstered dashboard.

For once, my mind wasn't on renovation. I was preoccupied with the rich neighbor, and confused. Zohra had tried to put my mind at rest, explaining that although the man was a gangster and a local Godfather, he wasn't involved in drug-dealing and gun-running. Moroccan gangsters, she insisted, were the kings of contraband, running empires built on illegal cigarettes, pirated movies, and stolen cars from Spain.

The Range Rover's monogrammed door swung open, and the architect's handmade shoe touched the ground. I welcomed him and showed him around.

"We'll take down some walls," he said casually, sucking at one of the cigars. "This one, that one, and that one over there. It'll be much better opened up. And over here, we'll cut arches so you'll be able to see right through the house. We'll rip out this old staircase and build a new one, gently curved. Then we'll extend the bedrooms upstairs and slot a huge roof terrace on the top. You'll get a fabulous view of the ocean from up there."

Despite my worries of how we would pay for all the work, I was impressed by his vision.

"My budget's very small," I mumbled yet again.

The architect swished my doubts away along with his smoke.

"Money," he said caustically. "It's just money."

FOUR

Every food has its flavor.

A MAJOR DILEMMA FACED US WITH the sewers. The fragile clay waste pipe laid to the Caliph's House had been designed to service a single lavatory. Over the years, as the house grew in size and the popularity of flush toilets spread, more and more of them were added. By the time we arrived at Dar Khalifa, there were a total of thirteen lavatories. The narrow clay sewage pipe running through the shantytown to the house was frequently shattered, as residents there attempted unsuccessfully to link their homemade sewers to our own. The problem was made all the worse by another modern innovation—toilet paper.

Add to the equation the stifling heat and drought of mid-August, and we were hit by an overwhelming wall of stench whenever we went outside. The matter was made all the more unbearable by the plague of biting flies that savaged us both night and day. Zohra said it was quite common for the primitive drains beneath Casablanca's shantytowns to explode in the night. Like many local people I met, she was something of an expert on sewers, but her casual interest didn't even come close to Hamza's preoccupation with the subject. His interest in sewers was equaled only by his obsession with the Jinns. Whenever I was doing my business, he would pound on the bathroom door.

"Not more than ten centimeters!" he would yell. "I beg you! Do not use any more paper than that!"

I assured him repeatedly through the keyhole that I was rationing the paper as best I could. I had never been so frugal. But still Hamza felt it necessary to patrol and to shout warnings of impending disaster through the door. We became so used to his intrusions that after a few weeks we grew concerned when they did not come.

ONE NIGHT AS WE were about to clamber into bed, the postman arrived. Ecstatic at finding the house at last, he thrust a clutch of letters into my hands and stood by the door meekly, inspecting his fingernails. I tipped him well and told him to remember me. He promised to do so and ran off into the night.

The next day, when I had opened the mail—most of it bills from England—I remembered my own promise, to Hicham the stamp collector. The guardians said he lived in the shantytown in a shed behind the mosque. They said I would know it because a dog with three legs would be sleeping outside. I strolled down the main track, slipped behind the mosque, and searched for a dog with three legs. In my hand was an envelope containing five postage stamps, all bearing Queen Elizabeth's head.

A large brindle dog was lying on its back in the dust. I

counted its legs. There was one missing. I stepped over it and knocked at the tin door. Hicham the stamp collector appeared, called out greetings, and invited me to come inside. The one-room shack had a neatness about it, the kind that only a stamp collector knows. Dustcovers had been laid meticulously over the prized artifacts—a carriage clock, a tea set with matching plates, a portable television wired up to a car battery. A faded photograph of King Hassan II loomed down from the far wall, and an impressively large copy of the Qur'an stood on a carved wooden stand near the door.

I presented the postage stamps to Hicham, who hissed to his wife for tea. He thanked me once, and then again, before pulling out a wallet.

"I will pay you," he said, taking out a note.

I refused the money. He insisted. I raised my voice and refused a second time. Hicham Harass's pride was dented. His face fell.

"Then I cannot take them," he said.

We sat in silence, crippled by good manners. Tea was brought. It was hot, sweet, and served in miniature glasses with a gold pattern on the rim. I wondered how we might save the situation. Then the perfect solution struck me. Hicham wanted postage stamps for his collection, and I wanted to learn about Morocco from someone who knew it. I suggested we make a trade. Each week we could meet. I would part with my postage stamps and Hicham would pay me, not in money, but in conversation.

BEFORE MOVING TO MOROCCO, the fantasy of having a large retinue of staff to attend to my every whim was very pleasing indeed. I used to find myself daydreaming. I would have people waiting on me hand and foot, I thought, and would never have to lift a finger again. The reality was very different.

By the middle of summer, Zohra had found us a maid, a full-time cook, and a nanny with jade green eyes. Morocco has severe unemployment and as a result everyone does their best to get on someone else's payroll. There is no shortage of applicants for any job. Before we knew it, we had three inherited guardians, the maid, the cook, the nanny, the gardener, as well as Zohra to pay.

Individually, no one was given very much. The rate per hour was low. But together, their salaries were substantial—money that had to be earned by me, then handed out each Friday lunchtime in small-denomination bills. The second problem was that once someone was on the payroll, it was almost impossible ever to remove them. Their jobs were secure for life—a point that each of them was very well aware of. But the worst aspect of all was that the house was suddenly filled with people who were trying to control us.

At the top of the rigid pecking order was Zohra. She was sweetness personified to me, but everyone else was terrified of her. Below Zohra were Hamza, Osman, and the Bear. They had been at Dar Khalifa so long that they had earned the right to boss the other staff about. Below them was the maid, then the cook, and after her, the nanny. At the very bottom of the hierarchy was the gardener. I discovered later why he was regarded as such an object of ridicule. It was because his wife had run away with another man.

Everyone had their own way of achieving power. The most effective method was to do the opposite of what they were requested to do. If I asked the cook to prepare a certain dish, she would sweep me out of the kitchen with her broom and make something quite different. When I asked the maid to make my bed, she cleaned the windows, and when I asked the gardener to cut the lawn, he pruned the hedges instead. The guardians were no better. Their longtime service had made them expert at evading orders. They could tell when I wanted something done—they could hear it in the way I walked—and they would vanish into the stables and bolt the door behind them.

Nothing gave the workforce more pleasure than taking up my time with their own requests. These usually included a petition to hire their brother or cousin, or to bestow charity on a long-lost uncle or aunt. At first I would um and er, blush, and mumble hollow promises. Then one morning I thought of the answer. It was simple. I would agree enthusiastically to hiring the person in question, so long as he or she was taken on as a replacement to the person making the request. It worked like a dream.

Even more irritating was the constant bickering and petty squabbles between the guardians and the other workers. I would sit down to write, and within minutes, the maid would come to say that Hamza had taken her brush, or that Osman was pouring her bleach into the drains. The gardener would complain about the nanny, because she let Ariane throw snails into the swimming pool, and the cook would rant on about the Bear for glancing at her in a lustful way.

IN THE LAST WEEK of August, the crag-faced imam from the mosque ambled over to the house and rubbed his thumb and forefinger together again. He needed cash, he said, because the mosque was very poor. As the owner of the largest house in the shantytown, it was my responsibility, he informed me, to pay for its upkeep. I asked Zohra what to do.

"The worst thing is to give money," she said. "If you hand cash to the imam today, tomorrow you'll have a line of people three miles long."

"Then what do I do?"

"You can support the shantytown's school."

A small windowless classroom was attached to the mosque.

Inside, there were a few battered chairs, homemade desks, a handful of copies of the Qur'an, and an elderly schoolmistress armed with an orange rubber hose. There were no blackboards or pictures, and no electric light. From eight-thirty in the morning until three each afternoon, the dark classroom was filled with forty children. Twice a day, when I strolled by, I would hear the whoosh of the rubber hose, followed by the shrill sound of a small child weeping.

Zohra said corporal punishment made children strong, but that they only understood the good it did them in later life. She told me her brothers had been beaten senseless at school, and it had made them saints in adulthood. They still had the scars, she said, as we went downtown in search of school supplies.

"You mean they're mentally scarred?" I asked.

"No, no," said Zohra, "I'm talking about their backs."

IN THE OLD ART Deco quarter stood the colossal Bessonneau Apartment Building, with HOTEL LINCOLN bolted onto the side. A forlorn reminder of the French era, it spanned an entire block of Boulevard Mohammed V, and was constructed in the very grandest Franco-Moorish style. Every technique of the day had been employed—arabesque arches and filigree iron-work, subtle cornicing, and miles of exquisite fretwork adorning the façade. But the golden age of Casablanca was a faded memory, and the Bessonneau building was a fragment left behind. It was derelict, unloved, and awaiting demolition. Behind it stood the great Derb Omar Bazaar.

The shops there were packed with cheap cardboard boxes piled up to the rafters. The boxes were filled with Chinese vases and gunpowder tea, with ornamental figurines, chrome chandeliers, pink plastic dolls, and school supplies. I spent an entire afternoon buying colored pencils and chalks, felt-tips, paints, exercise books, notebooks, and pens. I purchased forty sturdy schoolbags, too, and posters and maps for the classroom walls, and a blackboard for the teacher with the orange hose.

The next morning we delivered the boxes to the class, to the delight of the children and to the fury of the imam. He poked a wrinkled finger at me and rubbed it to his thumb. As Zohra and I dragged the blackboard into the class, the architect's Range Rover came purring down the trail through the shantytown. It was followed by a shabby Japanese truck with balding tires and a windshield cloaked in a spider's web of cracks. In the back were perched a dozen of the wildest men I had ever seen. They were scarred from head to toe, had unnaturally developed shoulder muscles and a brutal, sadistic look in their eyes. They resembled convicts sentenced to hard labor, and were armed with hammers—not the petite kind we use to do jobs around the home, but industrial sledgehammers.

Mohammed the architect extended his velvety hand for me to shake. It was soft and warm like a new chamois. As he marched in the door, he slipped me the details of his bank in Paris and asked me to deposit a very large sum of money into his account. Make the transaction, he said, and all my problems would be over.

Rachana and I watched as he glided through the house, with the rowdy hammer-wielding demolition crew heavy in his footsteps. In his right hand was a red china marker, and in his left, a cellular phone. He paused before each wall, inspecting it for a moment before either scratching an X with the pencil or walking on to the next wall. While he walked, he talked, or rather listened, to an angry voice at the other end of the telephone.

The moment he had finished, the wrecking crew began their horrible work. They savaged one wall after the next with their sledgehammers, their eyes glazed with indifference. I called out for them to halt, so that we could discuss the radical modifications, but no one could hear me. The architect had moved into the garden, away from the clamor of steel smashing stone. The angry voice was still berating him. I ran out and motioned for his attention. He flipped the phone shut.

"*Oui?*"

"Those madmen are breaking down the house!" I roared. "Tell them to stop."

The architect took a leather wallet from his breast pocket, slipped out a Cohiba cigar, and lit it. Sucking hard, he shook his head.

"Alas, I wish I could," he said calmly. "But once these men begin, no one can stop them."

THAT NIGHT THE GUARDIANS came to me to protest. They were very agitated indeed, and wanted to know why a dozen musclemen had smashed down so many walls. I described my own shock, but assured them the architect had everything under control.

"He studied in Paris," I said, as if it explained everything.

"But you do not understand," said Osman.

"I don't understand what?"

"That you are upsetting Qandisha."

The following afternoon, Zohra spent an hour soothing the guardians' worry. She promised them on the grave of her grandmother we would have a ceremony in honor of the Jinns. She promised, too, that we would all shout out our names when we entered a room—so that Qandisha and his fiendish kin would hear us and have a chance to move out of the way. The guardians perked up a little. They said they would be happier if we would sprinkle salt over our bedroom floor before we slept each night. Then they asked me to start leaving food out again. I told them I would see what I could do, but that there wasn't money for extra food, as I had to pay the architect so much cold, hard cash.

Two days passed. Work at the house began in earnest, fueled by my bank transaction to Paris. The wrecking crew ran off whooping into the dusk of the third day. They had exacted what seemed like a truly terrible toll. When the dust settled, I went to tour the destruction. Things were grim. Ten walls had been hammered down, and others were peppered with gaping holes. Ariane asked me why the bad men had caused so much damage. I told her it was for the best, so that she and Timur could one day run through the house unhindered by so many walls.

"Baba," she said, "you are not telling the truth."

AFTER THE 9/11 ATTACKS, and Casablanca's own suicide bombings the previous May, I had been wary of patronizing outwardly American institutions. François, my French expatriate acquaintance, had warned me to stay away from McDonald's in particular. The chain of fast-food restaurants were found all over Casablanca and were popular with young Moroccan families.

"They'll be hit first by the suicide squads when the meltdown comes," he said.

"But Ariane likes McDonald's."

"If you must go to them," François replied, "make sure you sit well inside. If a bomber strikes, he's likely to be nervous. He'll pull the pin when he's just got in the door."

At the end of August, when it came to enrolling Ariane in school, we were uneasy about sending her to one of the three American schools. Like McDonald's, they were potential terrorist targets. Then we heard that a new school was about to open near the house. It taught classes in English, Arabic, and

French, and aimed to have all its pupils fully trilingual by the age of six. From the first moment she entered its doors, Ariane loved it. She made friends fast and developed a passion for tortoises.

ONE EVENING IN EARLY September we invited Zohra to dinner as a way of thanks for all her work. She suggested an excellent restaurant called Sqala, set in a former Portuguese fortress on the cusp of the medina. Moroccan food tends to be as inferior in restaurants as it is superior in the home. To achieve the subtle flavors takes an astonishing amount of care and time. The ambience is important as the food itself, as is the attention lavished on a guest. As you gorge yourself on the delicacies, with your hosts whispering flattery, it's very hard not to give in to delusion.

The meal reintroduced me to the sensory marvels of real Moroccan cuisine. We ordered a selection of dishes. There was chicken tagine flavored with turmeric, honey, and apricots; a pair of sea bream marinated in a saffron sauce and served on a bed of couscous. After that came *bistiya,* a vast platter of sweet pastry, beneath which lay wafer-thin layers of pigeons, almonds, and egg.

Zohra said the family was the center of Moroccan life, and that food was at the center of the family.

"If only we could do everything as well as we cook," she said with a smile, "we would be rulers of the world."

The conversation moved away from food and on to love.

"When I am married to Yusuf," Zohra said, "we will live in a little house, with small red flowers around the door. We will have two children a boy and a girl, and , , ," she said, pausing to sip her orange juice, "and we will never be apart, not even for a night."

"It sounds idyllic," I said.

"Oh, it will be, it will be," said Zohra dreamily.

I asked how she felt when they met for the first time.

"I told you," she said, "we met on the Internet."

"But how was it when you first met in person, face to face?"

Zohra swallowed hard and blushed.

"Yusuf and I have never met," she said.

ARIANE WAS STILL VERY small, but she pleaded with me to buy her a tortoise. She wanted one like the tortoise at school. I fended off the request for as long as I could, as all my energy was taken up dealing with the problems brought to me morning and night by the guardians. Most of these centered around the well-being of Qandisha the Jinn and the trail of destruction left by the wrecking crew. Ariane begged and begged for the tortoise, until I could stand it no more. Hamza had got wind of her wish and insisted that nothing would bring more *baraka* to the house than a strong, healthy tortoise. The reptiles, he insisted, were the luckiest of all ever created by Allah. I asked Zohra to find out where to buy them. Two days later she reported. The only place to look was, she said, in Tan-Tan.

I looked at my wall map of Morocco. I couldn't see Tan-Tan.

"Move your finger down," said Zohra. "No, down much more."

Then I saw it.

"But that's way down south in the Sahara!"

"Of course," said Zohra.

"Can't you buy tortoises in Casablanca, in a pet shop?"

Zohra scoffed at the remark. "Do you want your little daughter to have low quality?" she said. "A tortoise that's been tortured and kept in a cage? Or do you want to be proud that you've given her the best, one that will really bless the house?"

I was sick of Casablanca, of talk of tortoises, and of the

Jinns, and so I packed Rachana and the children into the car. We loaded suitcases on the roof, and we headed south, in search of tortoises with divine spirit. We hadn't left the city limits of Casablanca when Ariane threw up all over her lap. Her Moroccan childhood had begun.

We shunned the highway and took the old, disintegrating road that ran along the coast as far as Agadir. Beyond it, we were in the desert. After many hours in the wretched butcher's car, I swore I'd buy my own vehicle as soon as we got home. The only things to take our minds off the rotting seats were the sand and the dust, and the boys swinging squirrels. There were just one or two at first, standing on the side of the road. As soon as they saw a car, they would whip their arms up, whirling strings around their heads like lassos. At the end of each string was a terrified ball of fur. I slammed on the breaks, cursed the boys, bought their squirrels, and released them a few miles on—just in time to meet another group of boys with another clutch of squirrels. The more damn squirrels I rescued, the more there were being tortured, waiting for a stupid foreigner to save them.

The journey revealed to Rachana, Ariane, and baby Timur the raw North African beauty I had known myself as a child. We had rumbled down the same roads then in a red Ford Cortina the fearful family gardener at the wheel. Very little had changed. The butcher's car was built in about the same year as our Cortina and was crammed with luggage and vomiting kids. As we swerved to miss the potholes, the wild dogs, and donkey carts, I congratulated myself on coming full circle.

After two days of driving, we arrived at Tan-Tan exhausted and shaking from the road. It was a dusty encampment of a town of very little interest, built of cinder blocks, cheap cement, and sand. I vowed I would never drive anywhere again. Ariane was still moaning about her tortoise. I rolled up to the market and quizzed the first man I saw. He was a butcher. There was blood splattered down the front of his shirt, and his mouth was filled with a big toothy grin.

"We need to buy a tortoise," I said angrily.

"Why do you want it?"

"So that we can go home."

The butcher asked if we were planning to eat the tortoise.

"Certainly not!" I snapped.

"They make good broth," he said. "Good for lunch."

I covered Ariane's ears.

"It's not for eating," I mouthed. "It's for the little girl."

The butcher's expression changed. "Ah, a pet, a little pet for the little one."

"Yes, a little pet," I said.

"Not for lunch," the butcher confirmed.

"No, not lunch."

He nodded, his toothy gums grinning hard. "I will show you," he said.

Without another word he led the way to the far end of the bazaar, where a man with large watery eyes was holding a box. The butcher pointed to the box. The lid was removed and the contents ceremoniously displayed. Inside was a frail young tortoise. The man with watery eyes said the reptile had been savaged by a dog and should, therefore, not be eaten.

"Oh, we don't want to eat it," I repeated. "It is for my daughter. She will nurse it back to health. It will bring *baraka* to our house."

I took out my wallet and asked the price. I was prepared to pay anything. The man with watery eyes squinted at Ariane and then at the tortoise.

"It is a gift," he said, wiping a tear from the corner of his eye, "because nothing is so sweet as to make a child happy inside."

———

HAMZA WELCOMED US BACK to Dar Khalifa and exclaimed that a dreadful new affliction had descended. I prepared myself to hear about Qandisha or another dead cat, but for once, the guardian seemed to have forgotten about the Jinns.

"It is the *bidonville,*" he said, "the shantytown."

"What about it?"

"The government is going to knock it down."

For days there had been speculation that the May 16 suicide bombers had planned their attacks in the safety of a Casablanca slum. News reports on television had featured a selection of so-called bidonvilles much like our own, with a few low stalls and rough jumbled shacks, a modest whitewashed mosque, and a wrinkly-faced imam.

Since moving to Casablanca, I had secretly hoped that the shantytown that surrounded the oasis of Dar Khalifa would be bulldozed, and that upmarket villas would replace them. If there were villas, then there would be a new road, a supermarket, cafés, and shops. And if the shantytown vanished, so would the stagnant pools of water, the mosquitoes, the plagues of biting flies, the braying donkeys, the raw sewage, and the mountains of festering trash.

The head guardian leaned forward and tugged at my shirtsleeve.

"If they knock down the shantytown," he said very softly, "then we will have nowhere to live."

THE DAY AFTER WE returned from Tan-Tan, I called the architect and asked when his builders would arrive.

"Rats are running in through the holes made by your wrecking crew," I said as politely as I could.

"Get a dog," he said.

"Can you send your team over this week?"

The architect sighed as if I were asking an impossible favor. "The builders will come," he said.

"When?"

"They will come."

"But *when* will they come?" I asked again, more forcefully than before.

"When God wills it," he said.

A WEEK LATER THERE was still no sign of the builders. I called the architect again and again, but his cellular phone was switched off. At the gallery, his secretary said he had gone to Paris and no one knew when he would be back.

The problem of the rats got worse. It became so bad that they made a nest from our mattress, gnawed holes in my bookshelf, and chewed up my books. After that, they ate all the soap in the house. Rachana regarded them as a health hazard and ordered me to stop them before the children were bitten.

I consulted Osman. He smiled broadly and gave me a double thumbs-up.

"Don't put poison," I said.

"Not poison, Monsieur Tahir."

"And don't put traps!"

"No, Monsieur Tahir, no traps."

He sauntered off, returning that night with a sheet of cardboard and a tube of glue. The tube featured the adhesive's many varied applications. There was a picture of a house, a car, a boat, a child's toy and, below it, a small indistinct image of a rat.

Osman squeezed a quantity of the glue onto the cardboard and positioned it inside one of the holes in the wall. He gave another thumbs-up and hurried off to pray. Next morning, to my great surprise, he took me to see the haul—three good-sized rats stuck spread-eagled on the cardboard.

DAYS CONTINUED TO PASS, and still Hamza refused me entry into the locked room at the far end of the courtyard garden. I had tried to pick the lock and had even attempted to prise the slatted shutters open. Hamza had no sympathy. He urged me to stop thinking about the room and to start the popular tradition of putting out platters of food again, for Qandisha. He repeated for the tenth time that the key was lost. I suggested bringing a locksmith.

"He is a bad man, that locksmith!" the guardian barked.

"There must be more than one locksmith in Casablanca."

Hamza screwed up his face. "They are all bad men," he said. "They'll make copies of all the keys and will come and rob us in the night."

"But we have three men protecting the house," I said.

Again, the guardian cursed the locksmith and his profession.

"No locksmith can open that door," he said.

"Why not?"

"Because it is locked for a reason."

MY FATHER NEVER SAID it, but I think he was ashamed of raising his children in a quiet English village. His own childhood had been spent in the Hindu Kush and rambling through the foothills of the Himalayas. His unconventional upbringing began early—he was born at the Indian hill station of Simla while his father was on an expedition hunting markhor. Always the trouper, his Scottish mother had agreed to tag along despite being eight months pregnant. When he eventually had children of his own, my father found that their school life was not something he could easily understand. We were, as he frequently reminded us, the first children in the family's history ever to go to school. Every other generation had been tutored by an eclectic mix of poets, philosophers, mystics, and battle-hardened warriors. For my father, education had meant learning to ride and shoot gazelle at the same time by the age of nine, memorizing the works of Saadi, the Persian poet, by the age of twelve, and mastering championship chess. He scoffed when he heard that his only son was learning Latin, the long jump, and the flute.

"When are you going to learn to hunt game?" he asked me on my tenth birthday.

"But we don't have any wild animals at school, Baba," I replied limply.

My father glanced down at me, his long forehead a web of frowns. "Don't you?" he said distantly.

Morocco was the balance that compensated for his shame. His children might have been learning useless skills at school, but he hoped that our journeys to the mountain kingdom would reveal to us the order of the real world. Nothing was so important to my father as mountain life. We would rove through Morocco's fertile valleys searching for "Fantasia," displays of tribal bravado—a dozen charging horsemen, firing their ancient weapons and whooping into the air.

Whenever the family Ford Cortina reached a mountain village, my father would wave his arms and order the gardener to apply the brakes. He would open the doors and, like the Pied Piper, would lead my sisters and me into the nearest teahouse. His feet may have been in the Atlas Mountains, but his mind was back in the Hindu Kush. To him, the teahouse was an Afghan caravanserai, the mint tea was *chai sabs*, green tea, and the Berbers were shepherds from his beloved Nuristan.

"This is the heart of Morocco!" he would exclaim. "Forget all that rubbish they teach you at school. This is the place to learn."

"But what can we learn here, Baba?"

My father would pause, knock back his tea, and slam the empty glass down on the table.

"My children," he would say. "It is here that you can learn why the heart beats as it does."

ONE AFTERNOON IN EARLY September, I sent Zohra to the Land Registry to search for the missing file, and I went downtown to poke about behind Hotel Lincoln. The area felt to me like the nucleus of the city—the spot where the seed of Casablanca had fallen long ago. People there were different. The shopkeepers didn't really care if you bought anything at all. They were in no rush for customers to leave, and liked it best if you stayed and chatted. Conversation of the old days passed the afternoons.

I perched on a black-vinyl-covered stool in a grocer's shop, swishing at the flies with my hand, listening to a tale of life after the war. Ottoman, the grocer, was round, white-haired, and bespectacled, with an affliction of furry brown moles all over his face. He was talking about the days when Casablanca was famous throughout the world, its name synonymous with all that was modern and exotic.

"The shops were filled with expensive goods from Paris, from London and Rome," he said, running his hand over the sleek tabby cat curled up on his lap. "The men wore hats then, and the women walked tall in high-heeled shoes. They smelled of perfume." He paused to draw a breath for effect. "The streets were clean and bright, and everyone was confident. Casablanca was paradise."

"Why did the center of town move to Maarif?" I asked.

The grocer scratched a thumbnail down his nose. "Other Moroccans cherish what is old," he said, "they understand that old is good. But people in Casablanca are childlike. They are fickle. They only appreciate the shiny, the new. Down here it used to gleam like a diamond, but when the luster was lost, they hurried away, to Maarif."

"I heard Casablanca's restaurants were once the finest in the world," I said.

The grocer's face froze, his old eyes misting over. "Ah, yes," he said. "Yes, it's true! There was one just over there . . ." He paused mid-sentence to point out the window. "It was called Au Petit Poucet. What a place! What an ambience! I took my wife there when we were first married. She wore a black dress, and I, my wedding suit. I had saved up my money and we dined like kings. I can see it clearly now." Ottoman stopped again and stared into the pool of fly-infested sunlight at the back of his shop. "There was the scent of lilies and the soothing sound of a harp," he said. "The waiter wore the whitest apron I have ever seen. His cheeks were so clean, they were pink."

"How was the food?"

"Oh, the food, the food!" he said wistfully. "I can taste it now! My wife had the duck. It was served with petit pois, and asparagus that melted in her mouth." Again, the grocer paused as he peered to see the detail of his memories. "I ate a steak," he said gently. "It was rare in the middle with dauphin potatoes at the side."

FIVE

Tomorrow there will be apricots.

AUTUMN APPROACHED. THE CRUEL summer heat softened, and the garden erupted into a blaze of color—red hibiscus and subtle pink mimosas, yellow jasmine, and delicate passion flowers, all set against a backdrop of blinding crimson bougainvillea. Dar Khalifa was an oasis, a sanctuary encircled by reality. Ariane would prod her tortoise across the lawn after school, little Timur would slurp his milk in the shade, and I would sit there, watching them both, thankful. We may have been beset with local difficulties, but we were blissfully separated from our previous lives.

When the telephone rang, it would be our relatives or friends, rather than some annoying voice trying to sell a holiday or a pension. There were no computerized switchboards to deal with or parking meters, no gridlock traffic or triangular sandwiches with upmarket names. Certainly, there was a language barrier, and a cultural one, but I found myself happier than I had been in years.

Late one night a close friend called to say that his Californian home had burned to the ground. There was nothing left. A lifetime of papers and possessions were gone. Next morning, I asked Zohra to upgrade our fire insurance. The policy she found was astonishingly expensive, but, I reasoned, it was money well spent. When Osman heard how much the insurance cost, he howled with laughter.

"Everyone knows that fire insurance doesn't work," he said.

"What do you mean, it doesn't work?"

"The only way to keep the fire away," Osman maintained, "is with a frog."

I raised an eyebrow. "A frog?"

"*Oui,* Monsieur Tahir."

"Can you explain?"

Osman acted out the method with his hands. "First you catch a frog, then you kill it, dry it out, rub it in salt, and hang it outside the front door."

"But what good is that if the house catches fire?"

Osman seemed surprised at my question. "If the house starts to burn," he said matter-of-factly, "you pull down the frog and put it in your pocket."

"And?"

"And when you go into the building, the flames will not harm you."

A MAN WITH A donkey cart took to selling cactus fruit outside the house. You knew he was there when you heard his cricketlike cry. There was something comforting about it. We would take it in turns to mimic him as we sat out on the verandah, wondering if the architect's building team would ever arrive. Overhead, flocks of white ibis could be seen as the afternoons eased into dusk. They were flying out to sea, toward the setting sun, their wings tinged with gold. I have never seen anything quite so beautiful.

One autumn morning a thick salty mist blew in from the Atlantic like dragon's breath. It consumed the Caliph's House and the garden and muffled the commotion of the shantytown. Hamza wasted no time in running round opening all the doors and windows as wide as he could. The vapor seeped silently into the main body of the house. I was in the shower when he rushed in and thrust the window open.

"The fog will bring *baraka*," he said as he ran toward the next room. "It will purify the house! We are blessed!"

By midafternoon the mist was gone, scotched by the sun's warmth. It was as if a spell had been broken and reality returned. To me, the place seemed unchanged, but Hamza was certain a divine transformation had occurred.

"It smells different," he said. "I have worked here a long time and I can smell it."

I told him I didn't agree. I said the mist was just water vapor and it had nothing to do with purification, *baraka*, or Jinns.

The guardian was usually willing to argue his case. But on this occasion he slid his hands into his pockets, took a shallow breath, and said: "Of course, Monsieur Tahir. You are quite right."

ONE MORNING ZOHRA ARRIVED at Dar Khalifa in tears. Her eyes were bloodshot. I asked her what was the matter. She brushed me away.

"It's fine," she said, sniffing into a handkerchief. "There's nothing to worry about."

When I asked again, her grief overflowed.

"He left me," she said, weeping on my shoulder. "Yusuf has

broken up with me. He's ended the engagement and gone off with another girl."

I mumbled sympathies. Zohra mopped her face with her scarf.

"I shouldn't have trusted him," she said. "Amina warned me."

"Who's Amina?"

Zohra looked up at me and froze, as if she had let something slip out by mistake. "Oh, um, er," she said, flustered. "She's a friend, a very good friend."

I asked if she was from Casablanca. Again, Zohra appeared uncharacteristically knocked off guard.

"She's not a normal friend," she said.

"Not normal in what way?"

Zohra stopped crying. She held her breath for a moment. "She's not a normal friend," she repeated, "because she is a Jinn."

HICHAM HARASS HAD MOVED to Casablanca twenty years before, when his three children were grown up and his career as a postal clerk had come to an end. Over the years, he had developed an affection for the city, but like almost everyone else, he was embarrassed by it.

"It's a French creation," he told me in one of our first conversations. "Everything about it's French, from the bath taps to the long boulevards. It's amusing," he said, "but it's not really Morocco."

I asked him where to find real Morocco. Hicham's eyes lit up.

"Real Morocco," he said, moistening his lips with his tongue, "it's in the south, far down south, where I was born."

"Where was that?"

"Three days' walk from Agadir."

"Why did you leave?"

The stamp collector rubbed his swollen hands together. "Because of a witch," he said, breaking into a smile.

As a small child, Hicham Harass tended his family's sheep on a rough patch of dust encircled by cactus plants. He lived with his parents, five brothers, a sister, and three dogs in a house made from flotsam scavenged from the Atlantic shore. Their life was simple and uneventful. Then one day a *sehura,* a sorceress, arrived.

"She said I would die within the next cycle of the moon," Hicham explained, blinking, "unless my parents gave me away to the first stranger they met. They were very sad, of course, because I was only seven years old. But they believed the woman."

Hicham stopped talking and watched his three-legged dog amble in and collapse by his feet.

"So they gave me away," he said.

"Who to?"

"To a man called Ayman. He was passing our village, selling scrap metal from a cart. He needed someone to help him, so I went along."

Again, the stamp collector paused. He looked at me hard, as if he were about to say something important.

"The day I left my village on the back of the scrap metal cart was," he said, "the first day of my life."

LATE ONE SEPTEMBER MORNING I was staring out through the giant carved cedar doors from what was to be my library. The view of the courtyard garden could hold my attention for hours on end. I would watch how the light broke through the layers of palm fronds, how the vines had triumphed over every obstacle in their path. At the center of the garden stood a fine date palm. It towered up eighty foot or more, its great spray of fronds throwing zigzagged shade across the whitewashed walls.

The gardener was standing at the base of the palm tree waving an axe. He was shouting at the tree in Arabic.

"Don't you dare cut down that palm!" I yelled.

The gardener, who was the only person on the payroll with genuine fear of me, dropped the axe and waved both hands in front of his chest. "Monsieur Tahir," he whispered fretfully, "I am not going to cut the tree down—I am just threatening it."

"Whatever for?"

"I'm doing it for you," he said.

I didn't understand. "How will I benefit?"

"Because if the tree thinks it is to be chopped down," the gardener said cunningly, "to save itself it will grow the finest dates you have ever tasted."

Just then Hamza came running into the courtyard, hands cupped over his head.

"It's begun! It's begun!" he shouted.

"What has?"

"They have started to break down the shantytown!"

I climbed up onto the roof and surveyed the scene. A pair of dilapidated bulldozers were wheezing down the bidonville's central track. An official was following in a small white car with Arabic lettering on the doors. The usually peaceful residents of the slum had erupted into a frenzy of activity. Women were pulling down their washing at high speed, the vegetable sellers were packing up their stock, and all the schoolchildren were tearing through the narrow alleys, sounding the alert.

The wizened imam stood outside the mosque. His hands were raised in the air, as if someone was pointing a revolver at his chest. A few feet away, the bulldozers were poised to attack the first row of homes. The families who lived in them didn't know whether to run out with their belongings, or to stay inside, hoping it would lead to an act of clemency. The white car shuddered to a stop at the first shack; the official clambered out, a clipboard under his arm. A group of fifty or so men appeared from the alleyways and waved their fists at him. He held the clipboard in the air so that its papers rustled in the light breeze. Then he pointed to the bulldozers. The vehicles revved their engines as if cued to do so.

Somewhere in the fray were Hamza, Osman, and the Bear. I wasn't quite sure where they lived, but I knew very well the shantytown was their home. If the tin-roofed shacks were leveled, they and their families would be homeless. As their employer, it would then fall to me to find them all new places to live.

The standoff continued for an hour or more. The official's clipboard waving on one side, fists on the other, and the bulldozers revving between them. Luck was on the side of the posse. Somehow they managed to cajole the official into ordering the vehicles to retreat. Life in the bidonville instantly resumed its normal routine—women hanging out the clothes, old men crouching in the dust talking of the old days, dogs gnawing at the garbage, and small boys jabbing donkeys with sharpened sticks.

That night I met Hamza as he prowled through the garden with his homemade sword.

"They have given us a week to move away," he said stoically. "After that they are going to smash down our homes."

"Where will all the people go?" I asked.

Hamza cleared his throat. "They have offered us apartments on the outskirts of Casablanca," he said. "But no one has the deposit."

"How much is it?"

"Forty thousand dirhams."

"That's four thousand dollars," I said.

"We can't pay it," he repeated. "No one can. So we will refuse to move."

Owning the Caliph's House was a blessing, but at the same time it was a curse. We had dozens of rooms at our disposal, vast kitchens, many bedrooms with en suite bathrooms, piping-hot water and electricity, endless gardens, stables, a tennis court, and an impressively large swimming pool. I cringed with guilt that we owned so much. A stone's throw away, Hamza, Osman, the Bear, and hundreds of others lived in lean-tos lit by candles. They had no refrigerators or cooking stoves, no running water, proper toilets, or privacy. What little they did have was now under threat.

Before he melted away into the dark, moonless night, I went up to Hamza and asked him about the future.

"What will you all do?"

He clicked his tongue. "We are in God's hands," he said.

A FEW DAYS LATER I bought a dark green Korean-made Jeep. Upgrading from the butcher's car was indescribably pleasing. There was no longer the stink of rotting blood or the scourge of flies. I found that when we drove through the shantytown, people would stop what they were doing and stare. Zohra said the Jeep had *baraka* because it was green, the color of Islam. She said that was why people were looking at it. It was, she whispered, the wisest purchase of my life.

"How can you be so sure?" I asked doubtfully.

"Because Amina says so."

It was a good moment to find out more about the Jinns.

"Tell me, Zohra, where is Amina?" I asked.

"She lives on my left shoulder," she said.

"Can you see her?"

"Oh yes, of course I can."

"What does she look like?"

Zohra thought for a moment. "She's got a beautiful face," she said. "She looks like an angel, and . . ."

"And what?"

"And she's a hundred feet tall."

IN THE THIRD WEEK of September, I was sitting at a café on the Corniche waiting for Zohra when a spindly, earnest-looking foreigner sat down at the table next to mine. He had a slight hunch, and stooped his head as he walked, as if he was used to people being unkind to him. He ordered a cappuccino in dreadful French and pulled out a crumpled copy of the *Herald Tribune*. It was so unusual to meet an English-speaking foreigner that I felt drawn to speak to him. I leaned over and broke the ice.

"Have you been to the dog races?" I asked. "I hear they are very good."

The young man let the newspaper flop onto the table. "I don't have time for dogs," he replied in a soft Texan drawl.

"Oh," I said. "What a pity."

The American put a hand to his brow to shade the light, and looked at me hard. "I'm hoping not to be in Casablanca any longer than I need to," he said.

"Are you on business?"

The foreigner looked down. "Kinda."

I waited for him to elaborate.

"I'm looking for someone," he said.

"Oh."

"Yes, I'm looking for a girl."

I thought instantly of Zohra, who was in urgent need of a man now that Yusuf from cyberspace had deserted her.

"I may be able to help you," I said. "I have a friend—"

The American cut in: "You don't understand," he said quickly. "I'm searching for someone I knew back in the U.S." He licked the milk froth from his lips. "Well, actually I hardly knew her," he said.

"Morocco's a long way to come to find someone you hardly know."

He stretched out a hand. "I'm Pete," he said.

As I was still waiting for Zohra, I asked if I might hear more of the details of his search. The Texan drained his cappuccino and told the tale. It had begun at a crowded nightclub in Amarillo, Texas, where he had gone dancing with college friends. Across the crowded dance floor he set eyes on the most radiant girl he had ever seen. She had full lips, high cheekbones, and long auburn hair. Without wasting a moment, Pete had hurried over, and the two began to dance. The girl seemed to like him as much as he liked her. When they took a break to have a drink, she told him she was from Morocco, that her name was Yasmine, and that she would be returning home for good at the end of the week.

Pete took a photo of her with his cellular phone. Then the phone started ringing. He motioned for Yasmine to wait at the bar while he ran outside to take the call. When he was ready to come back in, the doorman barred his way. No amount of pleading worked.

"When I finally managed to slip through the bathroom window," said Pete, "Yasmine wasn't there. I looked everywhere. She must have left through the front while I was coming in the back." He wiped the thin chocolate mustache from his mouth. "I have to find her," he said.

"You've come all this way to find a girl you danced with once?"

He confirmed that he had. "If I don't try to find her," he said, "I'll never sleep soundly again."

"What are your leads, then?"

Pete pulled out an American cell phone and showed me the indistinct picture of a dark-haired girl.

"Do you know her last name?"

Pete shook his head. "Who gives out their last name in a disco?" he said.

"Do you have anything else to go on?"

Again, his head shook left, then right. "Nothing, except . . ."

"Except what?"

"It may sound crazy, but at the nightclub Yasmine ordered an orange juice. She said the most delicious oranges in the world came from her village in Morocco. If I find that village, then I'm sure I'll find Yasmine."

SHORTLY AFTER THE AFTERNOON call to prayer, there was a knock at the front door. Hamza always insisted vehemently that he, and only he, should ever let visitors into the house. Explaining this, he said that in Moroccan culture an important man would never stoop to perform such a lowly action as opening the door to his own home. By merely touching the handle, I was bringing shame on the house. As I made my way over to the entranceway, the guardian thrust me aside and lunged at the door's bolt.

A woman was standing on the other side, waiting to be received. I recognized her as the gangster's wife. She was wearing a tailored leopardskin coat with a matching hat, and knee-length ivory boots. Her eyelids were weighed down with furry fake lashes, and her face was so caked in makeup that it looked as if she had stepped from the lead role in a Kabuki play. She introduced herself as Madame Nafisa Maliki.

I would have asked why her husband had paid twenty thousand dollars to have our paperwork hidden or destroyed, but something stopped me. Instead, I welcomed her formally and led the way inside the house. Hamza hissed loudly as we walked into the empty salon. The woman's furry eyes scanned the room.

"I see you are doing some building work," she said coldly.

"Just a little," I replied.

"Do you have permission from the authorities?"

"Um, er, well," I fumbled, "yes, of course we do."

"That's good," she said, "because in Morocco the authorities are very strict." She cleared her throat forcefully as if to make a

point. "If your paperwork isn't in order, they can take away your house."

"I am sure that won't happen," I said.

There was a pause, in which the gangster's wife lit a cigarette and stuffed the end into an extra-long holder.

"You never know," she said.

AT DAWN THE NEXT day, forty workers arrived, led by a foreman who was at least eighty years old. The entire team were dressed in suits as if they were going to a wedding. I would normally have barked at anyone turning up so early, but I was so thrilled they had come, I took them into the kitchen and served them mint tea.

The workers set about smashing down the wooden staircase that led up to our bedroom. The planks were chopped into matchwood by an apprentice and stacked very neatly against the wall. A crude, homemade ladder was swung into place, to the fury of Rachana but to the delight of Ariane. Five of the men scaled the ladder, marched into the bedroom, and tossed our bedding out onto the terrace.

I went down to see what the rest of the workforce were up to. The ferocious sound of hammers soon lured me back upstairs. To my disbelief, the men—who said they were masons—were breaking down one of the bedroom's supporting walls. They indicated in primitive sign language that the room was to be enlarged, and so one wall had to go. We would have to find somewhere else to sleep, they said.

On the ground floor, another group had started ripping up the floors. I protested, saying that some of the tilework could stay.

"It's damaged," said the ancient foreman.

"Well, it is now that your men have hacked it up!"

By midday the interior of the house looked as if the Horde of Genghis Khan had stormed through. The floors were ripped up, broken tiles flung about in all directions, and most of the windows were smashed for no reason at all. Water pipes and electrical cables had been hunted down and chopped up, and any wall that had been intact that morning was damaged now. The builders appeared very satisfied with their efforts. In the afternoon, they lit a fire, fueled by the chopped-up staircase, and brewed a colossal urn of chicken stew. When the bones had been picked clean, they spread out in the salon and fell into a deep childlike sleep.

I plucked up courage to call the architect. His smooth voice inquired after my health and praised my good sense for staying calm.

"The first days can be a little disorderly," he said.

"Your men are doing a lot of damage," I protested. "They're smashing up the house."

"It's all in the name of renovation," came the reply. "Have faith in me. Don't worry about a thing."

THE BUILDERS WERE NOT my only concern. Since being ditched by her beloved Yusuf, Zohra had begun to behave in an increasingly peculiar way. She took to wearing black, ringed her eyes in kohl, and tied her hair back in a bun like an old matron. I assumed it was an expression of her grief. When I asked if she was coping, she lashed out.

"You can't understand!" she said. "You're a stupid man!"

She began to turn up less and less for work, and when I did ask her to do anything, she said she was busy. I didn't know what to do. The guardians were always eager to dish out suggestions, but their own rock-solid belief in the spirit world prejudiced their advice. So I met François for lunch. Through the main course he listened patiently to my problems with the workers, and the guardians' obsession with the Jinns. During dessert I explained about Zohra's hundred-foot friend.

"When you've got talk of Jinns," François said, "you've got nothing but trouble."

"What can I do?"

The Frenchman sighed. "You'll have to fire your assistant," he said. "Get rid of her right now. If you don't, the cancer will spread, and things will get much, much worse."

The timing of François's advice was curious. I had planned to meet Zohra that evening at a café to discuss the work at the house. She was often late, and so after forty minutes of waiting, I didn't think much of it. I was about to pay the bill and go home when I received a text message on my phone. It was from Zohra.

"You are a bad man," it read. "The Jinns will kill you. You have no luck. God help you."

I tried calling Zohra's number, but there was no reply. The next day she sent me an e-mail. It was six pages long, a rant about lies and deceit. It said she had informed the police that I was a terrorist, and that she had taken sanctuary in the mountains with what was "rightfully hers." "Amina knows the truth," it said ominously toward the end, "and the truth is clear like glass."

I went straight to my bank to check that no money was missing. But it was. A little over four thousand dollars was gone.

EARLY OCTOBER WAS A terrible time. Each day brought new problems, and I began to feel that moving to Morocco was the worst decision I had ever made. Doing the simplest things, like paying a bill or communicating with the authorities, was a further burden that made life exceedingly difficult. The missing paperwork was another dilemma, one that needed local know-how. As for the builders, they were proving to be hopeless. It was not that I was losing control, because I had never had control. I kicked myself for early kindness. I'd paid money in advance to anyone who asked for it, in the hope it would solve problems.

I reflected about Zohra a great deal, pondering why she had felt it necessary to run off. Rather than boiling over with anger, the episode had made me very sad. I found myself slipping into depression. I missed the ordinariness of England—the land where nothing extreme ever takes place. I missed the dreary gray skies, the drab conversations about nothing at all, and, to my own astonishment, I even missed the food.

AS THE FIRST WEEK of October came to an end, the Bear charged into the bedroom where we were now living like refugees. It was late morning, and I was still huddled under the duvet, reluctant to get up and face the world.

"Monsieur Tahir," he said fearfully, "there has been an accident."

I leapt out of bed and hurried down the long corridor to the verandah, where a group of workmen were clustered. In the middle of the pack, a man was lying on the ground on his side. He was still breathing, but it was clear that at least one of his legs was broken, and possibly an arm. The old foreman pointed up to a glass roof fifteen feet above. I could easily make out the shape of a man framed in broken glass. It looked like a cartoon.

"He fell through there," he said.

"It's a miracle he isn't dead," I replied. "You'd better call the architect."

"I already have," said the foreman.

Ten minutes later, we made out the purr of the Range Rover gliding through the shantytown. The architect stormed into the house and looked down at the injured worker. He roared at the foreman, clapped his hands until they were red, and fired off a salvo of orders.

"It's bad, isn't it?" I said weakly.

"Oh no," he replied. "Absolutely nothing to worry about, these little things happen from time to time."

I voiced my concern at the lack of safety measures. After all, there were no hard hats, or gloves, or goggles, nothing in the way of protection, and all the ladders were cobbled together from scrap wood as and when they were needed.

"This is the way we do things in Morocco," the architect said, smoothing back an eyebrow with his fingertip. "There are injuries, but they can't be helped."

"Won't the man sue?" I whispered anxiously.

"Of course not" was the casual riposte, "this is Casablanca, not Colorado."

"Well then, I'd like to buy him a radio or something," I said. "He'll be in hospital for a long time. I want to show that we care."

The architect's face quivered. "No, no, no, that would be a bad idea," he said. "If you do that, all the others will be throwing themselves off the roof. You don't understand the Moroccan mind."

THE WEEK THAT FOLLOWED was beset with more trouble. On the Monday, the cook managed to slash her wrist with a fruit knife. Gallons of blood spurted over the kitchen walls like a scene from a horror movie. Remarkably, she survived. The next day, the gardener fell off his ladder while pruning a hedge, and on the Wednesday, I got knocked off my feet by a powerful electric shock as I turned on the kitchen lights. The Thursday was quiet, although I did find a pool of blood in what was to be the dining room. Despite an investigation, no one owned up to having lost it. Then, on Friday, the pièce de résistance . . .

We had just finished eating lunch on the terrace when we heard the sound of a fist pounding at the garden door. It was followed by loud cries in Arabic, what sounded like threats. Hamza and Osman appeared from nowhere. They jumped at the door, held it shut, and sent the Bear to rally the workmen. A minute later there were twenty men on our side holding the door shut.

I went over and asked Hamza who was trying to break down the door from the other side.

"It's the police," he said.

"Shouldn't we let them in?" I said.

"Monsieur Tahir, *s'il vous plaît!*" he retorted. "Of course we should not let them in."

As we stood there blocking the path of the authorities, I realized I still had much to learn about Morocco and the way things were done. In England we are raised to have a certain respect for the police. We may not like them, but we feel bound to do as they ask, whether we like it or not. If a squad of English bobbies tried to knock down your door, most people would consider themselves obliged to open it and inquire why they had come.

"Hamza," I said, "why are the police trying to break down the door?"

The guardian looked askance. "You don't have permission to do building work," he said.

"Don't I?"

"No, of course you don't. No one ever does."

"Then is this normal, then, the police hammering at the door?"

Hamza's spirits rose. "Oh yes, Monsieur Tahir," he said, "it happens all the time."

Six

A lame crab walks straight.

MISFORTUNE CONTINUED TO hound us. Household accidents decreased, but other forms of ill fortune arrived. First came the locusts. Their camouflage made them hard to see. But when my eyes had adjusted to picking out their segmented forms, I saw them all over the garden. They covered the hedges and the shrubs, the vines and the low boughs of the trees, and they consumed whatever they could get into their miniature mouths. Their territory spread from the end of the garden to the top of the house. Before we knew it, they were in the store-room and in the cupboards and in our beds, in the laundry and even in the food.

The balance of nature prevailed, and the plague of locusts was slaughtered by the rise of the rats. At the end of the second week of October, the savage, thickset rodents were almost everywhere the locusts had been. An easy supply of locust meat had made them strong and brave. They caused extensive damage. My files and all my books were chewed to pieces, as were Ariane's toys and Timur's quilt, and almost all the food in the larder was destroyed. They gnawed holes in sacks of cement as well, and shredded our duvet to make a nest. Ariane's soft leather shoes were eaten in the night. All that was left were the buckles.

I told Hamza to go and buy ten tubes of the rat-catching glue. He shook his head and said the only way to dispose of a plague of rats was to get a fierce dog. The bigger the dog, he said, the better.

"Why do you think the bidonville has so many dogs?" he intoned.

"For the rats?" I guessed.

"Precisely."

"Can't we just get a cat?" I said. "Rats are scared of cats."

Hamza burst out laughing. "In Morocco," he said boastfully, "rats eat the cats for breakfast."

Again, I instructed him to put out more cardboard strips laden with glue. The method had already proved its effectiveness.

"I told you," he said. "It's too late for glue. We need to spray the garden in poison!" he exclaimed. "Every blade of grass must be covered, and every centimeter of the house!"

Mindful of the children's safety, I told him not to use poison. Instead, I promised to find the most ferocious dog money could buy.

THE SUBJECT OF CHILD safety reemerged the next day. Ariane was found under the kitchen table by the cook, vomiting uncontrollably. Her face was scarlet, her breathing strained. Beside her was an open tub of oily white cream. It had a pungent smell, like drain cleaner. The label's script was Arabic; it bore the image of a grinning, fair-faced woman in Moroccan dress. We set to work trying to get Ariane to throw up more while waiting for the pediatrician to arrive. The cook, who had bulbous eyes and a swarthy complexion, was pacing up and down on edge. I asked her what the cream was for.

"I want to be fair like you and Madame," she said.

I repeated my question: "Fatima, what's the cream for?"

"It's for bleaching my face," she said.

ALL THAT WEEK I searched for a dog. The pet stores offered prim little Pekinese, bichons frises, and jittery poodles with silk bows tied all over them.

"These won't do," I explained to the sales staff. "I'm not looking for a lapdog. I want a blood-crazed demon dog, wild enough to devour a plague of rats!"

After much searching, I was given the number of a man who was rumored to own a German shepherd. He lived in an apartment and felt bad keeping his animal cooped up all day. The dog was seven months old. I asked if it was ferocious. The owner's voice trembled on the telephone.

"Of course not, monsieur," he said reassuringly. "She has a lovely character."

"What a shame," I said. "You see, I want a vicious dog. The wilder, the better."

The man thought for a moment. "Well," he said acidly, "I suppose if you want her to be aggressive, you could treat her very badly."

In the afternoon, I tracked down the man's apartment in fashionable Maarif. The German shepherd was brought out. As soon as she saw me, she gave me her paw and licked my face. Then she rolled on her back and whimpered.

"I'm desperate," I said. "I'll take her."

BACK AT THE HOUSE, I let the new rat-killing hound into the garden. But the rats were already dead or dying—cut down in their prime by a mysterious affliction. The carnage made for a terrible sight. There were dying rats everywhere. You couldn't walk two yards without stepping on one. Ariane was bawling her eyes out. She had grown to like them.

I took Hamza aside and quizzed him.

"I sprinkled a few pellets of poison," he said.

"A few pellets could not have caused death on such a scale," I replied. "How much poison did you use?"

The guardian rubbed his eyes. "Five bags," he said.

At that moment, the German shepherd began chewing at something on the lawn. It was a dead rat. I lunged for her mouth and prised the jaws apart. Thankfully, her teeth hadn't reached the rodent's stomach. I ordered Hamza to pick out every pellet of poison and to burn the dead rats. He would rather have tossed them over the wall into the bidonville, as he did with the trash. Do that, and we would have killed all the dogs in the shantytown.

Hamza was about to ask me something when he slapped a hand to the back of his neck.

"It's a bee," he said. "It just stung me."

A moment later, the colonnaded corridor was filled with bees. They were swarming. I couldn't believe it. First locusts, then rats, and now bees—all in the same week.

"What's going on?" I said. "I've never known anything like this."

But Hamza wasn't listening. He was dancing.

"Have you been stung again?"

"No, Monsieur Tahir," he said, "I am happy. Bees are a blessing sent by Allah!"

A FEW DAYS LATER, peace began to return to Dar Khalifa. Gone were the locusts, the rats, and the bees. The only scourge left were the oversized mosquitoes. They infested the house, where they tormented Ariane the most. She had an allergy to them. Her eyes swelled up like tennis balls when she was bitten. The pediatrician suggested getting the garden sprayed with insecticide.

When we moved to Morocco, I was not overly superstitious, but as time went on, I found myself wondering if someone had put some kind of curse on us. It was the easiest way of explaining the run of bad luck. You can't live in North Africa without being affected by the ingrained belief in superstition. It's everywhere. The more you think about it, the more it seeps into your bones. I was used to hard luck, but there was usually a gap between the waves of misfortune. In Casablanca, bad luck came in three dimensions.

One evening I was pondering the subject when Osman approached my desk gingerly. We were all invited to his home the next day, he said. I thanked him.

"What is the occasion?"

The guardian ducked his head. "It's my son's circumcision."

THAT NIGHT I COULDN'T sleep. Perhaps it was a mixture of accident and pestilence, or the greater worry that someone was trying to frighten us away. My mind was entertained by images of pools of warm blood, dead rodents, and the gangster's wife. I sat up in bed. Ariane and Timur were sound asleep, but Rachana wasn't there. She wasn't in the bathroom either, so I crept through the house to the kitchen. It was empty.

The guardians took it in turns to patrol at night, armed

with Hamza's homemade sword. But they, too, seemed to have vanished. The moon was nearing fullness, and the warm night air was alive with bats and with nocturnal sounds from the shantytown—the savage dogs fighting, setting off the donkeys and the hobbled mules. I walked all around the house, calling Rachana's name. To my alarm, she didn't reply. I climbed the makeshift ladder and searched the upper floor and the terrace. After that I looked in the outbuildings and in the garden. I suddenly realized I had forgotten to look in the courtyard garden. I rushed over, my bare feet tramping through the dirt.

"Rach! Rach!" I called. "Are you there?"

On the verandah beside the locked door, a figure was standing very still in a flowing white robe. It was Rachana.

"I have to go in there," she said very softly.

"What are you doing here? Come back to bed."

She resisted my arm.

"No, you don't understand. I have to go in there."

"Why?"

"I don't know."

"The key's lost," I said.

"Then break open the door. Do it now."

I called out for the guardians. No one came at first. Then, after a few minutes I could hear the Bear's heavy step moving across the terrace outside.

"*Oui, monsieur,*" he said balefully. "What is it?"

"We have to go into this room right now," I said. "Get me the crowbar."

The Bear spat out excuses. "There is no key," he said. "Only Hamza can go in there."

"I don't care. I own this house and I am going in there, do you understand?"

The Bear swallowed hard. He disappeared, returning a minute later with a jimmy. In the beam of his flashlight, I wedged the end of the steel bar into the crack and levered as hard as I could. The lock snapped. I pushed the door inward. The lights weren't working. We crept inside and I shone the beam over the walls. They were discolored with algae. The room was freezing. It smelled of death.

"Can you smell that?" Rachana said.

I grunted. "Let's go," I said.

"No, not yet."

Rachana walked into the anteroom, to the left of the door. She took the light and shone it upward. The ceiling was high, at least twenty-five feet. Then she moved the beam down to the floor. I edged closer to get a better view.

"Do you see that?" she said.

"My God, there are steps going down."

THE CIRCUMCISION ATTRACTED ALL the main players from the shantytown to Osman's modest home. Hamza, the Bear, and the gardener were there, too, as were their wives. Osman's own wife was flustering about making sure that everyone had a glass of sweet mint tea. She had a checkered scarf tied over her head and was wearing her best jelaba. It was violet and had a trace of pink embroidery around the neck.

In the middle of the small room was Ahmed. Having recently reached the grand age of five, the boy was about to pass through Islamic ritual to manhood. He was dressed in a sky blue three-piece suit with matching bow tie and a pleated dress shirt. On his head was perched a green tarboosh, and on his feet were shiny black shoes.

Ahmed showed off a new bicycle his father had bought for him, before being prodded outside into the dusty street. In front of the tin-roofed shack, a man was holding the reins of a slender gray horse. I wondered where such a magnificent animal had come from. Osman lifted the boy up, and the horse was paraded about through the heaps of rotting garbage. Unsure of what to do, Rachana and I clapped.

"This will be the happiest day of his life," said Osman, the smile even broader than normal beneath his handlebar mustache.

Under the circumstances, I might have disagreed. A few seconds later, little Ahmed was wrenched from the horse's back and dragged into the house, where his miniature suit trousers were whipped down. An unshaven hulk of a man loomed over the child, who was now pinned out on a low table. I recognized him as the street-stall barber from the shantytown. Osman ordered his son to be brave. I gulped. Rachana gulped, and Ariane burst into tears as the infant's penis was remodeled by the barber's scissors.

The crowd of family and guests pressed in close to gain a good view as little Ahmed's lungs swelled with air. There was no sound at first. Then the screaming began. It went on and on, rising sharply in volume, as the boy understood the scope of the operation.

"Ah," Osman exclaimed as his son writhed in agony before him, "this surely is the finest day of his life."

AT FIRST, I COULD not bring myself to ask Rachana why she had wanted to go into the locked room. I feared what she would say. We didn't talk about it the next morning. When I saw Hamza raking leaves in the garden, he didn't mention it either. I went up to him and asked where the stairs led.

"You should not have gone in there," he replied.

"Why?"

The guardian didn't say. He looked down at the leaves and continued with his raking. Leaving him to it, I went back to the locked door. To my surprise, the lock had been replaced.

Rachana could tell I was thinking about what had happened the previous night. She wouldn't look me in the eye all day. At last, in the evening, when the children were asleep in bed, she turned to me.

"I had to go in there," she said in a trembling voice. "I don't know why, or what it was about. But something happened in there. Didn't you feel it?"

I said I had felt something, a coldness, a danger.

"That's it," she added. "It was danger. Pure fear."

"I'm sure Hamza knows about that room," I said after a long pause.

"He won't tell," she replied, "at least not until he's ready to."

I looked hard at Rachana, her long black hair framing the edges of her face.

"Are you frightened living here?" I asked.

She didn't reply at first, as if she was reflecting on the question.

"I don't know," she said. "I don't know."

TWO DAYS LATER, I received a postcard from Pete, the American who had fallen in love with the Moroccan girl he met in the Amarillo nightclub. The picture showed a grove of orange trees weighed down by fruit, and a dark-skinned man inspecting the crop. The black ballpoint script on the reverse read: *You will never believe it! Have found Yasmine! She loves me! See you. Pete. PS: Some problems with her family.*

THE NEXT WEEK WAS painfully slow to pass. The building team arrived at eight each morning. They were always dressed in suits and led into the house by their aged foreman. He would insist on smothering my cheeks in kisses while his men set about cooking an elaborate breakfast on a gas burner in the main salon. Whenever I drew their attention to the fire hazard, they would cackle menacingly. As far as they were concerned, safety was for wimps.

The extension of our bedroom was progressing at a snail's pace, but at least it was under way. A forest of wooden staves was now holding up the ceiling. Large quantities of low-grade bricks were being lugged up the homemade ladders by the apprentices.

"They're doing hard work," I said.

"They must know pain," said the old foreman gleefully. "Only a man who has tasted pain knows the value of life."

Downstairs in the salon the giant holes in the walls, created by the efficient wrecking crew, were being sculpted into rounded arches. A man in a red felt hat was overseeing the work. Each archway took about a week to complete and involved an army of masons. The process was remarkably complex. A positive form of the arch was first constructed. The archway was laid in around it, and the positive—a kind of mold—was then removed.

The architect's grand plan to build a sweeping staircase from the new bedrooms upstairs to the salon below was in progress as well. The feature had necessitated destroying a pair of sizeable storage rooms and the laundry room. I had questioned why such valuable rooms had to go. All doubts had been brushed away by the architect's manicured hand.

"Why do you need those useless spaces?" he had sniffed. "They just collect dust."

Once I had paid all the money in advance, the architect himself was an infrequent visitor to the Caliph's House. From time to time he would swoop down for fifteen minutes, roar at his workers, and reveal the next stage of his grand plan. None of them ever dared ask a question, and to my surprise, they were given no scaled drawings. There was no paperwork of any kind. I managed to collar the architect on one lightning visit.

"Don't your team need plans to work by?" I asked.

"In Morocco," the architect said with confidence, "we don't do it like that."

"Do you trust them so completely?"

Mohammed, the architect, opened the door of his vehicle and lit a cigar. "I don't trust any of them," he said. "They are a bunch of thieves."

"How do you know they're not robbing you?"

"Because I have a spy," he said.

"The old foreman?"

The architect laughed. "Not him. He's the worst of all. The man with the red cap. He tells me what's really going on."

The system of informants buoyed my flagging spirits. I went back into the salon and winked at the man in the red cap. He winked back, and was about to say something when the foreman slapped him on the back of the head and ordered him to get back to work.

The old man then strode over to the staircase, the curved form of which had taken shape. He pulled off his worn tweed hat and scratched his head. Five new walls had been constructed around the staircase, and the foreman gazed at them. He scratched again. Then he yelled at one of the apprentices. The boy handed him a hammer and chisel. With uncharacteristic care, the elderly foreman put the chisel to one of the walls and began to tap very gently. I was going to stop him from destroying the only satisfactory work the men had done. But as I opened my mouth to protest, the end of the chisel disappeared into the wall.

"What is it?" I asked anxiously. "What's there?"

The foreman peered into the opening, no larger than a key-hole. "There's a room in there," he said.

"You seem surprised."

"We didn't know about it," he replied.

Someone passed me a flashlight. My stomach knotted in anticipation. I held up the light and I had a look for myself. It was like peering into Tutankhamen's tomb. The beam disappeared into what was a considerable space.

"It's huge," I said.

"It was sent by God," said one of the apprentices.

"*Allahu akbar!*" cried another. "God is great!"

IN THE THIRD WEEK of October the rain began to fall. It rained and rained in a chill North African monsoon. The God who had sent us the miracle of the lost room was now trying to drown us. Dar Khalifa leaked like a sieve. Water streamed in through the open doorways and the broken windows, and surged down into the salon from the roof. The room in which Rachana, the children, and I slept flooded. We were forced to move to higher ground.

The constant rain made mixing and pouring the concrete almost impossible. I was surprised that the team bothered to go on. One morning they knocked away the wooden staves that were holding up the roof of our bedroom extension. It was a wildly optimistic move. The concrete ceiling held for about thirty seconds before crashing down.

Another police raid followed, and after it came a string of new injuries. And the rain fell day after day. I don't know why I didn't throw in the towel and lead us all back to England. It wasn't that I was fearful of the sneers and the jibes. Deep down I knew that it was a question of endurance. If I could keep going beyond the point of reason, then, as I saw it, there was a faint glimmer of hope. So I resigned myself to keep standing, like a punch-drunk boxer who simply had to stay upright to win. Keep on my feet and, I hoped, the dark days would eventually come to an end.

THE GREATEST DAILY CHALLENGE was trying to make myself understood. My French is not good. The guardians and some of the workers had learned to understand me, but a great deal of Casablancans spoke only Arabic and no French at all. So I decided to look for another assistant.

I placed an advertisement on a local website. It sought two qualities—the ability to solve problems and to be enthusiastic at all times. No one replied. I was going to drop the whole idea when a man called. It was three in the morning and the man wanted to know if the position had been filled. He had a composed voice, with the trace of an American accent.

"It's early," I said, fumbling for my watch.

"Actually, it's late," said the voice.

I saw the time. "It's very early!" I said coldly.

There was a silence.

"It's very late," the voice replied. "When can you meet?"

We arranged to meet at noon, near Dar Khalifa, at Hotel Suisse. I turned up on time, having trudged through the shantytown's mud in the torrential rain. There was no sign of the job applicant. I scribbled a page of interview questions to pass the time. After half an hour of waiting, I assumed he wasn't going to show up, and I went home.

HAMZA WAS CROUCHED OVER in the mud at the end of the garden, mixing a bag of sand with cement. Osman was standing beside him, holding an umbrella over them both. I went over and inquired what they were doing.

"It's a surprise," Hamza said bashfully.

In the house the workmen were sitting on the floor eating couscous. When he saw me, the foreman got up, staggered over, and kissed my cheeks.

"You are a good man," he said, kissing me again.

I thanked him for the compliment.

"May you have a thousand sons!" he exclaimed, with another kiss.

I thanked him again.

"May your feet always walk on rose petals!"

He stooped to kiss again. I covered my cheeks and narrowed my eyes.

"What do you want?" I said suspiciously.

The foreman tugged off his tweed cap and held it over his chest. "We want for you to like us," he said.

IN THE AFTERNOON, THE man with the American accent called once again. He said a drunk driver had smashed into his car on his way to the interview.

"Were you injured?"

"I wasn't in the car at the time," said the man.

"Oh," I said, confused.

We planned to meet at the same hotel in the early evening. Again, I waited for half an hour, and again, the man didn't turn up. I cursed him for wasting my time and trudged back through the mud.

It was dark but Hamza was still working at the end of the garden. The ochre-red mud was deep from all the rain. Hamza's clothes were covered in it, but he didn't care. He had made what looked like a section of wide concrete pipe. It was laid end down on the ground. Sitting across the top was a homemade turning mechanism and a rubber bucket.

"It's a well," he said.

I peered into it. "There's no water in there," I said. "There's not even a hole."

Hamza brushed my concerns aside. "It's for the Jinns," he said.

JUST BEFORE I GOT into bed, the job applicant called again. I was going to shout something rude and hang up. But before I could say a word, he asked for our address.

"I'll be there in ten minutes," he said.

"You'll never find it. We live in the middle of a shanty-town."

Precisely ten minutes later there was a rap at the door. The applicant stepped into the house calmly, shook my hand, and looked away as he did so. His name was Kamal Abdullah. He was thin, balding, and aged twenty-five. He looked at least ten years older. His eyes were deep-set and distant, his long face bisected by a pencil-line mustache. We sat in the salon on plastic garden chairs, listening to the downpour outside. I was waiting for an apology, but it didn't come.

"We're doing some building work," I said, glancing at the mess.

Kamal scanned the walls and then looked over at the pile of sacks. "They're using thirty-five-grade cement," he said. "They should be using the higher grade—forty-five. If they don't, the roof will collapse."

"It already did," I said.

I didn't demand Kamal's family tree. Instead, I asked him about his life.

"I'm from a small town in the east of Morocco," he said in a quiet voice. "But I grew up in Casablanca. I lived in the States for seven years, mostly in Atlanta and New York. I did a thousand jobs—Arby's, Hardee's, Dairy Queen. Thought I'd never come back."

"Why did you?"

"Circumstances." Kamal moistened his lips with the tip of his tongue. "You never know what life's going to throw at you," he said.

SEVEN

*An army of sheep led by a lion would defeat
an army of lions led by a sheep.*

A GANG OF MISCHIEVOUS BOYS BEGAN wreaking havoc in
the shantytown. They stole smaller boys' homemade toys, threw
stones at the limping dogs, jabbed sharpened sticks at the
donkeys, and tripped up the old women as they stumbled
home from the communal well. The schoolmistress said she
would beat them senseless with her orange hose if she caught
them. The furrow-faced imam slapped the backs of his hands
together.

"If I catch them," he said, "I'll hang them up by their ears."

As he was the only applicant for the position, I took Kamal
on. From the outset, it seemed to me as if there were an invisible expiration date tattooed on the back of his neck. I didn't
expect him to last very long. After the debacle with Zohra and
her Jinn, my expectations were very low.

To my surprise, Kamal was punctual on the first day. He arrived at the house wearing a charcoal gray suit and a bulky Italian-made diver's watch strapped to his left wrist. His lips were tight together. If I asked him anything, he responded with a carefully considered answer and closed his mouth again. He didn't seem fond of idle chatter. When presented with a problem, he thrived on it. My first impression was that he was a loner, someone whose eyes had seen too much.

I gave a string of orders.

"We need the garden sprayed for insects," I said, "that old windmill above the well has to be dismantled, and the heap of wood in the vegetable patch taken away."

Kamal didn't take notes. He followed me quietly, his mouth clenched shut, hands behind his back.

"What else?" he asked.

"Well, there's so much more," I said. "For a start, we need to buy a bath, and a satellite dish, and someone has to fix the pool. We have to get safety railing made, to buy fire extinguishers, and to get the windows fixed."

I had an appointment with an official from the British consulate, and so I left Kamal to it and traipsed through the shantytown's mud to find a cab. The Korean Jeep had ground to a halt. The engine had seized up.

When I got back to the house three hours later, there were people everywhere. More unusual was that they were doing things. Ten men were carting away the logs from the end of the garden; a team of soldiers had scaled the windmill with ropes and were dismantling it; an engineer was repairing the pool pump, someone else was installing a satellite dish, and another man was putting in new windowpanes. I called out to Kamal. His head popped up from the roof.

"Up here," he said.

A moment later he was standing to attention before me, mouth closed, hands behind his back.

"How's it going?" I asked.

"It's under control," he said. "I did a deal with the bakery in the shantytown. They are taking the wood for their oven. They'll pay two hundred dollars for the lot." He asked if that was satisfactory.

"They'll pay us?"

"Of course."

"What about the soldiers?"

Kamal squinted. "Everyone was going to charge a lot of cash," he said, "so I invited the army to remove the windmill as a military exercise. I've done a deal with a scrap metal guy, too. He'll buy the metal for a hundred and fifty bucks. That pays for fixing the pool."

"That's great," I said.

"Not as great as this . . ."

Kamal picked up the television's remote. He pressed a button. There was the grinding sound of a satellite dish rotating on the roof. When it stopped, the screen came alive with what looked like the news from Peru.

"You've got two thousand channels now," he said. "I had a guy hack them for you for free."

"What about the bath?"

Kamal pinched his mustache. "We'll do that later," he said.

The guardians were not impressed by the day's progress. I toured the place with them in tow, showing off the repaired swimming pool pump, the dismantled windmill, and the thousands of television channels. Their faces were long and cold, as if I had betrayed them.

"Monsieur Kamal is not a good man," Hamza said scornfully.

"He will steal the clothes from your back," added Osman.

"He'll steal the house from you," said the Bear.

"Then I'll have to be careful," I said. "But if he can get so many things done in a day, I can't do without him."

THAT NIGHT, WE WERE all kept awake by the sound of a donkey thrashing about in pain somewhere in the bidonville. The poor creature brayed and brayed, as if the end of the world had come. Suspecting the band of unruly boys out on a night journey, I crept into the garden and called to Hamza to go and chase them away. It was a dark night, no more than a sliver of moon hanging above in the cloudy sky. The guardian was down at his ornamental well. He was throwing handfuls of what looked like raw meat into it.

"It'll attract rats," I said, against the echo of the donkey's pain.

"It will protect us," he replied.

We both laughed. And, for the first time, I sensed a warmth between us. I did not believe in Jinns, but I respected the superstition as an expression of a mature culture.

"What are we to do about the Jinns?" I asked him.

Hamza tossed the last few chunks of meat into the waterless well. The sound of the donkey became muffled and then stopped altogether.

"They live at Dar Khalifa," he said. "They have always lived here."

"We could have an exorcism," I said. "We could kick them out."

"You do not chase your grandfather away just because he's old," he replied.

We both stopped speaking. Silence was more appropriate than sound. I breathed in the nocturnal scent of jasmine and listened to the haphazard chorus of the wild dogs. We were both blinkered by our upbringings. I was restricted by the West's scientific ideals, and Hamza by the traditions of his culture. His certainty that Jinns existed was mirrored by my own conviction that they did not. I wondered if we would ever reach a middle ground, a no-man's-land in which one believed but did not believe.

The noise of stray dogs fell away, and the light breeze hushed. I could not recall a moment more peaceful at Dar Khalifa. I treasured it. In the East, silence is regarded as golden, and not the awkward space between conversations, as it is to us. For me, a break in speaking is a fearful thing, a thing to be extinguished as rapidly as possible. But for the first time in a long while, I cherished it.

Eventually it was me who broke the silence.

"Why is the room always kept locked?"

Hamza wiped his hands on his shirt. "I can't say," he said.
"Why?"
"Some things we speak about, and others we do not."
"What happened in there? Did someone die? Is that it?
There was a coldness. A fear. A scent of death."
The guardian sighed. "I cannot talk about those things," he
said. "If you want to know about Dar Khalifa, live here. The
house itself will tell you."

A DAY OR TWO passed. Then one morning, as I staggered
blearily down the long corridor to the kitchen for breakfast, I
was accosted by a man wearing goggles, rubber gloves, and a
chemical suit. On his back was a pressurized tank, and in his
hands was a hose that ran back to the tank.
"Get inside," he said calmly. "This is poison."
He waved an arm vigorously at another man positioned at
the far end of the garden. He was wearing the same outfit, with
an identical tank on his back. The pair switched on their tanks,
and greasy black gas billowed out. They aimed it low at first
into the flowerbeds, then across the shrubs, and finally up into
the trees. Within three minutes it was impossible to see anything at all. It was like being at the center of an industrial accident. The birds fell from the trees and lay stunned on the
ground. I closed my eyes and fumbled back to our bedroom to
warn Rachana and the children not to move.
After we spent an hour cowering there, Kamal arrived. He
had got the pesticide team on the cheap, he said. They were
government employees, but had dropped by before work to
help us out.
Over the next few days, my now assistant solved one problem after the next. I found myself thanking providence for
causing Zohra to run off. Her replacement was far more efficient. He treated me with formality, always called me "Mister,"

and seemed quite unhappy when the day's work was at an end. "I learned to work hard in America," he said one afternoon. "Over there people just get on with it. They don't sit about making up excuses, feeling sorry for themselves, or drinking mint tea all day long. If you work hard in the U.S., you can make good money and," he added, "you can get respect."

But all the while I knew it couldn't last. Such efficiency never does.

We were in a cab, stuck in Casablanca's gridlock traffic, when I asked Kamal what had taken him to the United States in the first place. His glance didn't leave the road. I watched his profile. He swallowed hard.

"There was an accident," he said. "It was a bad one. My mother and my little sister were driving through Spain. A truck hit their car. They both died—my mother first and my sister a few days later."

I expressed sympathy.

"When I was told the news by my father," he went on, "I didn't cry or anything. I was too numb."

"When did it happen?"

"Nine years ago."

"And you left for the States?"

"My family was shattered," he said. "Its heart was ripped out. I didn't speak a word of English . . . but I had to get away. So I took a flight to Georgia—home of Southern hospitality."

THE RAIN BEGAN AGAIN, while the architect's team floundered about like Lotus Eaters in the sun. I dreaded walking through the main body of the house. Nothing there ever changed. The floors were broken up, and the doors had been yanked from their frames; the light switches were smashed, electrical wires hung from the ceiling and walls, a hint at the chaos that lay beneath. Only half the arches were finished, and there was no sign the others would ever be done.

From time to time the foreman would buttonhole me as I hurried through the salon, my eyes covered by my hands. He would smack his lips to my cheeks and wrestle my right hand away to fondle it in his. When Kamal saw the old man greeting me, he barked at him in Arabic.

"He only wants to be friendly," I said tenderly.

"He wants your cash," he quipped. "The holy month of Ramadan starts next week. He's hoping his groveling will be rewarded with your generosity."

Kamal asked about the architect. I said he was a good man with a fondness for fine Cuban cigars.

"Don't give him any money," he said.

"I paid him everything in advance," I muttered. "He asked for it."

"Did he give you a receipt?"

"No, I wired the money into his Paris account."

Kamal rolled his eyes. "Only pay a Moroccan," he said, "if you want to see the back of his head."

BEFORE I MOVED TO Casablanca, my morning bath was typically occupied by the question of how I might escape the shores of England. I like to spend a great deal of time soaking in a tub, controlling the hot tap with my big toe, reflecting on life. Now that we had made the great escape, I wanted a bath in which I could steep myself long and hard and consider the future. It would have to be grand, well made, and built in a time when people understood the glory of soaking.

When I asked Kamal where I could get an antique bathtub, he promised to take me to the best bath showroom in town. I asked if it was in fashionable Maarif. He crimped up his nose.

"Maarif is for hustlers," he said.

I took Kamal to see the Korean Jeep before tramping out in search of the bath. It had been shut up in the garage since the engine had seized. He opened the hood and examined the mechanics before checking the papers and the mileage. He sent for a mechanic—a well-built man with dark murderous eyes and a scraggly gray beard, dressed in overalls so covered in grease that it was impossible to make out their original color.

"Moroccan mechanics are the worst villains alive," Kamal said. "Most of them would kill you without a second thought."

"Are they all villains?" I asked.

Kamal lit a cigarette and nodded in the smoke. "All of them," he confirmed. "All except one."

He jabbed the glowing end of his Marlboro at the man with murderous eyes.

"Hussein here is the only one you can trust," he said.

"How did you find him?"

"He'd lost everything at cards," he said. "His family were staring starvation in the eye. Then my father set him up in business. There's no way he'd ever stab us in the back."

As the mechanic's cruel eyes inspected the engine, I asked about being stabbed in the back.

"It doesn't take much," said Kamal knowingly. "Someone may be jealous 'cause you've got more than them, or they could have a grudge against someone in your family. If that happens, you're in trouble."

"What sort of trouble?"

"You might think Casablanca's modern with its chichi stores and ritzy cars," he said, "but under that façade it's raw. It's African. It's tribal. Never forget that. Slip up, and you'll have the tribe at your heels."

I made a note to bear the warning in mind.

The mechanic's head reappeared. His dark eyes squinted at Kamal and his voice cackled some words.

"Just as I thought," Kamal said.

"What?"

"The engine doesn't match the car. This Jeep's three years old and the junk under the hood's ten years if it's a day."

Kamal took out another cigarette and slid the tip of his tongue down the edge.

"You took your eye off the ball," he said. "The last owner sold the real engine on the side for a load of cash, and he sold you this heap of junk."

He lit the cigarette and exhaled hard.

"It's a classic engine swap," he said.

"Engine swap?"

"Sure. It's the oldest trick in the book."

THE UNITED STATES HAD made a very great impact on Kamal. His return to Morocco in the months before the second Gulf conflict required readjustment. In the States, he had been used to getting things done fast and efficiently. He perfected the arts of wheeling, dealing, talking fast, and covering a lot of ground. Back in Morocco he found life was couched in inertia, as it has been for a thousand years. As I had discovered, if you didn't move forward like a rampaging bull, nothing ever got done at all. Even then, as you charged headlong through the day, you had to keep both eyes open wide.

"Take your eye off the ball," said Kamal often, "and you'll lose everything."

I was impressed by his foresight, especially as I hadn't yet told him of the problems with the neighbor and the missing paperwork. When I did sketch out the situation, he didn't seem surprised.

"That house was empty for years," he said. "It's amazing the wolves didn't rip it up."

"The Jinns kept them away," I said sarcastically.

"You may be right," he said. "I've asked people in the bidonville about Dar Khalifa. Everyone talks about it. They say it's infested with Jinns, hundreds of them. You can't imagine their fear. Without the Jinns it would have been stolen years ago."

MY CONVERSATIONS WITH HICHAM the stamp collector continued. Each week, I would turn up at his shack, step across the three-legged dog, and barter a handful of postage stamps for conversation. We talked about his childhood, and about the years he had spent on the road selling scrap metal from a donkey cart. We talked about Morocco's past, the future, and about the dreams of youth.

Hicham was the kind of man who liked a conversation to have a beginning, a middle, and an end. He didn't approve of chatter for chatter's sake. I got the feeling he took our conversations all the more seriously because they were his side of a strange business contract. He weighed his words against the value of the postage stamps I brought, fragments of colored paper glued to the top right edge of an envelope.

One week I asked if he believed in Jinns.

"Of course I do," he said without a thought. "They are all around us. Their world shapes our own."

"Do you like them?"

The old man looked at me with disbelief. "If they could, they would slit our throats," he said. He scooped a stamp album from the floor and opened it.

"Would they kill us all?"

"Yes, that's why we protect ourselves!" he exclaimed. "We say *Bismillah,* 'in the name of God,' before beginning an action."

That explained why I heard the phrase a thousand times a day. Moroccans utter it before getting into a car, before eating, drinking, even before they sit down.

"Our Jinn is called Qandisha," I said. "He's got the guardians terrified. It's making life difficult."

"They have a good reason to have fear," said Hicham, arranging his stamps. "I've heard Qandisha's very strong, and likes human children. Your children are not safe. They could be snatched at any moment. That is why the guardians are so frightened."

Hicham said Jinns were known for stealing human children in the night, sometimes substituting a Jinn-child in place of the one they take.

"The Jinn-child grows up like one of your own," he said. "You don't suspect anything. Then one night he shakes off his human disguise, rears up as a hideous creature three hundred meters high, and swallows your family whole. Believe me, I tell you the truth."

"What can you do to prevent it?"

The old man put the stamp album down. "There's one way," he said in a grave voice.

"How?"

"You can trick the Jinns. You put mannequins in the children's beds, and tell your children to sleep in the oven each night. Do that, and you will all be safe."

WHENEVER I BEGGED KAMAL to take me to the bath shop, he would insist I was in far too much of a hurry. A bath was a finishing touch, he would say, and we were nowhere near ready for finishing touches. He was right. Throughout the renovations at the Caliph's House, I had a hard time with perspective. I am good at grasping details, but find it near impossible to envisage a project as a whole. I had filled an entire storeroom at Dar Khalifa with finishing touches. They were ready and waiting. There was a championship tennis net, although the tennis court was wasteland covered in rubble, broken bottles, and rotting rats. Beside the tennis net stood a stack of thirty framed paintings of Indian maharajahs ready for the dining room walls, and near to them was a trunk full of cushion covers, and a second brimming with light fixtures, bath soaps, and telephones. But the worst finishing touch of all was a twenty-foot container of Indian furniture I had ordered a few months before. It was on the high seas en route to Casablanca.

A GENUINE ENTHUSIASM TO make use of my finishing touches coaxed me to call the architect. I pleaded with him to send more men, men with the ability to finish the job. I told him about the ship's container filled with furniture that was about to arrive, and about the thousand final details ready for use. As far as he was concerned, I had become just another angry voice on the end of his cellular phone, an angry voice stupid enough to have paid in advance. During our brief conversation, I sensed the architect had moved on, to new, richer pickings of another foreign client.

"Don't worry, my old friend," he said cheerily. "Just relax. The work is wonderful."

"When will they start laying the floor tiles?"

The architect shouted that his car was heading into a tunnel. His phone went dead.

THE NEXT MORNING A team of shabby artisans arrived at the house. They weren't wearing suits like the others. As a result, they appeared rather underdressed. I asked the foreman who they were.

"The tile men for the floors," he said.

My dream was to restore the Caliph's House to its former glory, to a time when it would have been decorated in traditional Arab styles. The wrecking crew had assisted in stripping out any trace of European detail. On this blank canvas, I planned to reinstate the ancient crafts of Morocco—terracotta tiled floors from Fès, known as bejmat; fragments of colored mosaics called zelij, and tadelakt, the fabulous marble-dust-and-egg-white plaster from Marrakech.

As a foreigner learning about Morocco, you quickly get a sense that the place is a treasure trove of tradition, bursting with artistic skill. Western bookstores overflow with beautifully produced photographic books showcasing the arts and crafts of the kingdom. It's easy to imagine that everyone is making use of these age-old crafts, just as they have done for a thousand years. Nothing could be further from the truth.

For generations, the royal family of Morocco have patronized the kingdom's crafts. In succession, they have created astonishing mosques and public gardens and sumptuous palaces. By funding such projects, they have kept the flame of apprenticeship alive and ensured that the traditions are not lost—as they have been across most of the Arab world.

While they revere their cultural heritage, the majority of Moroccans these days go for modern decor. They embellish their houses with wall-to-wall carpets and glittering factory-made tiles, with mass-produced lighting and prefab furniture. Their homes are cozy and easy to clean. And, as I was finding out, the new decor from the West saved them plenty of money and time.

THAT WEEK WHEN I found Hicham Harass sitting alone in his shack behind the mosque, he was despondent. I asked what was wrong.

"Life is wrong," he said grimly. "My son has been killed. He was about your age. He was so alive, so full of life. Then in an instant a car swerved and my boy had the life sucked from his lungs. He is dead. Nothing. Just dead."

Hicham wiped a hand to the tears. They say the only time an Arab man can weep with honor is at the death of his son. I leaned over and held his hand in mine. He reached out and clasped my shoulder.

"We will talk soon," he said.

THE MEN WHO ARRIVED to lay the terracotta floors heaved twenty sacks into the salon and threw them on the floor. The sound of tiles shattering echoed around the unfinished rooms. The artisans declared that they were master craftsmen, the sons of master craftsmen, the grandsons of master craftsmen. Each one, they boasted, was from a line of craftsmen twenty generations long. I was delighted to hear it, and I welcomed them with small patterned glasses of extra-sweet mint tea. The aged foreman seemed unhappy at my display of hospitality. He marched over, wrenched the glasses away, and snarled at the newcomers in Arabic. Then he bore the tray of tea to his own grubby suit-clad team across the room and lurched over to kiss me on the cheeks.

"You're going to have more than problems," said Kamal. "You're going to have meltdown."

A FEW DAYS AFTER the death of Hicham Harass's son, the old stamp collector called unexpectedly at the house. He was dressed in his formal wear—tweed jacket and faded cloth cap. I welcomed him inside and dusted off a green plastic chair in the freezing salon. We sat quietly for about ten minutes. I didn't know what to say. I am awkward when it comes to offering condolences. Sometimes silence with a friend is more memorable than the most animated conversation. Hicham glanced up at me once or twice and strained to smile.

"You may think me strange," he said at length. "But I have a request."

"Of course, anything."

"I hoped I could hold little Timur, as I held my son so many years ago."

I went into our room where Timur was sleeping, fished him out from the cot, and handed him to the old man. He cupped the baby to his heart and closed his eyes.

"You must value every moment," he said.

THAT NIGHT, THE NEW moon was sighted in a cloudless sky, and the holy month of Ramadan began. For Muslims, observing Ramadan is one of the central pillars of faith. It is a time of prayer and strict fasting during daylight hours, when the gates of Heaven are open and those of Hell are shut. During Ramadan, Muslims are forbidden to tell a lie or to think unclean thoughts, and their actions must be cloaked in purity at all times.

No one living in Morocco can escape the holy month, and nowhere is the contrast with regular life greater than in Casablanca. Many of the city's young women preferred to swan about with faces caked in makeup, their youthful bodies stuffed into the skimpiest outfits imaginable. They would spend all day lounging in street-side cafés, preening their hair, gossiping, and smoking imported cigarettes. With the shroud of Ramadan hanging over them, they were forced to do away with makeup and the racy clothing and move around in billowing jelabas, their tasseled hoods dangling down behind. During the day, the cafés were closed, and smoking was forbidden for all.

The French expat, François, had been quick to warn me on the hazards of Ramadan. He said it was thirty days of anguish, when every Moroccan was twice as grumpy as the day before. But worst of all, he said, was that nothing got done.

"What about the building work?" I asked limply.

"Forget it!" he yelled. "You might as well pack up and go home."

"But this is my home."

"Well," said François acerbically, "stay home!"

Like everyone else, Kamal was abstaining from the vices that formed the bedrock of his life. He wasn't drinking, and the cloud of cigarette smoke that normally followed him was gone. He was abstaining from food and drink from before dawn until dusk, and was trying his level best to entertain clean thoughts. At the start of the holy month, he arrived at the Caliph's House in a chauffeured black Mercedes limousine. It had yellow diplomatic license plates and a miniature flagpole on the offside wing.

"I called in a favor," he said by way of explanation.

"Who from?"

"From the ambassador of Mauritania."

I asked Kamal for a rundown on Ramadan.

"It's the lack of sleep that gets to you first," he said. "You eat dinner at midnight, sleep for three hours, then go to the mosque, eat a mouthful of food, sleep a little more, and then get up."

"Ramadan's going to finish off the workers," I said.

"It does have some advantages," Kamal replied.

"Like what?"

"Like when you want to buy a bath."

THE BLACK LIMOUSINE ROLLED up the hill away from the ocean and turned right toward the sprawling new residential zone of Hay Hassani. Hundreds of plain, whitewashed apartment blocks lingered there, crisscrossed with washing lines and filled with people who had realized their universal dream.

"My uncle was mayor of this area," said Kamal as the stretched Mercedes swerved to miss the potholes. "He built the entire place from scratch."

"What kind of people live here?"

"People who have broken free and escaped the slums."

The limousine veered left off the main drag and descended a slope. We passed a man with a homemade cart on which was heaped a pyramid of odds and ends. There was a coffeemaker and a tangle of ropes, a crate of onions and a box of springs. At the apex of the pyramid was a large glass fish tank. It caught my eye. The tank was still filled with splashing water and fearful fish.

On one side of the street stood more low carts arranged in a line. At each one, energetic men were touting bruised vegetables and fruit. On the far side of the street lay a flea market of astonishing size. Kamal ordered the chauffeur to stop. We got down and he led the way into the souq. Every inch of the place was taken up with secondhand bric-a-brac. There were heaps of televisions with their guts ripped out, stacks of smashed VCRs twenty feet tall, industrial welding gear, and giant balls of barbed wire. There were bales of old magazines, too, a thousand doorframes and toilet bowls, spiral staircases, marble fountains, and mounds of old shoes.

I voiced surprise at the sheer quantity of stuff on offer. Kamal motioned for me to keep silent.

"Speak English," he said, "and the prices will quadruple."

"But we don't need any of this stuff," I said.

We turned down an alley and walked through cool shadows thrown by what looked like a row of ships' boilers. At the end of the track was a mountain of rotting bread. Rats the size of house cats were running over it, gorging themselves. Beyond the bread lay a cornucopia of old clothes, more shoes, and a sea of broken glass. We kept going. More televisions, more bread, boots, and magazines, then, at the end of the alley, we spotted an elderly man asleep. He was lying back in a rolltop bath, with a ginger cat asleep on his chest.

The bath was French cast iron, with a slow curve to the back and attractive clawed feet. It was Art Deco, about eighty years old. In London such a gem would have been in the window of a swish store on the King's Road.

I whispered for Kamal to check the price. He tugged at the salesman's sleeve. The cat woke up and flexed out its claws. There were groans of pain followed by conversation. The salesman was tired, hungry, and wanted to go back to sleep. He asked us to come back in the night. But, as Kamal was about to demonstrate, the one advantage of Ramadan was that Moroccan traders had no energy for the fierce bargaining that has made them famous. At the same time they were desperate for cash. During Ramadan nagging wives nag all the more.

"The price is two hundred dirhams," the man croaked, the lids hanging heavy over his grapelike eyes.

"I'll give you half that," said Kamal.

"No," said the salesman, "I always charge two hundred for baths like this."

Kamal nudged me to hand over the money. The salesman breathed in deep, swished the cat from his chest, and clambered out of the tub. He kissed the bills and thanked God. The bath was loaded onto a cart. Three men set off pushing it toward Dar Khalifa. We walked with them, with the Mercedes crawling behind. The sun was searing down, and the men pushing the cart were very soon drenched in sweat. After thirty minutes we were nearing the house. I was startled by the sound of small feet shuffling behind us. It was the tradesman who had sold us the bath. He was extremely agitated.

"Stop! Stop! Please stop!" he called.

"What is it?"

The man waved a fist of worn bills. I prepared myself to hear we had cheated him.

"I had to come after you," he said. "I ran all the way. I had to stop you."

"Why?"

The salesman seemed embarrassed. "I told you the bath

should cost two hundred dirhams," he said, mopping his brow with his sleeve, "but that was not true. They are always a hundred dirhams. So please, take back this hundred dirhams and forgive me."

"Why the sudden honesty?"

"It's Ramadan," said the man, "and I'm forbidden to lie."

EIGHT

Rain came, wind came, a lot of troubles came.

AT THE END OF THE FIRST week of Ramadan, I received another postcard from Pete. His spidery black writing announced that progress was being made. *The father's telling me to convert*, he wrote. *He wants me to have the chop below the belt. He says he'll do it himself. He's got a sharp penknife. It's a small sacrifice if it means I can be with Yasmine.*

The thought of adult circumcision being performed by a future father-in-law put me off my lunch. I was in the kitchen, crouching under the dining table, with a plate of cold couscous on my knees. The house was full of workers. They leered poisonously at anyone who entered the kitchen during daylight. As they rightly knew, the kitchen meant eating, and eating during Ramadan was a blasphemous act beyond all comprehension. The workers noticed that I went in and out of the kitchen frequently. They had taken to peering in through the windows. I was quite happy to be open—to tell them that I was not observing the fast, but they didn't want to hear the truth.

THE WORKMEN HAD SLID into a Ramadan routine of doing even less work than usual. They reeled about, their faces rapt with self-pity, hoping to win sympathy. François called me on the Thursday of the first week. There was an urgent tone in his voice.

"I have to warn you," he said, "you've got to tread carefully in Ramadan. Don't push people around. They could snap and run amok. You see, they're not getting any nicotine. Their chemicals are all screwed up."

I could make out shouting in the background, as if a disgruntled employee was picking a fight. François cried out once, then again, before the line cut.

The bejmat team had gone against my wishes and started to lay tiles in the library. I had asked them to begin anywhere but there, as it was the last room we needed finished. As the weeks of renovation passed, I learned that ignoring the client's wishes was a method of control perfected by Moroccan artisans, as it was by the guardians and everyone else.

Every so often, I would walk past the library and glance at the zigzagged tiles. The workers were laying beige bejmat, made from Fès clay in a herringbone design. The pattern is known locally as palmeraie, as in the zigzags created when palm fronds are laid one against the next. The artisans had started at the far end of the library, a room fifty feet in length. The original floor had been torn up and a new foundation of cement slapped down. A great heap of terracotta tiles had been towered up in one corner. I noticed that many of them were badly chipped or broken in half. The system seemed to lack the precision more usually associated with Moroccan tilework. Handfuls of the rectangular tiles were grabbed from the heap, casually tossed down into the cement, and poked into a crude herring-bone arrangement.

I stopped the team leader and asked him about quality control, or the apparent lack of it.

He jabbed an index finger at the work, then gave an assertive thumbs-up.

"*Très bien, non?*"

I shook my head. "*Non, pas bien.*"

The leader thumped both hands to his chest, like a primate attracting a mate. "*Je suis un expert,*" he said.

I am naturally a calm person, but at that moment I felt inspired to rip up the tiles and hurl them across the room. But François's caution held me back. I fought the anger, and instead of shouting, I blew a kiss at the artisan, backed out of the library, and phoned the architect.

"The work's not good," I said coldly. "It's not good at all."

"My friend," came the silken reply, "trust me. We are brothers."

Again, another unforeseen road tunnel, and the line went dead.

THE NEXT DAY A new team arrived: six men with dark, morose eyes, torn clothes, and matching maroon hats made from felt. They said that they had been sent to prepare samples of tadelakt, the plaster for the walls. After a few hours, they had pasted up a dozen swatches in what was to be the children's nursery. Their work looked good at first, applied with broad, flat trowels, like frosting on Christmas cake. But by the next morning, the plaster was cracked with a thousand miniature lines. Kamal shouted at me when he saw it.

"You have to fire the architect," he said. "You need craftsmen, and he's sending you clowns."

"Teething problems," I replied. "He'll sort them out."

Kamal grabbed my arm and marched me into the library. The workers were sprawling on the floor telling jokes. Some of them had taken off their trousers.

"Look at this work," he said. "Ariane could lay better bejmat than that!"

He hadn't been working with me long, but I could see Kamal was the sort of person who was always right. It was in his character to be so. You could fight his opinions, but in the end you found yourself giving in. However optimistic I tried to be, I saw that the architect's men were not up to scratch.

"Fire the architect," Kamal said again.

"But I paid in advance."

"Walk away from it," he said. "Risk not getting the money back and you will be stronger for it."

I dialed the architect's office. His silky voice cooed pleasantries.

"You're fired," I said. "Your men are clowns and I'm not running a circus."

The architect choked on his excuses. Kamal snatched the phone, barked, "We're going into a tunnel," and hung up. Fifteen minutes later he had rounded up the three teams of workers and their motley possessions and had routed them from the building. As they ran down the lane fearfully, some clutching their trousers to their chests, with Kamal chasing them, I said a prayer. I prayed that goodness would emerge from the chaos.

DURING RAMADAN THE SHANTYTOWN became more lively in the night. To say there was a carnival atmosphere would be an exaggeration. But the usual stalls —peddling third-hand clothes and vegetables—were joined by half a dozen more. An old woman started selling pink boiled sweets in clusters of three. Beside her sat a man with a crate of chickens, a scale, and a knife. You chose your chicken by weight, its head was then lopped off, and it fell into a box on the ground. The sea of blood attracted the limping dogs.

One morning a donkey hauled a well-built trailer into the slum and deposited it opposite the mosque. It was painted white, with go-faster stripes on the sides. A crowd of children gathered expectantly to see what tempting sweetmeats would be offered. Two men jumped from the trailer and swished them away with sticks. They had long black beards, teaseled out at the edges, and they wore the flowing robes of the Arabian Gulf. I asked the secondhand shoe seller about the newcomers and their trailer. He seemed very agitated.

"Go to your house," he said, "lock the door, and don't think about those men. They're trouble."

"Who are they?"

The man stuffed the assortment of shoes into a sack and staggered away. A moment later I saw the sweet-selling woman hurry off home. Ten minutes after that the bidonville had become a ghost town. I went back to Dar Khalifa and asked Hamza what was going on.

"They're bad men," he said. "They'll cut out your tongue and feed it to the dogs."

"Why would they do such a thing?"

Hamza rubbed his coarse hands together. "We are not rich," he said. "But we are Muslims, real Muslims. We read the Qur'an, and we understand it. The words of Allah are clear to us. But those other people . . ." The guardian stopped mid-sentence. He breathed in, then out in a deep sigh. "Those other people are hijacking our religion. They don't understand the Qur'an."

"Where are they from?"

"From the Arabian Gulf. They come here from time to time and try to win supporters for their vision."

"What is their vision?"

"Islamic anarchy."

WITH NO CAFFEINE TO power his bloodstream, Kamal's Ramadan mornings were almost unendurable. I could hardly remember ever seeing a man so despondent. But as a problem solver par excellence, he came up with an ingenious way of kick-starting the day. The secret was adrenaline. Each morning, after he picked me up, Kamal steered his cousin's pickup to the top of Anfa hill and pulled over to the side to mutter a short prayer. There was a clear view down to Maarif and to the old city. I would take in the sights as Kamal prepared for the contest. Swelling his lungs with air, he would rev the engine until the car was consumed in a thundercloud of oily diesel fumes. Against a backdrop of noise and smoke, he would jerk out the clutch. The tired old pickup would be propelled downhill. Kamal's method of producing maximum adrenaline was to swerve the wheel to the left. In an instant the odds of survival were slashed as we fought to dodge the stream of oncoming traffic. After a mile, Kamal would be drenched in sweat, panting, whooping with elation, ready to face the day.

THE HOUSE WAS SILENT. I wandered through it, depressed beyond words. The workmen had broken everything their unskilled hands had touched. The wiring and the plumbing were a disaster, the arches were a mess, and the terracotta tiles looked as if a monkey had laid them. I didn't understand. On television and in books, other people managed to renovate houses effortlessly. For them, there was nothing to it. They didn't have problems with slothful, ghoulish workmen. Their laborers were always cheery, fresh-faced, and incapable of making a mistake.

Kamal arrived in the evening. He said in Morocco only fools worked during the day, that all the serious employment was done at night, especially during the weeks of Ramadan.

"What about office hours?" I said.

"Pah! I never meet people in offices," he said curtly.

"Why not?"

"Too many ears."

I asked him how we could get new workers, men with the skill necessary to turn the house around.

"Don't be in a rush," said Kamal. "If you rush, you'll fall into the hole."

"Where's the hole?"

"It's all around you."

THE NEXT DAY, KAMAL borrowed the Mercedes limousine again. We drove across Casablanca in search of a new engine for my Jeep. It was a cool, bright day, with a strong breeze chasing in from the west. I could smell winter approaching. The only consolation was that by now London would be in the grip of black ice and freezing fog.

Kamal told me that to get an engine on the cheap, we would have to tell the vultures. Only the vultures, he said darkly, knew where to look.

"Tell them what you want, and they'll get it," he said.

"How do they do that?"

"They have their methods. If you have the cash to pay, they'll run a car off the road and track what's left to a scrap yard."

"That sounds illegal to me," I said. "In any case, I don't have much cash."

Kamal clicked his tongue. "Don't worry," he said, "I know a vulture with a conscience."

Far from the palm-edged avenues of the Corniche, we came to a fearful, ramshackle place. The sky was drab and gray, even though it was only late morning; the tin-roofed buildings were masked in decades of grime. The road had been torn up, and the smell of raw sewage hung in the air, a warning to the honest to stay away. The place was an automobile graveyard. They lay everywhere, carved up and contorted, ripped down the welding lines, despised heaps of steel.

From time to time a man would descend from the mountain of wrecks, clasping a trophy—a steering wheel, part of an engine, a fragment of indescribable metal. He would hand it to another man, who would count out a stack of tattered bills and leave with the trophy. We approached cautiously. My eyes were streaming from the rank smell of sewage. Kamal asked one of the vultures a question. The man pointed to the left, to a squat shed made from beaten sheets of tin. We went over. Another man came out and kissed Kamal three times on each cheek. He was average height, with a thick mane of orange hair and long sideburns that met beneath his chin. He was the vulture with a conscience.

Kamal described what we needed, stressing that the engine had to be in good condition. He didn't mention our budget. When I asked him about this on the way home, he said: "In the States, the first thing they ask about is the price. How much is this? What does that cost? But in Morocco, the very last thing you talk about is money. First you choose the thing you want to buy. You make sure it's just right. Then you fix the price."

The system seemed back to front.

"How do you know if you can afford it?" I asked.

"You don't," Kamal replied. "But that's what bargaining's for."

AT THE HOUSE, HAMZA and Osman were pacing up and down waiting for me. They said that there was something important for me to attend to.

"Has there been another accident?"

"No, no, not an accident."

"Thank God for that. Then what is it?"

"Follow me."

We walked across the terrace and into the courtyard garden. Hamza extended an arm, jabbed his index finger to the top of the great palm tree.

"See," he said.

I didn't see anything abnormal. "It looks fine to me."

Hamza and Osman clapped their hands to their faces. "What do you mean?" they said at once.

"Well, I can't see anything strange."

Osman prodded a finger at the tree. "Up there!" he said.

I looked up, peering into the afternoon light. I squinted, tilted my head. Squinted again. Then, gradually, I saw what they were pointing to. Hanging on a string by the cluster of dates was a small, lifeless, ratlike creature.

"It's a hedgehog," said Osman.

"What's it doing up there?"

Hamza ushered me from the courtyard, across the verandah, and out of the house. He led me through the shantytown, where the fanatics' trailer was still parked, and down the hill toward the ocean. I asked again and again where he was taking me. He didn't reply, except to say that we needed a safe place to talk.

"Isn't the house safe?" I asked.

An expression of absolute fear swept across Hamza's face. His tanned complexion seemed to turn ivory with fright. "No," he said once, and then again. "No, Monsieur Tahir, it is not safe."

At the end of the main road, Hamza crossed the Corniche and led the way down over the fence to the beach. Bitter winter waves were breaking on the sand. The guardian stopped and stared me in the eye.

"There is bad news," he said.

"Is it with the workmen? That they left?"

Hamza frowned. "No, no, not with the workers," he said. "Something far more grave. Someone is trying to hurt you."

"Qandisha and the Jinns?"

The guardian glanced down at his feet. "I will tell you," he said quietly.

We sat down on the sand and Hamza stared out at the waves.

"Once there was a man who fell in love with the wife of another man," he said without looking at me. "He would meet her secretly under a palm tree on the first night of each month. He would give her little gifts—a rose, a pastry, something like that. The woman fell in love with the man and they ran away together. The husband of the woman swore that he would kill them both. His family had been dishonored. He hunted them for weeks, then months, and years."

Hamza drew a square in the sand with his finger.

"When he eventually found them," he said, "they were living in a house near the ocean. They had a child, and were happy. The woman's husband broke down the door. He was about to kill the couple when something stopped him. He turned around, went back to his own house, and killed himself."

I wondered what the story had to do with the dead hedgehog.

"There was something that neither man knew about the woman," Hamza said.

"What?"

"That she was a Jinn, and her name was Qandisha."

"Qandisha's a female Jinn?"

"Yes."

I asked where the hedgehog fitted in.

"It's a sign," he said. "A sign that Qandisha doesn't like people living in her house."

"Well, what should I do?"

Hamza stared out at the water. He opened his mouth but no words came out. I repeated my question.

"Tell me, what should I do?"

"You should take your family, leave Dar Khalifa, and never come back."

I FOUND MYSELF TRAPPED in an awkward position. On my assistant's orders I had fired my workforce, and lost a fortune in the process, with little hope of recovering any of the money. I had a gangster for a neighbor, a house marooned in a shanty-town with no title deeds, and the weather was getting bad. And I was now being told that I should abandon the house because an invisible spirit was angry at us living there.

The next day, I asked Kamal for his opinion. He was quite certain the dead hedgehog and tales of Qandisha were part of an elaborate ruse to scare us away.

"Do you think the guardians were trying to take the house?" I asked.

Kamal pondered the question for a while.

"It's not the guardians," he said at length. "Someone else wants the house, not them."

"How can you be so sure?"

Again Kamal felt silent.

"Because," he said at last, "Dar Khalifa means too much to them."

IN THE SHANTYTOWN, THE imam was looking worried. As I walked past the mosque he smiled fretfully, but for once, he didn't ask me for money. It was then I realized something was very wrong. There was a tension in the alleyways and in the small shops that faced out onto the main track. I could feel it. Everyone could.

At dusk on the second day after its arrival, the windows of the white trailer flapped down. The two bearded men were sitting primly in the window on stools. They had donned white crocheted skullcaps and were wearing matching blue sweaters over their robes. Anyone who walked past the trailer seemed to do so at speed, as if the bearded men were waiting to reach out, grab them, and slit their throats.

"The bombers were men like that," Osman whispered to me that night. "Having them here doesn't do us any good. If the government sees them, they'll tear down our houses. They'll say that we support the radicals."

"Why don't you all chase them away? This is your bidonville, not theirs."

Osman's ready smile froze, then became a scowl. "If we throw them out," he said, "they'll burn our houses down."

RAMADAN CONTINUED. AS IT did so, the façade—that everyone was enjoying the strict routine of fasting—wore thinner and thinner still. Each day, Kamal would meet me at the house later than the day before, until one day he didn't turn up at all. I was worried. I thought he might have been killed on his morning adrenaline run or knocked down by a nicotine-starved driver running amok.

By late afternoon the streets of Casablanca were a terrifying place. Cars swerved about even more randomly than normal, veering from one lane to the next, as if the drivers didn't care whether they collided or not. Everyone had their windows open. Not for air, but so that they could yell abuse at anyone they passed. By five o'clock, Boulevard d'Anfa, a main thoroughfare, was a carnage of crashes, scrapes, and feuding motorists.

Another day slipped by, and still no sign of Kamal. I called his cell phone, but it was switched off. So I griped to Rachana, then ranted with anger, asking how anyone could be so irresponsible. Two more days passed, and with each, my fury mounted even more.

By the fourth day I had decided to fire Kamal, if I ever saw him again. There was no question about it. I lined up the guardians and told them of my decision. They were delighted. Hamza said Kamal was nothing but trouble, that he was trying to get his hands on my money. The Bear broke with formality and slapped me on the back. Cackling to himself, he made for the stables to celebrate with the others.

At seven that evening, I received a text message on my cell phone. It read: "Come to big police station on Zerktouni Blvd. Now." I ran through the shantytown, my heart pumping, and took a taxi into the center of town. A policeman shooed me away from the gates of the precinct. He told me to wait at the corner.

I waited and waited. Then, at nine-fifteen, Kamal appeared. He was dressed in the same clothes he had been wearing five days before. His head was low, his confidence broken.

"Where have you been?"

"In jail," he said.

NINE

A one-eyed man is king in the land of the blind.

THE WORST THING ABOUT RAMADAN WERE the thieves. They were everywhere. You couldn't leave anything unattended for a minute without having it stolen. Thieves preyed on honest folk, whose hunger made them easy targets. Morocco is usually a safe country with very little crime. But as soon as the holy month arrived, everyone we met cautioned us to lock up or tie down anything we owned. We scoffed at their warnings. By the second week of Ramadan, my wallet was gone; so was Rachana's, as well as Ariane's schoolbag, my new camera, and even our groceries. The local newspapers were packed with tales of daring theft—of cars and donkeys; briefcases filled with cash; jewelry, furniture, and even household pets.

The holy month was supposed to be a time of pious reflection. But, like Christmas in the West, it was tinged by commercial-

ization. Every evening families spent fortunes on providing delicacies for *iftour,* the breaking of the fast. There were trays of
macaroons and a hundred varieties of biscuit, pastries, and
sweetmeats, and dates from oases in the south, juicy figs from
the mountains, honeydew melons, fresh yogurt, and plums.

Each evening as the day's fast was broken by the muezzin,
the guardians would nibble a handful of dates, sip a little milk,
and rush out on patrol. For them, it wasn't a time for gorging
oneself on food; rather, it was the time to go hunting—for
thieves.

"They come while people are eating iftour," said the Bear.

"Yes, and they creep about like foxes," Osman said.

"Like young, cunning foxes," Hamza added.

"What would you do if you caught one?"

The three guardians looked at each other furtively, then at
me. Then they guffawed.

"We would trap him in a corner and throw stones at him,"
said Hamza. "Then we would beat him with long sticks, until he
cried out like a woman."

"Would you give him to the police?"

The guardians scoffed at the suggestion.

"That would be no fun," said the Bear, grinning.

KAMAL DIDN'T SAY A word until after he had eaten his way
through an entire dish of couscous piled high with pumpkin,
potatoes, and succulent lamb. He wasn't his usual self. For the
first time, he was meek.

"What happened?"

"It was bad," he said, picking at the lamb's shoulder bone.
"Very bad."

"Did you steal something?"

"No!"

"Then what?"

He leaned back and lit a cigarette. "I was at a government office checking some papers," he said, "and the clerk insulted me. It's Ramadan and his temper cracked. He called me the son of a noseless whore!"

Kamal paused to exhale.

"No one calls my mother a noseless whore," he said.

"What did you do?"

"I saw a big metal vase on a shelf. I picked it up and hit him with it in the face."

IT WAS TWO DAYS before Kamal was back to normal, although there was no such thing as normal in Ramadan. His eyes were circled by black rings, his complexion pasty and white. He said the clerk had dropped charges against him. They had come to an understanding of some kind. It was good news. But there was better news to follow. The vulture had located an engine. Kamal claimed it was pristine as the day it was built and had been ripped out from a freshly injured Korean-made Jeep.

"What luck that an identical car to yours crashed just when we needed it to."

It sounded too good to be true.

"Are you sure the car wasn't hunted down on my behalf?"

Kamal looked at the floor timidly. "Don't ask me that question," he said. "You know it's Ramadan and I cannot tell a lie."

I HAD BEEN SO ready to fire Kamal, but having him back meant we could start solving problems once again. I scribbled down a new list of things to do. The first was to find a net to cover the swimming pool. A few weeks before, Zohra had managed to get a quote from the leading pool company in Casablanca. Their price was close to three thousand dollars. Kamal said he could get a net made for almost nothing. He asked for the second problem.

"The staircase is a death trap," I said. "It's got no banisters. We need a mason to build some, and a carpenter, too."

Next morning, Kamal arrived at Dar Khalifa with two plump men carrying two plump sacks. They looked like brothers and were wearing thick rubber aprons and gumboots, the kind worn by fishermen. Kamal led them to the swimming pool and motioned to it. He took time to explain something carefully in Arabic. The men nodded, opened their sacks, and dumped out two heaps of brown nylon cord as thick as a child's finger. They folded the sacks and sat on them, took a handful of cord, and started to knit.

A few minutes later, there was a scratch at the front door. Hamza hurried over. In the frame was standing a tall, thickset man with rounded shoulders and a wild growth of beard. He looked like a hit man. I assumed he was in the employ of the shantytown's gangster.

"I think he's got the wrong house," I said.

"No, no," Kamal said, greeting the man, "he's the mason."

"What about a carpenter? We need one to make doors and windows for our bedroom."

The winter rains had transformed the windowless hulk of a room into a lake complete with a family of ducks.

"In Morocco, carpenters are all drug addicts," said Kamal.

"That's a sweeping generalization."

"It's not. They are bad men—all of them."

"There must be one honest carpenter. I'm sure we can find him if we look very hard."

Kamal suddenly tapped a finger to his temple. "Of course," he said. "There is one."

THE FISHERMEN KNITTED AND knitted, and as they did so, a great brown blanket of net billowed out over the garden. They claimed there was no finer net in all Casablanca, that it was strong enough to catch a whale.

"I don't want it to catch a whale," I said.

The plump fishermen seemed displeased for a moment. They glanced at each other, and one of them said, "This net has *baraka*. It can protect life as well as taking it."

By the afternoon of the next day, they had knitted a net thirty feet long. They were halfway done, their nimble fingers knotting the nylon cord at an astonishing speed. I was admiring their work when Kamal rolled up in my Jeep. The vulture's engine had been fitted.

Wasting no time, we trundled through the shantytown and out to the open road, in search of the clean-living carpenter. Kamal recounted his exploits in America as we drove. Nothing gave him more pleasure than talking of the times he had spent in the bosom of Southern hospitality. He said that when he first got to Atlanta, he went to a supermarket and fell backward at seeing such packed shelves.

"It was like a dream. There was such wealth. Such glamour."

"Glamour? In a supermarket?"

"Yes!" said Kamal in an excited tone. "I met my first American love right then, right on that first day."

"Where?"

"In Safeway, at the frozen peas."

The Jeep rattled southward out of Casablanca toward Marrakech. The villas were replaced by shantytowns, and then by open fields. Farmers were tending their crops of onions, melons, and maize. I asked Kamal about the girl.

"She was beautiful," he said, a hint of lost passion in his voice. "Her skin was the color of walnuts, her eyes green, like apples hanging in an orchard's shade. We stood there, staring at each other at the refrigerator filled with frozen peas. It was love."

I burst out laughing.

"You don't believe me," Kamal said desolately. "But it's true. We had so much in common. She gave me her picture. I pressed it to my heart. By the time I left Safeway, we were engaged."

"That's crazy!"

"What's crazy about it? It was love."

"Did you marry her?"

Kamal glowered at the road. "Allah did not want it," he said.

"How do you know?"

"I left her phone number in my jeans when I went to the laundrette. It was washed clean away."

Kamal eased the car into fourth gear.

"There was only one thing to do," he said.

"What was that?"

"I went back to Safeway and waited. I waited and waited, but she never came back."

"How long did you wait?"

"For a week."

"You wasted a week waiting for a girl you'd met for a few minutes at the frozen peas?"

Kamal sniffed, as if he felt genuine pain at the loss. "You don't understand," he said. "We were engaged."

THE CARPENTER'S WORKSHOP WAS set off the road, opposite Casablanca's main garbage dump. Refuse trucks from across the city would end up there day and night. A pack of scrawny dogs were picking their way through the trash.

The workshop was a one-room shed with a wooden roof. There was nothing remarkable about it. A man inside had heard the car approaching. He was aged and crooked, like a warped old post of pine. His head was completely bald, his eyes small, as if they had been shrunk in some way by time. As we neared him, he squinted at us through a large magnifying lens held in his left hand.

When he saw Kamal, the crooked man almost jumped for joy. He let the lens fall on its cord around his neck, and he staggered forward to press his old lips to Kamal's cheeks.

An hour of inquiries slipped by. The carpenter asked after each member of Kamal's family. He knew them all—brothers, cousins and aunts, nephews, nieces, uncles, and grandparents. The name of each one was spoken, praised, and blessed. He begged our forgiveness.

Were it not Ramadan, he said, he would have served us a banquet. Next time, there would be a couscous cooked with raisins and tender meat, trays of pastries flavored with orange blossom, and gallons of sweet mint tea.

"Next time, *inshallah*, if God wills it," I said.

After two hours, we still hadn't brought up the subject of work. I nudged Kamal.

"The old generation can't be hurried," he whispered.

Another half hour elapsed. I couldn't stand waiting any longer, especially because the wind had changed and we were all choking on the air gusting off the garbage mountain. At last, when every relative living and dead had been praised once and praised again, the old carpenter fell silent. He prayed for a few moments, his hands cupped on his lap.

Kamal explained that we had a favor to ask him. We needed a set of windows and a door to be made. The carpenter leapt to his feet. Pulling the magnifying glass up to his eye, he moved in close to me, the lens a window between us.

"I will do the finest work that has ever been made!" he shouted at the top of his voice. "The wood will be fragrant and strong. I will sculpt it, lovingly, caressing it with my fingers."

"That sounds very good," I said. "Just what we need."

The dimensions were scratched down on a splinter of pine. And, after more prolonged formalities, we made our escape. On the way back, I asked Kamal how he had come to know the carpenter. He said he would show me. We drove back past the open fields and the shantytowns, past the villas and the office blocks, into the center of Casablanca.

Kamal stopped the car outside an apartment building. On the ground floor was a *hammam,* a Turkish-style steam bath, with an entrance for men and another for women.

"I live in this building," he said, "and my family own the hammam."

He opened a steel door on the street level and led the way into a dark basement. When my eyes had adjusted to the dimness, I made out someone crouching against one wall, near a boiler. He was completely bald and had no eyebrows. Kamal called out. The figure opened a hatch on the side of the boiler and tossed a handful of something into the inferno.

"What's that?"

"This is the boiler that heats the hammam," Kamal said. "All day and all night a guy crouches here, throwing handfuls of sawdust into the fire. The sawdust is brought each morning from the carpenter we just met. We've been buying it from his family for fifty years."

Again, Kamal warned me about taking my eye from the ball.

"We used to own dozens of buildings in Casablanca," he said. "We had factories, too, and farms. But now all we have is this hammam."

"What happened to the rest?"

"After the accident," Kamal said, "my father lost interest in life. His wife and his only daughter were dead, so he took a backseat and everyone walked over him. When they saw he didn't put up a fight, they took everything. It was like wolves ripping a carcass apart."

Kamal led me back up to the street.

"Beware," he said, "the same could happen to you. There are wolves all around you. Blink once and the Caliph's House will be gone."

THE ONLY PROGRESS AT the house was the fishermen's net. There was miles of it. Hamza and his fellow guardians considered it a needless expense. They said I could have spent the money pleasing the Jinns instead. By doing so, they insisted, the house and all who lived inside it would be protected by a cloak of invisible energy. To the Western mind, it sounded like lunacy   rely alone on prayer, offerings, and tokens of superstition. But if I did so, the guardians promised, I could live without any safety features at all.

"You mean I wouldn't even need locks on the doors?" I said.

"No," replied the Bear.

"What about fire insurance?"

"Not that either," quipped Hamza.

"If I indulged the Jinns and got their protection," I said, "then surely I wouldn't need guardians."

Hamza, Osman, and the Bear fell into line, shoulder to shoulder. A great fear descended across their faces. It was the fear of unemployment. I could feel them fumbling desperately for an answer.

"You do need guardians," said Hamza at length.

"Why?"

"Because it's us who communicate with the Jinns."

BY THIRD WEEK OF Ramadan there was still no sign of the new team of artisans frequently promised by Kamal. Whenever I asked after them, he would caution me. Hurry to find craftsmen and, he said, the mess would get even worse.

"These people are not like builders," he declared, "they are artists. Hurry an artist and he'll chop you in two with his knife."

"But I don't want any more psychos," I said anxiously. "It's bad enough already."

Kamal waved a finger at my face. "You have it quite wrong," he replied. "In Morocco, the more insane the artist, the better he knows his craft. It will take time to find a truly disturbed team to work here at the Caliph's House."

FRANÇOIS HAD TOLD ME that Casablanca's old quarter of Habous was the place to find real craftsmen. I didn't believe him for a minute, but forcing Kamal to drive me there on the Friday morning was a way of exacting my authority.

The last Friday in Ramadan was a day when no work at all was done. For three weeks I had been ever more scathing about the artisans' output, but I hadn't seen anything yet. People should have been thinking about prayer, but their minds were all on the same mirage—a giant plate of couscous and lamb with all the trimmings.

Kamal didn't speak on the drive to Habous. He was barely functioning. The lack of sleep, nicotine, and alcohol, and the adrenaline overload, had taken a heavy toll on his system. The last thing he wanted was to chauffeur me to the stone-built bazaar in search of workers. Fortunately, his weakened condition made it easy to take control. Unlike him, and everyone else, I was eating three meals a day and sleeping seven hours a night. By the final days of Ramadan, I felt like king of the world.

Habous was quite different from the ritzy French villas and the apartment blocks more normally found in Casablanca. Its buildings were crafted almost entirely of granite, rather than concrete, so favored elsewhere. Pointed arches led to dozens of small shops, set back off stone colonnades. It looked as if the neighborhood had stood there for centuries, and so I was all the more surprised to learn that Habous was constructed by the French in the 1930s.

The shops were packed with wares—colorful jelabas edged in silky brocade, tarboosh hats made from fine red felt, yellow *barboush* slippers, caftans embroidered with sequins, and wedding regalia lavish enough for any bride. One entire street was devoted to Moroccan furniture, while another sold only brassware, and a third perfumes and beauty products—rose water and antimony, jasmine oil, sandalwood and musk.

We searched for craftsmen, but could find none. Everyone we asked either scowled or suggested returning after Ramadan. They thought I was mad to be thinking of such things on the final stretch of the fast. As we wandered through the porticoes, I spied a courtyard behind one of the arches. Inside was a cluster of antique shops. Each one sold the usual assortment of Art Deco bronzes and prewar furniture and prints. Everything in Casablanca's antique stores, without exception, dates from the first half of the last century, a legacy of the French.

But there was an exception. At the back of one shop, I set eyes on an exquisite dining table. It was veneered in walnut, with gently bowed sides and cabriole legs. The detailing, the choice of wood, and the style suggested it was not French, but Spanish. To my inexpert eye, it looked as if it dated to the early nineteenth century, long before the French annexed the kingdom of Morocco.

I pushed Kamal forward and urged him to ask the price.

The shop's owner was too ravenous to bother with a sales spiel. He sat doubled over in an old wicker chair, as if his stomach was giving him pain. His head was in his hands. Kamal inquired the price of the table.

"*C'est cinq milles dirhams,*" he said.

"Five hundred dollars," said Kamal. "That's far too much."

"We can bargain," I said brightly.

Kamal led the way out of the shop. "Ramadan has made the shopkeepers greedy," he said.

"That man's starving," I said, "he's putty in my hands."

"We are leaving," said Kamal sternly.

OUT ON THE STREET, I noticed a woman begging. She was elderly, her face a maze of shadowed wrinkles, her bent form shrouded in a dark green jelaba. She caught my attention not because of what she was wearing, or the way she looked, but because of what she was holding.

In her basket was a collection of the very finest fruit I had seen in Casablanca. I took a moment to watch as she went from stall to stall. The shopkeepers would spend time selecting the very best apple, orange, or plum, before handing it to the woman with their blessing. I was surprised, for in the West we reserve second-rate goods for people without the money to pay for them. I stepped up to one of the fruit stalls and asked the owner why he had presented his very best peach to the beggar. The shopkeeper groomed his beard with his hand.

"Just because someone is begging," he replied, "does that mean they should be given items of low quality? We are not like that here in Morocco."

TWO DAYS MORE AND the holy month was at an end. The severity of Ramadan was suddenly replaced by the excess of the Eid celebration. There was a palpable sense of delight on every Moroccan face. Teenagers raced their parents' cars up and down the Corniche, hanging out the windows, horns blaring, hands waving. Middle-class families strolled up and down, fathers smoking, children slurping pink ice cream. Music blared from every restaurant and café, each one overwhelmed with a tidal wave of customers.

I gave the guardians a week's pay as a bonus. Their mouths grinned wide, and they hurried home to hand the cash over to their wives. That night the shantytown was bursting with life. On the main track sheep were roasting on low charcoal braziers, sparks shooting like tracer fire up to the stars. A group of musicians were weaving down the alleyways, the soft lilt of their tune rising over the rusting tin roofs. In the middle of the main street, the imam was making the most of the season's charity. Across from his mosque, the white trailer was shut up for the night. Its resident fanatics had disappeared.

At midnight, Osman knocked at our bedroom door. His three small children had been coaxed forward, bearing homemade gifts for Ariane and Timur. Their father poked them in the shoulder blades, and, reluctantly, they hummed a Moroccan nursery rhyme. In the West, nothing is so sacred as the ritual of putting kids to bed on time; while in the East, no evening is complete unless the children have been stirred from deep sleep and cajoled to entertain.

When Osman had gone, and our own children were snoring loud, I went down to the verandah and sat on a wicker bench. The bidonville's celebrations were still raging on, the sound of music and laughter warming the night air. Around me, the Caliph's House was sleeping. I thought about what Hamza had said—that only the house could give up its secrets, only it could tell me about its past.

As I sat there, I sensed very strongly that Dar Khalifa had a soul of its own. It seemed far more than the stone and mortar in its walls, as if it knew clearly who we were and why we were there. Maybe, I thought to myself, it wasn't the spirit of the house I was sensing, but Qandisha and her fraternity of Jinns.

TWO DAYS AFTER THE end of Ramadan, Kamal arrived. He was bright-eyed and confident again.

"I have found you a *moualem,* a master craftsman, to lay the terracotta tiles," he said.

"How do you know he's good?"

"Because he's a madman," said Kamal.

That night I slept well. It was as if we had turned the corner on our bad luck. I had talked my bank in London into loaning me some money, and Ramadan was now a distant memory. I nestled my head into the pillow and thanked God for good fortune, and the Jinns for leaving us alone.

At that moment, as I drifted into a deep, pleasing slumber, I felt a hand on my shoulder. I jerked upright.

"Who is it?"

"It's me," said a voice.

"Who?"

"Me . . . Kamal."

I fumbled for my watch. "It's three A.M."

"I know."

"Well, what's your problem?"

"Put on your clothes," said Kamal, "we have to go and buy sand."

In any other country in the world, people buy sand when the shops are open. This doesn't usually include the middle of the night. I drew this point to Kamal's attention as we drove out through the suburbs and along the coast road.

"No one ever got a good deal buying anything in a store," he said.

"Why do we need sand anyway?"

"For the bejmat."

Another feature curious to Morocco is the purchasing of building merchandise. Anywhere else, the builder buys what he needs for the job and then bills you for it. But as Kamal explained, in Morocco only a fool would let someone else buy sand, cement, metal girders, pipes, or wood.

"But the architect bought all that stuff for me," I said.

Kamal lit a cigarette and sucked at it hard. "Then you're a fool for letting him," he said.

The first reason to buy your own merchandise was to get a good price. The second was to ensure quality. When we had driven for more than an hour, Kamal showed me what he meant. His contact was waiting in a turnout. His truck was old and wounded by years on the road. It was leaking oil, and its lights were all smashed. The driver was a silhouette in the cab. It appeared he wasn't alone. As we approached I made out passionate groaning sounds.

"Is there a woman in there with him?" I said.

"He's a trucker," said Kamal.

"So?"

"So he's doing what truckers do best."

"What's that?"

"He's whoring."

TEN

Trust in God but tie your camel well.

KAMAL TAPPED HARD ON THE DRIVER'S door. There was a rustling inside, sounds of commotion, then of fear, followed by urgent clambering. The passenger door was flung open and a girl of about fifteen leapt out. She was veiled in black and ran very fast.

An oily, bearded face appeared at the window.

"It's me," said Kamal hoarsely.

The man inside glared out at us with anger. "I paid for her in advance!" he shouted.

"We've come for the sand."

Kamal pulled the tarpaulin back and pointed to the load. "Feel that," he said.

I did. It was slightly moist, cool to the touch.

"Top quality," said Kamal, "and half the going price."

WHEN HE SET EYES on the sand, Hamza said it was the lowest quality he had ever seen. He boasted that he'd been born in the desert, a fact that enabled him to tell good sand from bad merely by the smell. The other two guardians were equally scathing when they saw the giant dark mound now sitting outside the house.

"It will give you trouble," said the Bear.

"And it'll bring bad luck into the house," said Osman.

It was obvious the guardians were disparaging because Kamal had brought the sand to Dar Khalifa. As far as they were concerned, anything my assistant did was part of a grand scheming plan to relieve me of all I owned. They hated everything about him. Most of all, they hated that I listened when he spoke.

For my part, I really could not work Kamal out. He was an impossible person to pigeonhole—capable of brilliant thought one minute, and utterly reckless behavior the next. While I had him working, I valued his know-how, his ability to get difficult things done. At the same time, I was still unsure of his real motives.

ONE MORNING IN EARLY December we drove back out to see the carpenter. It was the middle of the week, and we went to check on the windows he was making. The carpenter kissed Kamal's cheeks, praised his ancestors, and ushered us to seats in the shade. A pot of mint tea was brought, glasses poured out once, then poured back into the pot before being poured out a second time. A team of boys fetched the windows and held them up like oils at a fine-art sale. They looked very good. The carpenter was pleased when I praised the work. He exclaimed something in Arabic.

Kamal translated.

"He said, 'Through these windows, your eyes will separate reality from illusion.' "

I pondered the comment as we drove back toward Casablanca. It was a dazzling morning, far cooler than previous days. The road was lined with hawkers selling cactus fruit and plums. Kamal didn't say anything on the way home. His mouth was clenched tight. He breathed through his nose, huffing like a stallion before the race, as if he were overcome with anger. I asked if something was on his mind. He didn't reply. Then, suddenly, he swerved off the main road onto a dirt track, dust enveloping us. I was taken by surprise.

"Where are we going?"

"Shortcut," he said.

We drove for thirty minutes in the opposite direction from Casablanca. On either side of the track, there was open farmland, rich red African soil, peppered with crows. I kept silent. As far as I was concerned, it was the middle of nowhere.

At a place where the tracks converged and then crossed, Kamal hit the brakes. The Jeep skidded to a halt, sending dust sideways like talc cast into the wind. Kamal got out of the car. He said he wanted to check the exhaust. At that moment, two men appeared from behind a bush. They looked like laborers from the city. Kamal greeted them as if they were old friends. A surge of adrenaline welled through me. For the first time, I was frightened of Kamal. I thought he was going to kill me right there and then. The car key was still in the ignition. I was about to jump into the driver's seat, throw the car in gear, and charge away. But at that moment, he ambled back to the car, started the engine, and headed for town.

"Who were they?" I asked.

"They wanted a ride to Casa," he said.

"It looked like you knew them."

Kamal turned to face me. His distant brown eyes locked

onto mine. His mouth was tight shut, jaws clenched. He stared at me for so long as to make me uncomfortable. It was not the time for speaking. He could feel my fear, I was sure of it. I hoped he would burst out laughing, slap me on the back, or let me in on a secret. But he didn't speak.

IN THE SAME WEEK, I received another postcard from Pete. The writing was more obscure this time, as if it was written by someone who had come to know pain. It said: *Had the chop. Now I'm learning the Path to Allah.* The note was followed by an address in Chefchouen, a small town south of Tangier. I showed it to Rachana.

"I think you better go and see if he's okay," she said.

"But I hardly know the guy."

"So what?"

There was a far stronger reason to venture north. I wanted to track down the house in which my grandfather had lived for the last decade of his life.

Kamal's team of artisans were about to turn up at Dar Khalifa. I couldn't face them. I don't know why, perhaps because I was so sure they would create more problems than they solved.

I took the morning train from Casa Voyageurs and was soon trundling north along the coast. Leaving Casablanca and the Caliph's House behind filled me with new energy. It was as if a burden had been eased from my shoulders. I stared out at the groves of cork oaks and breathed long and hard. If I could keep standing a little longer, I thought to myself, we would have a chance at weathering the storm.

I planned to go straight to Tangier, to spend a night or two ferreting out the riddle of my grandfather's last years. After that, I would head down to Chefchouen, to find the newly circumcised American.

MY GRANDFATHER WAS SIRDAR Ikbal Ali Shah. He was the son of an Afghan chieftain, raised in a tribal fiefdom in the Hindu Kush. As is traditional in our family, he was encouraged to master many fields of study, to live many lives in one. He was a medical doctor and a diplomat, a professor of philosophy, an expert on folklore, mysticism, and political science. He was an adviser and confidant to half a dozen heads of state, and the author of more than sixty books—on poetry, politics, biography, literature, religion, and travel.

At twenty-three he was sent to Edinburgh to study medicine. He was very taken with Scotland, and wrote later that the mountains, the castles, and the strict system of clans reminded him of his Afghan homeland. It was 1917, and the Great War raged on. A generation of young men were being slaughtered in the trenches of Flanders and France.

One spring day, my grandfather was invited to a charity tea, where a group of young women were raising funds for the war effort. Across the crowded room, he spotted a prim Scottish girl standing alone, china cup poised to her lips. Her nickname was Bobo, and her family came from the Edinburgh elite. She was only seventeen. Her brother had just been killed fighting in France, and she was distraught at his loss.

Bobo spied Ikbal gazing across at her. She stared back with nervous anticipation, and they fell in love. The next day, she asked her father if she might meet the Afghan chieftain's son for tea. The request was refused, and she was locked in her room. Allowing her heart to rule her mind, Bobo escaped, eloped with Ikbal, and together they traveled to his ancestral fortress in the Hindu Kush.

Their marriage endured more than forty years, until the day of Bobo's death. They lived in Central Asia, the Middle East, and in Europe. Then, in 1960, Bobo died suddenly of cancer, weeks before her sixtieth birthday. My grandfather could hardly contain his grief. He vowed that he would not return to any place they had been together, or look at anything that would remind him of his beloved wife.

Morocco was a country where they had never traveled. My grandfather had heard of the kingdom's mountains, its kasbahs, and the proud tribal traditions. The sound of such a place was alluring. So, that summer, he packed his sea trunk with some books and a few clothes and set sail for Tangier.

THERE IS NO BETTER way to travel through Morocco than by train. The journey from Casablanca to Tangier takes about six hours, sometimes longer, depending on whether the driver takes a long lunch or a short one at Sidi Kacem. In the winter, the travelers are bundled up in heavy woolen jelabas worn as overcoats, as if a searing arctic wind is about to tear through. But it never does.

The man sitting opposite me in the compartment noticed the calfskin amulet around my neck. He was in his sixties, dressed in a pale jelaba with black trim, and brown barboush on his feet. His face was swollen, scattered with patchy beard and sores. I explained to him that the amulet was given to me by a friend.

"What for?"

"For the Jinns," I said.

The man scratched his face. "Let them into your head and you'll have trouble," he replied.

"They're not up here," I said, tapping my temple, "but in my house." I laughed. "Anyway, it's not the Jinns who are a problem," I said, "but the people working for me."

"What's wrong with them?"

"They believe in the Jinns," I explained. "That's the problem."

The man didn't say anything else for a long while. I stared

out the window at the plowed fields edged in cactus plants. I thought our chat was at an end. But a traveler's conversation can be disjointed, strung out along miles of railway line. The man cleared his throat.

"Across from me," he said, "I see a sheet of white paper. There is no writing upon it, nothing at all. The paper has just been made. It's new. There's great hope for it. A beautiful poem could be written on it—something inspiring, something wonderful. Or a fabulous picture could be drawn on its surface, the face of a child perhaps."

I looked at the man, and took in his sores and his tired face, and I wondered what he was going on about.

"But the great shame is that the sheet of paper will never know beauty," he said. "Why? Because it doesn't believe."

MY ONLY CLUES WERE a few letters written by my grandfather to my parents during the last years of his life. They were always composed in dark blue fountain pen on lightweight writing paper, in a precise, sensible hand. They spoke of a life of solitude, of modesty, a life waiting to be reunited with Bobo. At the top of each was printed an address at 21 rue de la Plage.

Once in Tangier, I bought a street map from a tobacconist and found rue de la Plage running inland from the port. The nearest hotel was Cecil's. I was acquainted with it from my grandfather's letters. He waxed lyrical about the place, suggesting it was palatial in the extreme, an outpost of true luxury. I walked from the train station down to the waterfront. A group of children were playing marbles on the pavement, in the yellow light of afternoon. I asked them for the direction of Cecil's. Without looking up, one of the boys pointed over his shoulder.

I had not noticed the whitewashed hotel perched there behind him, set back on the far side of the esplanade. It was easy to see its original appeal. The building was wide but not high, two stories clinging to the ground floor's roof. There were steps up from the street, a sheltered entrance, above it an expansive balcony. All the windows had slatted jalousie shutters; some were blown open by the wind, others bolted shut. The place resembled one of those solid, compelling gems found in the novels of Graham Greene.

Time had not been kind to Cecil's. Even in the sugar-sweet light of late afternoon, it was hard to lavish praise on the current condition. Washing lines crisscrossed the balconies, and the whitewash was dirt gray and blistered with damp. I walked up to the entrance and climbed the steps.

Inside, the receptionist was watching television with his left eye; the other was covered by a homemade patch. He was holding the TV antenna in one hand, jiggling it to make sense of an Egyptian soap opera. Beside him, a squat man was smoking hashish. Both figures looked up in amazement. It was clear that no one had ventured there in years.

The entrance was gloomy, the walls waxy and damp. The only decorations were tourist posters from the 1970s and a cardboard cutout of an Aeroflot stewardess. There was a sense that at one time, perhaps long ago, something very evil had taken place within the walls.

I inquired if there was a single room, for a night or two. The hashish smoker cackled with laughter; his friend dropped the antenna and shuttled over to a desk diary. His fingers began in January, turning over a week at a time. They made their way through many months of blank paper, until they arrived at December.

"*Oui,* monsieur," he said hesitantly, "I think we have space."

He led the way up an attractive double staircase, no doubt quite a feature in its day. On the first floor were yet more mildewed posters of Moroccan highlights and innumerable ice buckets on stands, filled with cigarette ends.

After wrestling with a Chinese padlock on door number three, the manager swung the door inward. He winked with his one good eye, as if to prepare me for the opulence inside. I stepped across the threshold. Not since my travels in search of India's underbelly had I seen such impressive wear and tear.

All the windows were cracked or missing entirely, half-concealed behind rotting curtains. The linoleum floor was mottled with dark spots where previous guests had stamped out their cigarettes, and the bed was a ramp, collapsed at one end. There was no bathroom. It was explained in a mumble that the hotel had a problem with its water supply.

"There are no toilets at all?"

The manager replied in the negative. He suggested the place was far better off without the toilets, sticking his nose up at the very thought of them. Then he held out a palm and asked for payment in advance. I counted out some banknotes and passed them over.

"Where can I take a shower?" I asked.

"In the kitchen of the restaurant next door."

THE LAST TIME I had come to Tangier was thirty-five years before, aged three. My strongest memory of the city was the scent of orange blossom. I can smell it now. It was pungent, intoxicating. I had spent days running through the public gardens, dressed in my itchy camel-wool jelaba, sniffing the air. I remember, too, the warmth of the sun on my back, the crowded cafés, and the people. There were so many people then.

In the 1960s, Tangier was famed for the foreign writers who took refuge there, away from the more rigid conventions of Europe and the United States. The most celebrated was author Paul Bowles, who moved to Tangier after the war and resided there until his death in 1999.

Wandering the streets, it seemed to me that the vibrancy of

Tangier had been replaced with gloom, a melancholy, as if the party had moved on elsewhere. The buildings reflected it. They were no longer loved. Fabulous villas and theaters, hotels and cafés, were all boarded up, or fallen into a limbo like Cecil's.

It was dusk by the time I reached rue de la Plage. I stood at the bottom of the hill, staring up at the narrow street. I admit it—I was apprehensive. I was fearful, too. I am not certain why. Sometimes it's like that, when you have traveled far to be somewhere or to meet someone very special. You pause at the last step. There was a temptation to turn on my heel and take the next train back to Casablanca. My grandfather had been a figure of inspiration, an example, as well as a myth. And this was reality—the place where he lived, and where he died.

Keeping well to the side of the road, I started walking up the hill. There were small shops on both sides—each one offered the same selection of knickknacks and razor blades, toothpaste, boot polish, and canned cheese. I checked the square enamel numbers outside the shops. As I did so, I felt my heart in my chest. There was 17, then 18, 19, and after it 20 . . . one more to go . . . 21 rue de la Plage.

I had arrived. My feet were pressed together outside the doorway, on the very spot my grandfather had been struck by the reversing Coca-Cola truck back in 1969. The road was two-way then, astonishingly, as it was barely wide enough for a single car. It was so steep that vehicles were challenged to get all the way up to the top. The local taxis had perfected a way of revving their engines, racing headlong, swerving from side to side so that their bald tires could maintain traction.

I turned my back to the lane and stared up at the building. The outer wall was made from large square blocks of stone. It went straight up and gave no sign of what lay behind. The doorway was arched, filled with a blue wrought-iron gate backed by a sheet of steel. Above it was a modest marble plaque, inscribed with the words *Villa Andalus*.

I took a deep breath and rang the bell. I waited. No answer. I rang again. Still no answer. I was about to leave and walk back down the hill to Cecil's when a woman arrived at the front door. She was in her fifties, with a mass of gray hair knotted up in a bun. Her face was kind and motherly, dominated by wide-rimmed glasses. I was struck by a warmth, a generosity of spirit. It seemed to radiate all around her. She was carrying a basket. In it was a Siamese cat.

It was a difficult moment. I began to explain in my limited French that I was the grandson of an Afghan chieftain's son who had once lived at Villa Andalus.

"Do you speak English?" the woman asked in an American voice.

"Yes."

"Then you had better come inside."

A STEEP BANK OF steps ran up to the villa. It was cobbled at the edges in rounded pebbles, stone slabs in the middle. A nervous old Alsatian charged down to the door and was called sharply to heel. On the right of the entrance was an outbuilding. It looked down onto the street. The American woman, whose name was Pamela, lived there. At the top of the steps was the villa itself; the walk up to it was shaded by a canopy of vines.

Pamela said that the landlord lived in the villa. She offered to arrange for me to meet him the next morning. We chatted about books for a moment or two. Pamela was well-read. She knew my book on Ethiopia, my quest for King Solomon's Mines, and she had read my grandfather's books on Afghanistan, and even knew my grandmother's autobiography—the tale of how she abandoned Scotland for the Hindu Kush.

Twenty minutes after our doorstep meeting, I was sitting with Pamela in a small café, eating barbecued fish. I asked how long she had lived at rue de la Plage.

"It's been twelve years," she said.

"Do you live alone?"

"No," she replied, "I share it with my cats, and with five hundred caftans."

"What brought you here?"

Pamela stared into a glass of local red wine. "The wanderlust of youth," she said, her gaze unflinching. "I was living in Brooklyn, in 1965, when I heard a Yugoslav cargo ship was about to leave for Eastern Europe. Without giving it a moment's thought, I talked my way aboard. The first stop was Tangier. For me it was the exotic East. I planned to be onshore two days, but stayed two months. The smells and sounds, the blaze of color—I was knocked down by it all."

Pamela said she had spent years living and traveling through the Mediterranean and North Africa. Much land passed beneath her feet, but her first love was always Morocco. She returned to the United States and opened a Moroccan restaurant in Los Angeles, but even that wasn't enough to satisfy her heart.

"One morning I packed it in," she said quietly. "I bought a one-way ticket, and arrived here with a pair of suitcases and my favorite traveling cat. I have never looked back."

I told her about my grandfather, who had come to Tangier after the death of his wife.

"Whoever you are," she said, "Morocco takes you in. Before you know it, you have a home and friends, and you've forgotten your troubles."

I asked Pamela what her friends had thought when she had set up home in Tangier.

"They tried to hold me back," she said.

"Why?"

She looked across at me and sighed. "Because of their own fear," she said.

THE NEXT MORNING, I was up early. Sleeping at a forty-five-degree angle had been uncomfortable, but nothing in comparison to the desperate nocturnal urge to pee in a hotel without toilets. I sponged myself down as directed in the roach-infested restaurant kitchen next door. It is a memory I hope, someday, to forget.

Pamela had told me to come to the villa at nine-thirty to meet the landlord. She had set up the rendezvous and gone off to work with her favorite traveling cat.

The doorbell was answered by a slim, straight-backed man aged about sixty. His hair was dyed black and glistened in the light. It was combed carefully to the left side of his square head. He introduced himself as David Rebibo. He said he was one of Morocco's last remaining Jews, that his family had owned Villa Andalus for more than a hundred years. I asked if he remembered my grandfather.

"How could anyone forget such a man?" he replied swiftly. "It was a long time ago, and I was much younger, but we would sit together on the balcony, and he would tell me of his travels."

Mr. Rebibo led the way to the villa. As I passed under the canopy of wisteria vines, I first set eyes on the building's extraordinary façade. It was arranged on two floors, linked by a curved double stairway, rising from a patio in front of the house. Wherever I looked, there were flowers and ferns erupting from terracotta pots.

I was led inside. The rooms were small but well appointed. There were long mirrors to give an extra dimension, and a great many pictures—some Indian, others European and Chinese. On every windowsill and table there were orchids. I found it intensely moving to be in the house where my grandfather had spent his last years. I took in the details, which his own meticulous eye would have treasured—the coving on the ceilings, the sconces on the bedroom wall, and the patterned brass handles on the doors. But my delight at being there was tinged with sadness, for it was here that he lived a life waiting for death, pining for his beloved Bobo.

We went back out onto the patio and sat at a wrought-iron table, the winter sun quite dazzling above. The landlord pressed a hand to his glistening hair, unsure perhaps whether the dye could take the sun.

"Your grandfather would sit here in the mornings," he said. "He would read and write letters. He used a fountain pen, on onionskin paper."

I pulled out a clutch of the letters. "Here are some of them," I said.

Mr. Rebibo leaned over and glanced at the sheets.

"That's his hand," he said calmly. "Look at the precision. He was the most conscientious man I have ever met."

A maid descended from the first floor, a headscarf knotted at the back of her head. She slid a silver tray with tea onto the table.

"Did he ever have visitors?" I asked.

The landlord poured me a porcelain cup and slid it over.

"Oh yes," he said. "Some very important people indeed. He knew the late king, and his father, too. And, of course, I remember you and your two sisters coming. You were very small. Your father brought you."

I stirred my tea and breathed in the steam.

"The first time I met your father," he said, "he had recently returned from Arabia, where he had been the guest of King Ibn Saud. He was sitting where you are sitting now. I remember it so clearly."

Mr. Rebibo called his elderly Alsatian to heel.

"He told me a story that has stayed in my mind," he said.

I asked what it was.

"Your father was welcomed at the palace in Mecca," he said. "He had forgotten to bring a gift. Suddenly he found himself in the throne room before the old king. He bowed low and kissed Ibn Saud's right hand and said, 'Your Majesty, I would like to present you with a gift. Here it is before you. It is I. I give myself to you as your servant until the end of my days.'

"Ibn Saud looked down and said, 'I thank you for your fine gift, and I give you back to yourself. Now come and sit here, and we will talk.' "

The landlord laughed, sipped his tea, and laughed again.

"I can't tell you how sad we were when the accident happened," he said. "Your grandfather was walking back down the hill from Café de France, as he did each morning. He had reached the door and was taking out his key when the truck reversed. He was knocked unconscious."

"Did you see it happen?"

"No, I was away on that day. When I returned, your grandfather was dead."

We sat in silence for a few moments. The vines around the villa's door were alive with shadows and birdsong.

"Now," said the landlord in a serious voice, "I'll give you what you came for. I am surprised that no one from your family has come to collect them until now."

"Come to collect what?" I said, confused.

"Your grandfather's diaries, of course."

ELEVEN

The value of the dwelling is in the dweller.

THE DIARIES SAT SQUARELY ON MY lap as the bus rumbled south toward Chefchouen. There were two of them—both bound in faded red cloth, filled with the unmistakable dark blue lettering of my grandfather's hand. It was far too bumpy to read, and so I gazed out the window. The landscape of northern Morocco slipped slowly by—small fields scattered with cactus and sheep, wizened men perched on donkeys, orange groves, farmsteads, and translucent winter streams.

As the afternoon light waned and dusk approached, I caught my first glimpse of Chefchouen. It was set on a hillside, all rocky and bleak like the end of the world. The foothills of the Rif hung about it in a dark curtain. The buildings were white, their roofs red terracotta; they were quite unlike any

others I had seen in Morocco. A man on the bus said the town
had been settled by the Muslim refugees fleeing Andalucía five
centuries ago.

I took a room in a gloomy guesthouse on a backstreet of the
medina, attracted to the place by the name—Hotel Paradise.
Dusk had brought a sudden chill. The lanes were packed with
people, all of them trussed up in woolen jelabas. I dug out
Pete's postcard, handed it to the first child I met, and touched
the address at the bottom of the card. The boy nodded. He led
the way up flights of awkward mule steps and through whitewashed alleyways where the aroma of roasting meat mingled
with the scent of jasmine flowers. After fifteen minutes of
walking, the boy stopped. He pointed to the card and then at a
low entrance plugged by a battered wooden door. I gave him a
coin, and he ran off back into the maze. I wondered if it really
was the place where the Texan had found true love. I knocked
hard. There was shuffling inside, as if someone old and tired
was moving forward. The sounds were followed by those of
a bolt sliding back and of unoiled hinges moving against each
other.

A bearded man was standing in the doorway, the right side
of his face illuminated by a stub of candle. He was aged and
wore a turban. The smell of putrid fish emanated from the
darkness behind. I hoped very earnestly that I was at the wrong
address.

"Peter Williams?" I said.

The man gasped. I said the name again.

"*Nam*, yes," he said in Arabic, "*bienvenue*, welcome."

The smell of fish got stronger as I followed the flickering
candle wick into the body of the house. The walls were black, as
if a fire had taken hold at some time in the recent past. I could
hear chanting. It was close—a male voice, hypnotic against the
shadows. The bearded figure pushed at a door. It didn't open at

first. He pushed again. A key turned in a lock, and the door opened inward.

Inside, seven men were sitting cross-legged, chanting verses from the Qur'an. The only light came from a single candle placed in the middle of the floor. It was hard to say how large the room was, as it was so dark. The figures didn't look up when I entered. They were lost in their own world. I scanned their faces. All had beards. They ranged from old age to youth.

I crouched on the floor, waiting for something to happen. I would have left had there been an easy way to do so. Calling out for the American would have broken the concentration. So I sat and waited.

After an hour of chanting, the figures disbanded. Six of the men filed off. The last one looked at me through the dimness. He was lanky and hunched.

"Pete?" I said softly.

"Yeah?"

"It's Tahir," I said.

The figure moved closer. *"Allahu akbar!"* he said. "God is great."

I was very eager to get out of the house. I mumbled something about claustrophobia and led Pete into the street. Five minutes later we were at a café, drinking glasses of mint tea. I looked at him long and very hard, as if to try and understand how he got into such a mess. His face was bronzed and bearded and had been savaged by mosquitoes. His head was crowned by a lacy white skullcap; his eyes were somehow clouded and cold.

"I wanted to check if everything was okay," I said. "I was worried."

"Praise Allah for bringing you here," he said. "I am well. You can see for yourself."

"How is Yasmine?"

"*Alhamdulillah,* thanks be to God," he replied, "she is well. We were married last month."

I gave congratulations. "Do you plan to go back to Texas now?"

Pete pulled the hood of his jelaba over his head. "I am a Muslim," he said. "I will never go back to the States."

"Why not?"

"The American Dream," he said. "It's propaganda, it's bullshit!" Pete swirled the tea leaves in his glass. "Allah has shown me the Path."

"What is it?"

"A world without America," he said.

LATE THE NEXT DAY, I arrived back at the Caliph's House. The guardians swarmed round to greet me as I entered the garden door. I had only been gone two nights, but a great deal had happened in my absence. Ariane had been stung by wasps, the house had been flooded in a thunderstorm, and the shantytown's gangster had called the police again.

"Where's Kamal?" I asked Rachana.

"Probably at a bar," she said. "He's been drunk since you left."

I said something in reply, but my mind was not on Kamal. I was thinking about Pete and his descent into fanaticism. He had come to Morocco in search of true love and had fallen victim to the embrace of a misguided brotherhood. I hardly knew him, but for some reason, I felt obliged to become involved.

A LETTER HAD COME from Thailand, sent by a student who had read my books and wanted a job. The envelope was adorned with an ornate stamp bearing the image of a ruby-colored rose.

I hurried over to Hicham's house with it. The old man held the stamp in his palm and gazed at it lovingly. He didn't speak for a long time. Then, slowly, he put it down and thanked me.

"What conversation could ever pay for such a beautiful thing?" he asked.

I said I hoped we could talk about fanatics.

Hicham called for his wife, Khadija, to make a pot of sweet tea. He nestled in his favorite chair, rubbed his hands together, and looked at the floor.

"They think they can see clearly," he said, "but they are blind men. Blind men who understand nothing but death."

The old stamp collector put a hand on his chest. "I will die soon," he said plainly, "my heart is bad. But I fear the future. It's for your generation to deal with, for you to solve. It's a war. You must understand that. It's not the time for kind words. These people must be found and killed. That is the only way."

Hicham's wife brought over the tray of tea, served it, and slipped back into the shadows.

"When there is rabies in a village," said the old man, "you don't think twice. You kill the rabid dog. It whimpers and looks sad, but you don't pay attention. You shoot it. If you don't, it will threaten the society. The same goes for fanatics. Kill them or be killed by them. As I see it, there's no choice."

KAMAL DIDN'T TURN UP for three days. He kept his cell phone off, a practice he knew infuriated me. When he disappeared, I could never be sure if he would ever return. I would wonder if he had been thrown in jail again. Eventually he would slink into Dar Khalifa without a word of explanation.

The longer I spent in Morocco, the more I found that explanations were rarely given. If anything at all was said, it was to pass the blame onto someone or something else. The cook was an expert at it. Every week, she smashed a variety of serving dishes and plates. The first time she broke a china teapot, she blamed the soap on her hands—it was bad quality, she said, more slippery than usual. When she smashed a new earthenware *tajine*, she blamed me for buying such an inferior one. And after that, when she dropped a glass vase, she said it was the Jinns.

In the West, we try to work out a logical cause when an accident occurs. The vase breaks because it's knocked by a careless hand. The car crashes because the road is wet. The dog bites a child because it's savage and a danger to honest society. But I found in Morocco that these everyday mishaps were treated in a very different way. They were frequently put down to the work of supernatural forces, with the Jinns at the center of the belief system.

Although I was intrigued by the idea of invisible spirits and their parallel world, I found myself cursing them every day. They were a back door by which all blame could be neatly side-stepped, shifted onto someone else. The guardians had mastered the technique of using Jinns to blame-shift. They lived in a world in which any blunder could be instantly brushed aside. Any mistake was explainable, from chopping down the wrong tree to setting fire to the lawn mower. The explanation was always the same: "It was not my fault. It was the work of the Jinns."

At last, when Kamal finally arrived, I launched into a scathing attack on the supernatural as a method of shifting blame. I couldn't control myself.

"There's no way Morocco will progress," I said accusingly, "until people lose the superstitious thought. It's crippling them."

Kamal didn't reply until my storm of anger had passed. Then, after a long gap in conversation, he said, "The Jinns are at the heart of Moroccan culture. Pretending they don't exist won't help you."

"You lived in the United States," I said. "You're a modern guy. Don't tell me you believe in Jinns."

"Of course I do," he said. "They're the backbone of our culture. They are part of the Islamic faith."

At that moment it seemed to me as if the Jinns were in league with the fanatics—both sideshows to the genuine message. The encounter with Pete was still fresh in my mind. I told Kamal what I had seen.

"He was brainwashed," I said. "He's a fanatic, for God's sake."

"That's not real Islam," Kamal replied. "It's a hoax, an illusion. It's anarchy."

"Well, Islamic anarchy is how the West sees the Arab world."

Kamal bit his lower lip. His expression was cold. "You don't know what it's like to enter the United States with a passport covered in Arabic writing," he said. "One look at it, and the flags go up. They're thinking 'terrorist.' There's nothing you can say. You can just pray they'll let you in."

"But how do you expect the Americans to behave after 9/11?"

"With suspicion, of course," he replied. "But not with hatred against all Muslims."

Kamal was right. Of course only a fraction of Muslims are fanatics. But their voices are loud and getting louder all the time. Worse still, their actions speak far louder than their words. Every morning before breakfast I would check the news on the Internet. My great fear was seeing the word "Morocco" for the wrong reasons. The Casablanca bombings earlier in the year had been a terrible reminder that Islamic extremism was spreading like wildfire.

A COUPLE OF DAYS later, Hamza asked very politely if he could have two hundred dirhams. He said the money, about

twenty dollars, was not a loan, but to perform an act of charity. The good deed, he assured me, would raise my standing in the eyes of God.

"Give it to me," he said with conviction, "and you will be forgiven your sins on Judgment Day."

I frowned hard, gave him the money, and went back to the top terrace to read. Later that afternoon, I found Hamza digging a hole in the middle of the lawn. He was sweating profusely, his eyes bloodshot from the stream of perspiration. I couldn't understand what he was doing. Unable to hold in my curiosity, I went down from the terrace. By that time, the hole on the lawn was about three feet deep, and half as wide. Beside it was a pile of straw. I was about to ruffle about in the straw when Hamza stopped me.

"Be careful!" he said brusquely, "that's very delicate."

"It's only straw," I said.

"No, it is not!"

The guardian tossed down the shovel and dipped his hands

into the straw. He pulled out an ostrich egg. I looked at him, at the oversized egg, and then the hole, hoping a natural connection would present itself. Hamza smiled.

"The two hundred dirhams," he said shrewdly, "I spent it on this."

"An ostrich egg?" I said. "The act of charity?"

"Yes, yes, that's it!"

Hamza placed a nest of straw into the hole, put the egg on it, and filled it in with soil. I waited for an explanation. It didn't come.

"How will that help anyone?" I asked.

"You gave me the money without asking what it was for," the guardian said. "You trusted me. Your trust will be repaid on Judgment Day."

"But who is the egg going to help?"

"You, of course!" said Hamza. "It's to help you."

THERE IS NO SUCH thing as building renovation that runs on time. But I find it hard to believe there has ever been a project more delayed than our own. We continued to camp in one room on the ground floor of a large house. The rest of Dar Khalifa was unfit for human habitation or was downright unsafe.

The architect's teams had done some passable building work, but they left a wake of destruction and chaos. Despite Kamal's promises, his master craftsman didn't turn up until the third week of December. Whenever I asked what had happened to the new team, he enthused that they were led by the maddest, and therefore the most gifted, moualem this side of Marrakech. And, as he declared very frequently, a madman could not be rushed.

The craftsman's small, ordinary pickup arrived three days before Christmas. There was a soft scratch at the front door, and a minute later, Hamza was leading the artisan into the house. He was very reserved, with the build of a sumo wrestler, a great hulk of a body poised above a pair of nimble feet. He didn't look very mad to me.

I drew this point to Kamal's attention later in the day.

"Don't be fooled," he said. "Aziz is madder than a rabid dog. But he channels his madness into his work."

I sat for an entire afternoon drinking mint tea, discussing the various types of bejmat and the patterns to be used. A box of tiles was brought out and a handful of samples laid out on the floor. Aziz talked about the color and consistency of the different clays.

"This is the red clay from Meknes," he said, holding up a square of rose-tinted terracotta. "And this is the clay from Fès, much paler, the color of fresh-baked bread."

The master's assistant delved his rough hand into the box again.

"The bejmat can either be used like this in its raw state," Aziz continued, "or it can be fired again with one of a hundred glazes—blues, greens, yellows, reds." Aziz paused to sip his tea. "Until recently," he said, "unglazed terracotta was not used inside a home. It was considered too crude. But now there is something of a fashion for it."

The simple terracotta reminded me of Mexico, where haciendas are tiled with them on the inside and roofed with them on the outside. This is no coincidence, of course, as the know-how to make terracotta was transported to the New World by Spanish conquistadores five centuries ago. The Spanish had themselves acquired the techniques from the Moors of Andalucía, who had brought it to Europe from Morocco.

Visit any important building in the kingdom, and you will never see unglazed terracotta used anywhere but on the outside, where it adorns verandahs and garden paths. For Rachana and me, there was something very wonderful about it, a stark

beauty whose simplicity could be complemented with a scat-
tering of zelij mosaics.

Aziz and his team may have been mad, but they were not
stupid. They encouraged me in ever more piercing tones to let
them demonstrate the limits of their skill. Naturally, the more
intricate the work, the more elaborate the price.

"We can create for you a labyrinth of color and design,"
Aziz said. "You will be blinded when you enter your bedroom,
dazzled when you go into the salon. By the end of each day,
your head will pound like a steam train charging through the
night!"

The first day of discussions ended very late, and talk began
again the next afternoon. Aziz sat before me, his portly form
shrouded in a pure white jelaba, his head covered by the hood.
Apart from the odd outburst of tempered enthusiasm, he was a
calm man who took his work very seriously indeed. We talked
all through the second afternoon, considering the many samples of tile. When the time for decisions came, we decided on
the simplest patterns, which would be enhanced by a chiseled
border around each room. Through the many hours of conversation, money had not been mentioned once. There was something very civilized about choosing work because you wanted
it, rather than because it is all you can afford. But as always, I
was racked with fear at what it would cost.

I prodded Kamal. "Ask him for the price."

"Hush," he said.

"I'm sure I can't afford Aziz," I whispered. "Should we find
a man a little less mad?"

My assistant didn't reply. But when the matter of money
was eventually brought up, as if it were a final detail, Aziz
gave me a scribbled list of figures. The sum was surprisingly
affordable.

"Try and get the price down anyway," I said to Kamal.

He and Aziz deliberated for a moment or two.

"Aziz is an honest moualem," he said. "And as such his price is his price. He will not raise it, nor will he lower it."

The master craftsman gulped down his tea, and we shook hands, before placing them on our hearts.

EVERY TIME I REMINDED Kamal we had to get the money back from the architect, he brushed the subject aside. I began to get the feeling he didn't care. I pleaded with him. Without the money, I said, I would have to cut his salary. Kamal looked worried. A single bead of sweat welled up on his forehead and rolled down his nose.

I suggested we hire a lawyer to write an official-looking letter.

"The architect will drop dead laughing," he said. "There's only one way to get the money."

"How?"

"We'll hold a feast."

THAT NIGHT, THERE WAS the rumble of thunder. I rushed to the window, only to find the sky quite clear. The sound came again, low and deep. On its tail were screams, then shouts, from the bidonville. The shouts were followed by the scurry of a man's feet and a pounding at our bedroom door.

"The bulldozers are back! Come quickly!" said the voice.

It was Hamza. He was hysterical. His house was being torn to pieces. I put on my shoes and ran with him to the far side of the shantytown. A crowd had gathered—men and women, small children held tight in their arms. A pair of yellow bulldozers had started to demolish a wall against which shacks had been built. There was rubble everywhere, clouds of dust, and hastily gathered possessions tied up in sacks.

I had not met Hamza's family before, even though we were

neighbors. The customary formality between employer and employee had kept us apart. His wife and five children were ferrying a lifetime of belongings into an open space at the side of the crowd. Hamza's face was ashen, his head stooped, his self-assurance shattered. I tried to comfort him.

"It will be all right," I said pathetically.

The guardian was far too polite to strike me with his fist. But had I been in his position, I would have felt tempted to do just that. I owned an oasis an acre in size, and he a modest two-room shanty, now being torn up by government machines.

My friend François had warned me time and again about being too helpful to the guardians. He recounted endless tales in which a naive expatriate gave shelter to a forlorn Moroccan family. The stories always had the same punch line—"So-and-so made the biggest mistake of his life."

We stood there, the cold winter night cloaking us like a burial shroud, Hamza's belongings stacked up in a heap nearby. I breathed in hard. As the employer, I was more than the man who handed out cash every Friday. I was the man expected to come to their aid when his own men were in need. I saw François's face in my mind. He was wagging a finger, shouting cautions. I brushed him away. Only an expatriate would shy from his responsibilities, I thought.

Within an hour, Hamza and his family were installed in the guesthouse at the far end of the vegetable patch. There were two bedrooms, a toilet, and a shower. The place was rundown, but no more so than the main house. I welcomed the family and said they were free to stay until they found their feet. Hamza's face broke into an ample smile. He jerked my hand up and down, pulled me to his chest, and pressed his lips to my cheeks.

ACROSS THE ARAB WORLD, Friday prayers are followed by the heaviest lunch of the week. Moroccan families come together, cluster around communal platters of couscous and lamb, and feast. It's the one time when all employers are generous, treating their workers to great salvers of food. Those without families or jobs hurry to the mosques in search of charity.

On Friday morning, Kamal asked me for money to buy ingredients. He bought three sacks of assorted vegetables, fifteen chickens, couscous, and fresh fruit. The food was taken to his grandmother, who prepared a banquet fit for a king. The platters were loaded into my car, which was then parked outside a mosque near Maarif, in time for Friday prayers.

At the end of the service, as the worshippers exited, Kamal approached a huddle of beggars with outstretched hands. He talked to them for a few minutes, motioned directions, and came back to the Jeep. We sped into the traffic.

"Where are we going with all this food?" I said.

"To the architect's office," he replied.

At the gallery, a fresh exhibition of abstract art had been hung—giant canvases splattered with multicolored spots. The prim receptionist was sitting alone, filing her nails. She said the architect was not there.

"We are not looking for him," said Kamal as he blustered in with the food.

He ferried the platters into the main gallery and put them down in the middle of the floor. The receptionist asked what was going on. Kamal smiled.

"A feast," he said.

Five minutes later, the first of the beggars turned up. They bustled in nervously, thanked God, and dug into the food. Fifteen minutes after that, there were sixty or more, gorging themselves, tossing the chicken bones on the ground. The architect's assistant chattered to her boss excitedly on the phone. As word of the banquet spread, more and more homeless souls arrived to eat.

Kamal seemed pleased. "He'll be here any minute," he said.

A second later, we made out the architect's Range Rover, and the sound of Italian shoes moving swiftly to the door. A string of insults followed, then threats. The architect's face became so ferociously red that I feared he might keel over.

I asked for my money. He fired off a salvo of excuses.

"Our friends want to touch the paintings," Kamal said.

The architect glanced at the beggars' oily fingers, the mess on the floor, and clapped his hands to his cheeks. He strode over to his desk and wrote me out a check.

CHRISTMAS WAS COMING. I was not brought up as a Christian, but I was raised to appreciate the consumerist trappings of the holiday season. Now that Ariane was almost three, I wanted to buy her a Christmas tree. Kamal was solemn when he heard of the plan.

"This is an Islamic country," he said, "Santa doesn't come here."

I held Ariane's ears and gave him a cold look.

"Santa comes to all boys and girls," I quipped. "It doesn't matter where they live!"

We set off in search of a Christmas tree. First we drove to fashionable Maarif. If Christmas was going to happen anywhere, it would surely be there. The week before the holiday, the Western world is a frenzied meltdown of gift buying, dangerously large meals, and endless TV reruns. During Christmas week, the streets of London are usually so crowded that you can't even get into the stores. If you do manage to prise your way inside one, you find everything's been picked clean, as if vultures have descended.

I braced myself for some of the same in Maarif. To my surprise, there was nothing in the way of festive cheer—no synthetic snow or carol singers, no Santa or reindeer, or turkeys hanging in butcher's windows, and absolutely no Christmas trees in sight. The streets were empty.

"If you want Christmas," said Kamal, "go back to Europe."

"I'm not going home without a tree," I said. "I'd never be able to look Ariane in the eye again."

Kamal swung the wheel and stepped hard on the gas. We rolled out of Maarif and into a plush residential area. A few minutes later, Kamal was leading me into a haphazard garden nursery, where a man with one hand was sleeping in a chair.

"Do you have any Christmas trees?" Kamal asked, prodding him awake.

The man opened one eye, rubbed his nose with his stump, and motioned toward a clutch of frail young trees.

"That one," he said. "That one's a Christmas tree."

I followed the line of the man's stump. He was pointing to a palm tree.

"That's not a Christmas tree," I said. "It's a date palm. I'm desperate, but I'm not that desperate!"

The man closed his eyes, and by the time we were out the door, he was snoring again.

Back in the Jeep, the tension was rising. I had promised Ariane a tall, fragrant fir tree. She was young but her tiny mind had already been corrupted concerning the whole concept of Christmas. As far as she was concerned, the tree was the center of it all. Without it, there could be no reindeer, no stockings, no Santa, no gifts.

"There is a place," said Kamal, forcing the accelerator down again. "It's a last chance."

We slalomed across Casablanca, back through the suburbs and the well-to-do new town. The modern sprawl was replaced by the Art Deco quarter. Kamal applied the brakes hard. The Jeep jolted to a stop. Wherever I looked, men were unloading nondescript boxes. There were thousands of them, all bearing

Chinese characters. The area looked like the backdrop for a 1970s martial arts movie. I recognized it as the place I had bought the school supplies with Zohra.

Kamal disappeared and, a moment later, he reappeared clutching a flat cardboard box. There were Chinese characters at one end of the package. At the other was a skull and cross-bones with almond eyes. We opened it up. Inside was the scruffiest, lowest-quality synthetic Christmas tree imaginable. Kamal threw his cigarette out the window.

"One spark," he said, "and you'll have an inferno on your hands."

ON THE WAY HOME to present Ariane with her festive fire hazard, we stopped at Habous. I wanted to buy the children jelabas. The outfits are of universal use. You can wear them out-doors as overcoats, as daytime clothing, or even as bathrobes. We hurried through a row of jelaba shops, looking at colors and trying to gauge prices. Whenever I found one that looked good and was soft to the touch, Kamal would storm out, screaming insults at the shopkeeper.

"That man's a thief!" he would yell, or, "May his tongue be ripped out by demons for asking so much!"

In the East, the tradition of bargaining is an honorable one, and Moroccan society has one of the most developed bartering economies I have come across. I am usually satisfied with chip-ping in a few cents more if it saves time and secures the pur-chase. But to a native Moroccan, shirking on the bargaining front is seen as falling short of responsibility. There is honor at stake. Forget the bargaining and you are bringing shame on the shop.

The guidebooks always say it's best to take a local person with you when you go shopping in Morocco. But they don't tell you that the local is likely to veto all purchases, and even liable to get you into a fistfight with the shopkeeper as he strives to protect your honor.

Kamal refused to let me buy any jelabas that afternoon. He warned the stallholders that he would injure any of them who went behind his back and sold me a jelaba without his permission.

"Once I have beaten them up," he said, "I'll go after their families. I'll attack them, and then I'll find their friends!"

I liked Kamal and found him useful, but he was becoming a control freak. I told him to relax.

"You don't understand," he said. "This is the way our society's stayed on track for a thousand years. If you let one shopkeeper get away with overpricing, the whole country will collapse like a house of cards."

Before we left Habous, I made excuses and slipped into the courtyard where I remembered seeing the fine Spanish dining table during Ramadan. I peered into the back of the shop and spied it sitting there piled high with junk. It was no good getting Kamal involved. He was in far too foul a mood. So I asked the price myself. The shopkeeper sat forward in his wicker chair and coughed.

"You like it very much," he said.

"Oh yes," I said, "owning it would make me the happiest man in Morocco."

The tradesman rubbed the tips of his fingers together.

"Because you love it so, the price has gone up," he sniffed. "It's now *six milles* dirhams, six hundred dollars."

TWELVE

The dog barked, but the caravan moved on.

NEW YEAR'S EVE WAS A DAY filled with hope. Like a snake sloughing an old, tired skin, it seemed that we were leaving the problems behind us, pushing forward into a new year of possibility. My resolution for the coming twelve months was to be the master of my own decisions, and top dog in the Caliph's House. As the final few minutes of December ebbed away, I ranted at Rachana how I would no longer be pushed around by the guardians, by the imam, by Kamal, or any artisans.

Midnight came. We clinked glasses, swilled a mouthful of rough Moroccan wine, and said our prayers. I prayed for an uneventful year, with no surprises.

Ten minutes later we were ready for bed. I slipped under the duvet and closed my eyes. Outside, the bidonville was silent. Even the donkeys were hushed. All I could hear was the ocean breeze rustling through eucalyptus leaves and the sound of an owl pining for its mate. No one in the shantytown bothered with New Year celebrations. Such festivities are the preserve of people who already have too much.

Fifteen minutes into January, my cellular phone rang. It was Kamal. He sounded very drunk. There was a problem, he said.

"What is it?"

"The truck driver."

"What's wrong?"

"He's been arrested."

"So what?"

Kamal's voice trembled. "He's got our sand," he said.

Nothing would normally worry me less than hearing of a truck driver and his load impounded in the night. But, as Kamal made clear, the driver was the linchpin to my life. It was he who was keeping everything on track. Without him, we would have no cheap sand, and without the sand we would have no bejmat laid. Without the tiles for the floors, we would not be able to do the walls, and without the walls we couldn't plumb the bathrooms. Very soon, Kamal slurred, the renovation would fall to pieces. If that happened, he said, my children would fall sick and Rachana would end up divorcing me. It seemed a radical deduction.

"There's only one thing to do to prevent your divorce," he said grimly. "We have to get the truck driver out of jail."

An hour into the New Year, Kamal and I were in the Jeep driving out of Casablanca on the empty coast road. It was dark and windy, the kind of night when evil takes hold. Kamal was far too drunk to drive, but he did anyway. He boasted of knowing every bend and said he could drive it blindfolded. As we zigzagged south of the city, he told me about the truck driver, Abdul Haq.

"He's been working for our family since he was a child," he said. "His father worked for us, and his grandfather before him. There's a bond. If he's in trouble, we are bound by honor to help."

"Why's he in jail?"

"The usual," said Kamal.

"What's that?"

"Whoring."

Kamal staggered out of the Jeep and into the jail. I followed him timidly. The officer in charge said Abdul Haq was to be locked up for a month. His driving license was going to be impounded, his vehicle auctioned, and the precious cargo of sand sold. The circumstances looked bad, but in Morocco ill fortune can be overturned in the blink of an eye.

By the second hour of the New Year, we had paid off the guards, freed Abdul Haq, and recovered the sand. It was a high moment and one I think back to often. I hoped the year's early success was an omen of good fortune to come.

THE SECOND EVENT THAT faced us on New Year's Day surrounded Hamza. He and his family were now comfortably established in the outbuilding at the end of the vegetable patch. His wife spent half her time cooking up pots of stewed meat, and the other half slaving over a mountain of laundry. However hard she toiled, the mountain never seemed to decrease in size. Their five children ranged from about nine down to less than a year. All of them were boys, carbon copies of their father— minus the handlebar mustache.

On the night they first sought refuge at Dar Khalifa, I had strained to make it clear to Hamza that the accommodation was temporary, until he had built a new shack in the bidonville. He had promised to move out as soon as his family had regrouped.

But as the days passed, it was obvious he regarded the stone guesthouse, with its electricity, flush toilet, and private garden, as a permanent new home. He knocked a door in the wall so his friends could visit more easily from the slum. Before we knew it, wild dogs, donkeys, rats, and waves of street hawkers were drifting in and out. Each day, osmosis brought a little more of the bidonville into the garden and into our home. I bit my lip and held back until New Year's morning.

Rachana and I were sitting on the balcony in bright sunlight. I was relishing January's peace. But then, through the silence came a wild commotion. There were shrill banging sounds first, then shouts, and cries of great anguish.

"What's that?" asked Rachana.

Before I could answer, Osman came running up to the house. Hot on his heels was the Bear.

"Come quickly," they both said at once. "Our houses are being broken down."

We went to investigate. A small crowd had gathered in the area where both guardians lived. They were milling about, almost as if they had been told to do so. There wasn't the sense of urgency or fear that had sounded the destruction of Hamza's home.

Osman led the way to the ruins of his house. "This was my home," he said mournfully. "This is where I lived with my wife and four children. We were so happy here." He pointed to a heap of stones, bricks, and corrugated iron.

"And that's where I lived," said the Bear meekly.

I glanced over at an almost identical pile of debris. What struck me was the orderliness of both the heaps. They didn't have the random chaotic signature of a bulldozer strike. Rather, it looked as if the roof and walls had been taken down carefully, a piece at a time.

"Where are the bulldozers?" I said.

"Oh," said the Bear, "they came and went."

"I didn't hear them."

"They came in the night," said Osman. "It was terrible."

"I was up in the night," I replied. "I didn't hear bulldozers."

Osman and the Bear exchanged troubled looks.

"They were special ones," said Osman, after almost a minute of thought. "Their engines were wrapped in blankets so they wouldn't make a noise."

Outside the supposed ruins of the guardians' homes were two neat piles of belongings. There were rudimentary pieces of furniture, blankets and pillows, pots, pans, and a huddle of children's toys. Beside the first heap, Osman's family were standing to attention, and next to them was the Bear's own entourage. The wives looked sheepish and expectant, the rows of small children hopeful, as if a new world were about to open up to them.

I asked where they were all planning to live. It was a question with a ready answer. The guardians' families had already divided the territory between them.

"The building at the side of the garden is empty," said Osman.

"Yes, and so are the rooms near the tennis court," announced the Bear.

"Our wives are both pregnant," Osman said limply, drooping his head.

I looked hard at the two men, their families, and their worldly goods. Then I glanced over my shoulder at Dar Khalifa. The house seemed to rise up like a bastion of protection, a sanctuary for refugees. I cursed myself for being so weak.

"All right," I said, "you'd all better come in."

ON THE FOURTH OF January, Kamal rolled up. His eyes were bloodshot, his hands shaking. He said someone had sold him a bad bottle of rum.

"I've been knocked out for three days," he said feverishly. "Contraband from Spain . . . Casablanca's awash with it."

"While you've been sleeping, we've been taking in tenants," I said.

I took him up to the terrace. We looked down on the garden. There were children everywhere, boys fighting and throwing mud, and girls playing hopscotch on the shaded paths. The guardians' wives had turned the barbeque area into a communal laundry. They took it in turns to smash their lathered clothes onto the hearth. Nearby were an assortment of their extended families and friends. Some were peeling vegetables, others chatting or just sitting in the sun.

"What can I do?" I said anxiously.

"You have made a grave mistake," said Kamal. "Now that they're in, they'll never leave."

"But how can I get them out?"

Kamal rubbed his eyes and slumped on a chair. "I'll think of something," he said.

THE FIRST WEEK OF January was almost at an end when, at long last, I found the time to read my grandfather's diaries. Ariane was howling because the guardians' sons had taken her dolls and amputated their limbs. Rachana was furious that the house had been hijacked from under our noses. She shouted at me, scorning my guilt-fueled generosity. I crept from the Caliph's House, out through the shantytown, and took a seat in the nearest smoke-filled café.

I opened the first of the two cloth-backed books. The immaculate indigo script stared up at me, as if ready to impart its own cautionary tale. It began:

Afifa, the maid, is taking liberties again. She has been taking my vegetables home to her family, replacing them with her own

meager groceries. For some reason she thinks I don't notice.
That's the thing I find most insulting. I may be old and
myopic, but I am not blind!

I read on, through pages of hypochondriac detail, endless lists
of self-prescribed medicines, and more moaning about the
maid:

I heard her boasting to her friend how she bosses me about. She
said I was like a child who had to be treated firmly. Fancy
that! I would dispense with her, but she would surely exact
revenge.

There were more reports on his health, about the damp winter
climate in Tangier. Then this:

At last I have found Afifa's Achilles' heel. Only one thing fills
her with terror. True terror. I have found her trying to under-
stand this diary. But thank God she cannot speak a word of
English. She doesn't know that I know her fear—her fear of
the Jinns.

IN THE SECOND WEEK of January, our friends arrived from
London. I had pleaded with everyone I knew to stay away, citing
the appalling living conditions as the reason. I warned them
about the deficiency of habitable bedrooms, the lack of hot
water, the stalled building work, and the mud-stricken shantytown. And now, on top of everything else, we had the
guardians' families and friends to deal with.

I had left Europe to escape our pseudo-friends. Everyone in
London has them—people you don't really want to see, but
who never leave you alone. I had hundreds of them. In their

world, my stock value was high only because my face had appeared on television. Each month, we were trapped into a dozen or more unnecessary social engagements. I had made a list of random excuses and pasted it up next to the phone. But pseudo-friends have a sixth sense. They could always tell when an excuse was read off a list. Now that we had a large house and an exotic address near the sea, word spread at lightning speed.

Our real friends were far too well mannered to invite themselves. If they did ask to come, they always offered to stay at a local hotel. But the pseudos had no scruples. They tended to travel by road with a throng of offspring and suitcases, squashed into a minivan. They were all in search of the same ideal: free lodging with plenty of local food, wine, sun, sand, and sea. Worse still was that they expected us to put our lives on hold and attend to their every need.

The first of the New Year guests were Frank and Lulu. They had found me a few years before through my interest in shrunken heads, the handiwork of the Shuar tribe of Peru. Frank was a nervous Englishman, his wife a strict Bavarian woman with a limp. Together they had borne a crop of four blond daughters, all of them under the age of ten. They traveled everywhere in a Japanese-made minivan.

It was early morning and Rachana had gone shopping with the maid. Ariane and I were in the garden courtyard, hiding from the guardians' wicked progeny, when the sound of a Bavarian hausfrau could be heard above the din of the shantytown. A moment later, the sleek aerodynamic lines of the minivan turned onto our lane.

Lulu got out first. I opened the front door even before she had rung the bell. She pushed her way past me without any greeting, except to thrust a pair of baby bottles at my chest.

"Milk," she snapped. "Make it warm. Blood temperature!"

I gave muffled salutations, but Lulu had vanished into the

house, leading behind her a line of daughters decreasing in size, like Russian matryoshka dolls. Frank, the henpecked husband, didn't get out of the car. After driving through England, France, Spain, and half of Morocco with the pit bull at his throat, he was cherishing a moment of solitude. I opened the car door and he shook my hand.

"Hello, old boy," he said faintly. "Here we are, then."

I called for Osman to help us with the luggage, but he was too busy settling in with his family to respond. So we staggered into the house with the vast assortment of suitcases and travel cots, fishing tackle, deck chairs, golf clubs, and roller skates. After we had ferried about half the baggage into the salon, Lulu accosted me.

"This place is a dump," she snarled. "I don't know how you have the guts to invite guests when it's in such a state."

I was going to mutter something about us having not invited anyone, but broken Frank pulled me back with a frown.

"There's a lot of building work going on," I said, "but we've cleaned out a couple of rooms for you. It's camping, I'm afraid."

The pit bull smiled ferociously, revealing her back teeth. "I've looked around," she said, "and found a cozy little bedroom on the long corridor."

"That's where we stay," I said.

"Oh, is it?" growled Lulu. "Well, we are going to stay in there."

She beckoned to Frank to lug the bags forward. Five minutes later, Lulu, her daughters, half the luggage, and the long-suffering husband were blissfully settled in our room. I was wondering what to tell my wife. At that moment she arrived home.

"They're here," I said cheerily. "So many of them!"

"Are they comfortable?"

"Oh yes," I replied, "I think they're very comfortable."

There was a short pause.

"They've taken our room," I said.

Marriage is a succession of good and bad moments. You strive your hardest to maximize the good and to minimize the bad. But that moment, standing outside the locked door of our own bedroom, was one of the very worst I have encountered since our wedding day. Rachana looked at me so coldly that the air between us froze.

"She's frightening," I said. "She's taken over. There was nothing I could do."

"We're going to a hotel, right now," Rachana said.

While Lulu and Frank slept off the fatigue of the journey, we slunk out of the house. Thirty minutes later we were checked into a suite in a luxurious hotel down in the Art Deco quarter. There were soft beds and feather pillows, dainty bars of perfumed soap, monogrammed bathrobes, and an unending supply of boiling hot water.

"Let's stay here forever," I said.

"Well, at least until our guests have gone," said Rachana.

So we did.

AFTER FIVE DAYS AND nights of fitted carpets, hot bubble baths, and room service, we crept back to the Caliph's House. I went ahead to check that the sapphire blue minivan had departed. It had. There was no sign of Lulu, Frank, or the flaxen-haired girls. The only suggestion they had been there at all was a note. It was written in an angry hand.

Where are you??? This is Hell on Earth, it read. *There is shouting from the mosque all the time, the noise of dogs and donkeys, and the clang of hammers banging. There is no hot water either, and a garden filled with wild people. We will NEVER visit you again! Lulu.*

THE NEXT DAY, KAMAL appeared. I had not seen him for almost a week. As usual, he didn't say where he had been or why he hadn't called me. I found this strange at first, but later discovered it to be a characteristic common in Morocco. When someone did not turn up for work, they didn't feel obliged to give apologies and long, elaborate excuses for their absence. I told Kamal that in Europe we try our best to come up with an explanation, even if it is a lie. The longer the absence, I said, the more detailed the lie is expected to be. He nodded and promised to bear my advice in mind.

"What are we going to do about the guardians?" I probed. "Their families are driving us crazy."

Kamal cracked his knuckles. "I'm working on it," he said.

WITH THE GUARDIANS AND their extended families residing at Dar Khalifa, I began to witness firsthand the ancient employment system of the East. It's sometimes known as "living off Abdul's job." As soon as someone gets work, everyone else gives up their jobs and leeches off the employed member of the family. The result is a situation in which normal salaries are never enough. The longer you are employed, the more money you need, merely to support all the hangers-on. Anyone with a nice home and full-time job has a vast cast of characters living off them.

Each day that the guardians and their families stayed in our outbuildings, word of their good fortune spread a little further through the kingdom. Within two or three days, all their close relatives had come, poked around, and gone back to their own shacks in the bidonville.

By the end of the first week, news of their improved lodgings had reached far and wide. A trickle of relations began. Four of Osman's cousins arrived from Nador, a day's bus ride to the northeast. After that, Hamza's maternal uncle came from the High Atlas Mountains, and then Osman's wife's aunt turned up. A few more days passed, and word spread to all four corners of Morocco. The trickle of relations turned into a tidal wave. Every day dozens of distant relatives and friends came, lured by the myth of lavish lodgings. They traveled to Casablanca by rough country bus and by donkey cart, on the back of hay wagons and on foot.

The constant influx of guests meant the guardians had to provide board and lodging for them all. Not to have done so would have been a stain on their family honor. The flood of people affected not only the guardians, but their patron as well.

One of the unwritten rules of the Arab world is that an employer is expected to take care of his people. No great show of thanks is made or ever asked for. When the guardians needed to borrow money, they came to me and petitioned without embarrassment. It was their right to ask and their right to be given money on account. But now so many of their family members and friends had to be supplied with generous platters of food, they found themselves staring financial ruin in the face.

Days went by when I didn't see the guardians at all. They were so occupied by attending to familial demands that they had no time to carry out their normal duties. The perimeter of our oasis was left unguarded. The leaves were not raked, and the German shepherd was left unfed. I didn't say anything, because I had myself tasted the flavor of uninvited guests.

The same life that poses the problem tends to provide a solution. One glorious, dazzling morning in the third week of January, Hamza, Osman, and the Bear shuffled into the room I was using as an office. They announced that their fine new accommodation had attracted a growing stream of freeloaders.

"Word of Dar Khalifa is spreading far," said the Bear, waving an arm at the distance.

"First our close relations came," said Hamza.

"But now people we hardly know are arriving," said Osman. "Our wives are very angry. They have to cook day and night for the visitors. We're waiting on them like servants and have even given up our own beds to them."

"So," said Hamza. "We have decided to go back to the bidonville."

"Our lives were quiet there," said Osman.

"But you don't have houses," I said. "They were knocked down."

The guardians clicked their tongues.

"*Mishi mushkil*, no problem," they said. "We do not live in palaces. We can build new homes by nightfall."

THE NEXT MORNING, I looked down from the top terrace to see that the guardians and their hangers-on had departed. It was as if the circus had rolled out of town, leaving a vacuum. Dar Khalifa was bathed in a rare and pleasing silence. Rachana and I ate breakfast on the verandah, wondering aloud if the previous two weeks had been a dream.

In the afternoon I walked out into the bidonville to see the guardians' new houses. They had found a patch of land well away from where the bulldozers had begun clearing, and had put up three low rectangular homes. They were built from old bricks, doors, and tiles scavenged from Dar Khalifa's junk heap. Osman was standing outside his new home. He was beaming.

"It's very quiet now your relatives have gone," I said.

"Thank Allah for it," he replied. "There is pleasure in modesty."

TWO OR THREE DAYS passed. Then, one evening, Kamal's fist could be heard banging on the front door. I opened it and found him lolling there, his face pouring with sweat, his eyes scarlet. I feared he had been drinking again.

"I have news," he said.

"Bad news?"

"No, no! It couldn't be better."

"What?"

Kamal kissed the fingertips of his right hand. "The Land Registry," he said. "You remember the dossier was missing?"

"Yes."

"Well," said Kamal, "I knew a clerk had been told to hide or destroy the file. But he'd retired. So I went to find him. I only had his last name and the rough idea where he lived. I've spent the last four days searching for him."

"Did you find him?"

"Wait, I'll tell you." Kamal mopped his face with a corner of his shirt. "Eventually I found his house, but the man wasn't at home," he said. "His daughter was there. So I left some flour, some sugar, and cooking oil as a gift. It's a custom in Morocco to show you have come in peace. Then last night the clerk called me. We met and I asked what he knew about Dar Khalifa. As soon as he heard the name, his eyes lit up."

"What about the file?"

"I'm coming to that," said Kamal. "Today there was a strike at the Land Registry. The workers there are asking for more money. So the clerk took me over there. He was angry at being retired early, so he took a set of keys with him when he went. He opened the side door and we slipped in.

"He led me down into the basement, where all the files are kept. There are rows and rows of them—thousands and thousands—a file for every building in Casablanca. The clerk closed his eyes. Then he marched seven paces to the right and two paces to the left. He stopped, opened his eyes, and took out a small brass key. In front of him was a locked steel box. He put the key in the lock and turned it."

"What was inside?"

"Dar Khalifa's papers," bellowed Kamal, "the dossier for the Caliph's House!"

THIRTEEN

A stone from the hand of a friend is an apple.

THE ELATION AT FINDING DAR KHALIFA'S lost paperwork was intense but short-lived. It was followed by a new dilemma, one that the ordinarily calm Kamal said could wipe me out altogether.

"Residency," he said anxiously. "Without the local papers, you're an open target."

"What's the solution?"

Kamal cracked his knuckles once, then again. "Marriage," he said.

"But I'm already married."

"You don't understand," he said, wincing.

"Understand what?"

Kamal cracked his knuckles a third time, louder than before. "You're going to have to take a second wife," he said.

THAT AFTERNOON THERE WAS a violent rap at the front entrance. It was Madame Nafisa, the gangster's wife. She was smoking a cheroot and sporting a long French-cut fox fur. The animals' tails trailed behind her as she walked; a pair of miniature fox heads, replete with snarling mouths, had been sewn on as epaulettes. The gangster's wife took a puff of her cigar.

"The shantytown is going," she said. "It will be swept away."

"Where will they go to?"

"To another gutter."

"But they don't have any money."

"Who cares?"

I wondered where the conversation was leading.

Madame Nafisa dusted an imaginary speck of dust from the fox face on her shoulder.

"Once the vermin have scurried off," she said, "this land will be valuable, very valuable. You can sell and you will be very rich."

"We don't want to sell," I said. "We're happy living here."

The gangster's wife tapped the ash from her cheroot onto the floor. "Morocco's a dangerous country," she said, "especially for someone who doesn't know the system."

"Is it?"

Madame Nafisa narrowed her eyes, an action that tightened the skin of her cheeks so greatly I feared they might split like overripe tomatoes. I was waiting for her to say something else, but she swiveled on her high-heeled boot and strode off, fox tails sweeping the ground behind her.

I DIDN'T LIKE THE idea of getting married again, especially since I was already happily married to Rachana. It was a matter that so worried me I held back from mentioning it to her. I didn't know how to bring it up. But then, as Kamal explained, marriage to a Moroccan woman would set me on a fast track through the ocean of bureaucracy.

"I'm sure we can find someone very beautiful," Kamal said, "a girl from the mountains perhaps. Leave it to me."

"You have to understand something," I said. "Rachana won't like the idea."

"First wives never do," he said.

"If I'm going to have a hope," I whimpered, "the only chance is if she's so incredibly ugly that Rach won't see her as a threat."

Kamal rubbed his nose. "Why waste such an opportunity?" he said. "You could do very well out of this."

THE TERRACOTTA TILES ARRIVED in custom-made baskets, two hundred in each. They were dry, brittle, the blush pink of chilled rosé. Aziz shepherded the stock into the garage area. There must have been at least two hundred baskets, each one tenderly unloaded from a bright orange truck newly arrived from Meknes.

An army of apprentices started opening the baskets and sorting the tiles. They were square, a little more than three inches long, half an inch thick. Unlike regular machine-made tiles, handmade bejmat is anything but uniform. The exact color of each tile varied considerably from the palest pink to a deep, plum-color red. The apprentices soaked the first batch of tiles. Four 40-gallon oil drums had been rolled into the house and filled to their brims with water. The tiles were left to steep in the water for three or four days. In the meantime, the floors were leveled, laid with a veneer of cement, made ready for the terracotta.

The greatest distinction between building practices in the East and the West is the way tools are used. A century ago

Western craftsmen had almost no power tools. Instead, they relied on dexterity and skill of sight, developed through years of apprenticeship. Power tools have enabled us to cut corners, to undertake jobs that would be near impossible without them. In Morocco, artisans are almost never seen working with an electric saw, a drill, a polisher, or anything else with a power cable. They rely on their ability alone. The end result may have had a lack of uniformity, but there was a sense that it was quite unique. I adored the subtle unevenness and didn't regard it as a drawback. If there was one, it was that the manual labor took ten times as long.

Seeing Aziz's team at work was like witnessing the reenactment of a medieval woodcut. Their methods had remained unchanged for five centuries. The same simplicity and attention to detail created the palaces of Granada, of Fès and Marrakech, and, more recently, Casablanca's own great Mosque of Hassan II.

To ensure the floor surfaces were level, Aziz's apprentices used a simple U-tube—a clear plastic pipe half filled with water. The tube was stretched across the floor, held up on adjacent walls, and the water level measured. A British builder would have probably used a laser for the same job.

Once the floors were level, a thin sheet of cement was put down, and they were tested again with the U-tube. After that, the apprentices laid the first patch of dark, moist sand, mixed with powdered cement, spread flat with a long wooden baton. Laying terracotta tiles and Morocco's famous zelij mosaics calls for a level of precision that sets the craft apart as an art form. Just as the architect's team had struck me by their inexperience, Aziz's moualems, master craftsmen, impressed me by the sheer perfection they achieved with the simplest tools and materials. When I asked Aziz how such precision could be realized without electrical equipment and fancy gadgets, he said:

"If you want to kill a fly, you can make a poison gas from complicated chemicals, or you can develop a machine with a fast swatting mechanism. Or you can use another approach altogether. You can learn to think like a fly. It will take you years, of course, but once you understand how a fly thinks, you can control it in every way.

"Our tools are not impressive to look at, but they are used by moualems who have mastered how to use them. Like the man who learns to think like the fly, they have reached a level of advanced control. They can create perfection because they have inner knowledge."

———

THE GREATEST PROBLEM WITH Kamal was his habit of disappearing. He would go missing for days at a stretch. Each time, I was racked with worry, like the mother of a teenage girl who hadn't come home after a night out. My concern was not inspired by a great affection for him, but rather by a fear of being without him.

In the weeks he had worked with me, Kamal had demonstrated a rare originality of thinking. He could solve problems like no one I had met before, and he could tap into the dark underworld of Casablanca. When he was around, he would turn his mind to solving anything I threw in his direction—the need for cheap dog food, the problem of missing papers, a source for black-market sand. While he was beside me, I was calm and composed, assured that we could rise to any challenge. My great anxiety was that one day he would be gone— slain perhaps while driving home from a bar, drunk out of his mind, as he did on most nights.

With time, Kamal learned more and more about the paperwork of the Caliph's House. He understood the details better than anyone else and used his network of underworld contacts to move its situation forward. More often than not, I didn't know exactly what he was doing for me behind the scenes. He wasn't the kind of person who gave information easily. Ask him a question and, more likely than not, you would receive another question in reply.

My fear that Kamal might disappear for good was equaled only by my fear that he might somehow snatch Dar Khalifa away from me. The more I got to know him, the more I realized he was a man not to trust.

———

TOWARD THE END OF January, he sent me a message to meet him at a café opposite the crumbling Hotel Lincoln. It sounded urgent. The café was smothered in the afternoon fog of cigarette smoke, a smell so pungent it drowned out the aroma of the dark Arabian coffee served automatically to all who came. I peered through the smoke at the rows of mustached men wearing woolen jelabas and pointed yellow slippers. No sign of Kamal. I checked my watch. I was on time, and he was always late, despite my regular pleas for punctuality. I sat down, drank a glass of café noir, and stared out at the street. An hour passed. Then another. I would have gone back to the house, but something kept me there, a sense that it was in my interest to remain seated.

As I gulped back my fourth espresso, Kamal barged in. He was leading a short veiled woman and was grinning from ear to ear. Most Moroccan cafés are patronized by men, and by men alone. Women avoid them, regarding them with contempt as pitiable bastions of imagined machismo.

So the sight of a heavily veiled woman pushing through the cigarette smoke was something of a sensation. All the regular mustached customers looked up. Some dropped their newspapers. Others thumped their canes on the floor in objection. Kamal sat down beside me and pulled over a chair for his guest.

"Here she is," he said.

"Who?"

"The *chica*."

"Which *chica*?"

"The one you're going to marry."

Before I could say another word, the veil was drawn back. The face behind it was so hideous that I jolted sideways in an involuntary reaction. The woman's cheeks were scarred and emaciated, as if an illness had taken hold. Her nose was eroded; she was bald and was missing her right eye.

"Gosh," I said, struggling to exude warmth.

"You said you wanted someone ugly."

"I didn't say I wanted anyone at all!"

"She needs you as much as you need her," Kamal declared.

"What do you mean, she needs me?"

"She's got little kids, two of them. How will she support them without you?"

The woman, whose name was Kenza, smiled. I smiled back, so as not to upset her.

"She likes you," said Kamal.

"We are going to find another solution," I hissed. "I'm not taking a second wife."

"You're forgetting the fast track," he said.

"I don't care. I'll take it slow."

Kamal glowered at me, flipped the veil back across Kenza's face, and led her home to her children. An instant later, I was alone again, peering through the smog to the street. The rendezvous with the unwanted wife had filled me with a sense of melancholy. I sat there until darkness fell, reflecting on how we judge a person by a few square inches of skin on the front of their head.

BACK AT THE HOUSE, Hamza and the other guardians had caught wind of Kamal's plan for me to take a Moroccan wife. They gathered round, pinning me to the garden wall, eager for the details.

"Is she from the south?" Hamza asked. "Those women are best. They don't talk too much, and they do as they're told."

"Hamza's right," Osman confirmed, "a woman from the south is best, because you don't want to be nagged too much."

"I'm not going to take another wife," I said.

"Why not?"

"Because I'm already happy."

"You must consider it," exclaimed the Bear. "We would all take second, third, and fourth wives if we could afford them."

"Would you?"

"Of course!" the three guardians said in one voice.

"But it's so expensive," Osman added.

"You must give each one a house," said the Bear, "and a bed, blankets, pots and pans."

"That's just the start," said Hamza. "You see, when you have more than one wife, they get jealous of each other. It happens all the time. If you give one something, you have to give the same thing to the others."

"It sounds terrible," I said.

"Oh, no, it's wonderful," said Hamza, blushing. "If you had three wives, you would have six lips to kiss you good night."

KAMAL'S APARTMENT DOOR WAS always firmly bolted shut. Behind it lay a fraternity house of debauchery. The sitting room was large and empty except for a stack of inherited furniture and a heap of empty vodka bottles. Between the two there was a stained couch with broken springs. Every available receptacle had been used as an ashtray in times of drunken need—an egg cup, a soup spoon, an old tennis shoe. Kamal never opened the door to visitors, not even to his own family, who would call to him through the letter flap. The only people admitted were women, most of them of the professional variety, lured back from the alleys behind the Marché Central. The only way I ever got inside was when I brought him a set of green plastic chairs as a peace offering. He had often wished aloud how fine plastic garden chairs would look in his bachelor pad.

When they had been assembled, Kamal went into the bedroom to look for a match. I slipped in behind him, to his great annoyance. It is not easy to accurately describe the vileness of that room. Even though the curtains were drawn shut, I could make out the virulent growth of fungus sprouting from the far wall. The bed had no sheets and stank of excrement. Inside the door was a low bookshelf. I was surprised to see a cluster of books laid neatly along it. More surprising still were the titles. They were classics—the collected works of Aristotle, Plato, and Pliny, the Greek myths, *Les Misérables,* and an imposing biography of Einstein. I poked a finger toward the bookshelf.

"That's a bit out of place, isn't it?"

"What do you mean?"

"Well, they're the only high-quality things in this dump."

Kamal sniffed his nose in the air haughtily. "I use them," he said.

"You read them?"

"No, of course not!"

"Then?"

"I use them for impressing the *chicas.*"

WITH THE NEW YEAR had come a faint sense of hope. The weather had turned much colder, but at least it meant the flies had gone, as had the blight of cockroaches. The days were vivid, the sunshine dazzling, broken from time to time by a thunderstorm pushing in from the Atlantic coast. The sight of the craftsmen laying the floors buoyed my spirits like nothing else. I was euphoric that good work was at last being done.

Now that the guardians had built new shacks in the shantytown, they seemed much happier. They reported frequently their communal mistake of not marrying women from the desert. Their wives, they repeated over and over, were nagging, troublesome creatures, who deserved nothing at all.

It had taken a long time, but we were falling into a routine. Ariane would go to school each morning and return in the afternoon. Rachana would help me with chores in the morning and study French when she could find the time. Kamal blustered in and out, either drunk, hungover, or somewhere between the two. The gangster and his trophy wife were dormant, as were the fanatics in the shantytown. The guardians were quiet, too. They oversaw the craftsmen laying floors, raked leaves obsessively, and hardly ever mentioned the Jinns.

Then, early one morning, as the first strains of light tinted the clouds, Hamza thumped at our bedroom door.

"Monsieur Tahir, Monsieur Tahir!"

"What is it?" I whispered through the keyhole.

"You must come," he said.

Pulling a raincoat over my pajamas, I went outside.

"The big courtyard," said Hamza.

We paced down the long corridor, over the verandah, and into the courtyard. Hamza opened the door to the room he had always kept locked. I followed him inside. There was a scent of something citrus, tart on the nose. I sniffed it in once, then again.

"Look there," said Hamza.

He was pointing to the wall above the steps that went nowhere. A patch of mysterious cherry-pink slime covered one part of the wall, high up near the coving. It was the size of a pillowcase and appeared to be dripping.

"It is not of this world," said the guardian.

"There must be a scientific explanation," I replied. "I'm sure it's coming from outside. Later on I'll take the ladder and have a good look."

I expected Hamza to claim the slime was the work of Qandisha, that it was a sign of impending doom. But he didn't.

Instead, when I turned up at lunchtime, he was showing the patch to his two fellow guardians. By teatime their families had been smuggled in to have a look. I didn't approve, for the wall was part of our home and was not a tourist attraction. I went off to do some work. When I returned to the courtyard that evening, I found thirty or forty people milling about.

Hamza was giving them tours of the room with the mystery slime.

The last thing I wanted was another invasion of the guardians' families and friends. I took Hamza aside and asked him in a robust tone to send everyone away. He seemed disappointed.

"Everyone is interested," he said.

"In the pink slime?"

"Yes, you see, it's *baraka,* it's a blessing."

NEXT DAY, KAMAL TOOK me to meet his grandfather. He was an old man, in his mid-seventies, with a mane of white hair and the kind of face that once led empires into battle. Unfortunately, he had recently been afflicted by a stroke and was a shadow of his former self. We sat in the salon Moroccain at Kamal's family home, with lengthy fitted sofas set along three of the walls. Small silver-rimmed glasses of green tea were brought. We sat in silence, calm and respectful. Only when the old man had stretched out and fallen asleep did Kamal speak.

"To live in Morocco," he murmured, "you have to understand it. And to understand it, you have to talk to the old people. Only they can teach you about the traditions."

"But your grandfather's very quiet," I said.

"He's had a stroke. He lost his voice."

We sat in silence again. It was pleasant, as if the time really mattered.

"How can I learn about the traditions if I can't hear him talk about them?" I asked.

"Through osmosis," said Kamal. "Sit close up to him and you'll feel it."

So I pulled my chair closer and sat there. An old woman

bustled in and refilled our glasses. A few minutes passed and a second woman, much younger than the first, entered. She put down a tray of biscuits.

"They are my grandmothers," said Kamal at length. "See how well cared for my grandfather is—he was smart. He took two wives. It may have cost him more money, but he has known twice the joy."

We left the old man to sleep, and went down to the Jeep. I told Kamal about the incident with the pink slime. I was sure he could come up with a plausible explanation if anyone could.

"Hamza thinks it's *baraka*," I said, "a blessing from God. It's stupid, isn't it?"

"Where there is good there is evil," said Kamal thoughtfully, "and where there is evil there is good."

It sounded like a line from a third-rate Bollywood movie.

"It's nonsense," I said. "It's pink slime and it's come out of the walls. I'm sure I can prove it."

Kamal took a detour on the way to Dar Khalifa. He drove across railway tracks and into an area called l'Hermitage. There were rows of spacious villas dating back to the 1930s. Their lines were sleek, curved, the trees around them mature. We stopped outside one of the grander villas. It was encircled by a wall overgrown with tangled bougainvillea. The shutters were drawn down, the garden a mess of weeds.

"We own this house," Kamal said.

"But it's boarded up."

"There was a fear," he said.

"A fear of what?"

"You will laugh."

I promised not to.

"A fear of the Jinns," he said.

I fought back a smile.

"One day when my aunt was reading in bed," Kamal explained,

"a Jinn came into her room, grabbed the book, and tore out all the pages. Then the bathrooms flooded and no cause could be found. After that, strange writing was found on the walls."

"When did all that happen?"

"A long time ago, when I was seven or eight."

"So why didn't they just sell the house?"

"Because there was no *baraka*," he said. "No one dares sell a house with angry Jinns."

"Then why not exorcise them?"

"It was not the right time," he said.

As we drove back to the Caliph's House, I found myself wrestling with questions—How could Hamza be so sure that pink slime was a blessing? When was the right time to exorcise Jinns? How could such a modern man as Kamal believe in such nonsense? Had I been in Europe, I would have pursued these and other questions until I reached satisfactory answers. But the cultural divide ran deep. I knew now it wasn't the case that people were trying to deceive me by holding back the answers. Rather, it was that for some questions there were no answers.

THE ONLY WAY TO be taken seriously in Casablanca is to buy yourself a four-by-four with black smoked windows and extra-wide wheels. The richer you are, or the richer you want people to think you to be, the bigger the vehicle, the blacker the windows, and the wider the wheels.

One morning a deep rumbling sound was heard in the distance. It was so loud that it set off the donkeys and the dogs at the far end of the bidonville. I was unloading bricks from our war-wounded Korean Jeep—just in time to witness the launch of the gangster's newest toy. It was sleek, shimmering black, and as vast as an oceangoing ship. The Cadillac coat of arms was shining on the front grille like a medal of valor. The car crawled forward and paused level with our own abominable vehicle. I felt my heart beating faster, the instinct of fight or flight. As I stood there, my face mirrored in the glass, the rear passenger window slid down very slowly. It was as if a veil had been lowered for the first time. I found myself staring into the dark Gucci lenses of Morocco's Marlon Brando. I rubbed my filthy hands down my chest and stepped up to introduce myself. The Godfather remained motionless, like a figure in wax. His face was smooth and confident, his nostrils flared at the ends. He held out a hand. I leaned into the car to shake it. But as I did so, the gangster's fingers clicked in a signal to the chauffeur. The sheet of black glass slid up as I withdrew my arm and lurched backward. A second later the Cadillac was gone.

FOURTEEN

The fruit of silence is tranquillity.

TWO DAYS AFTER THE EPISODE WITH the rose-tinted slime, I was overcome by a strong suspicion of conspiracy. Veiled threats from the gangster's wife, talk of *baraka* and Jinns, and the slime itself lured me into a state of paranoia. I was certain dark forces were at work against us. But rather than ghosts, I felt sure it was the people all around who were conspiring to evict us from the Caliph's House.

The three guardians must have sensed my unease. They came to us that evening bearing gifts. Osman's wife sent a loaf of hard, round *khobz,* home-baked bread flavored with aniseed. Hamza gave Ariane and Timur fresh new amulets to replace the old ones. He whispered that the children would live a thousand years. And the Bear presented me with a paperweight he had made from a polished stone.

After the gifts came the warnings.

"Kamal is bad, very bad," said Osman, his ever-present smile fading for a moment.

"He is trying to take Dar Khalifa away from you," the Bear said. "He understands the paperwork."

"What about the Godfather?" I said. "Isn't he more dangerous?"

Hamza jabbed a finger in front of his nose. "A blind thief inside the house is worse than a one-eyed thief outside it," he said.

When Kamal turned up, he warned me about the guardians. He said they were in league with the gangster in the bidonville and kept him informed of the intricate details of our lives.

"Hamza and the others are the Trojan horse," he said.

I DIDN'T KNOW WHOM to trust, so I decided not to trust anyone at all. The gangster and his wife, the guardians and Kamal, began to seem like different parts of the same foe. I was certain they were all somehow conspiring together.

In the meantime, I found solace in my grandfather's journals. His maid, Afifa, was his own Trojan horse.

She is like a Burmese cat, he wrote. *Given food, shelter, and affection, you might think she would care for her master. But the opposite is true. The depth of her perfidy is unknown. She would take everything I owned if she could get away with it.*

The irony was not lost on me. On my grandfather's death, Afifa chose her moment. She stripped the villa bare of his possessions. She even took a pocket watch presented to him in the 1930s by Atatürk. Then she made for the hills, and, of course, she did get away with it.

I BEGAN SPENDING MORE time alone, away from Dar Khalifa. It was as if the house had too many eyes watching my movements, too many mouths whispering my news. Rachana couldn't understand what I was worrying about. She said she had never felt safer in her life. To calm myself, I would explore the Art Deco quarter downtown and seek out the lost jewels.

One old guide to Casablanca, written during the heyday of the French rule, swooned with praise for the Rialto Cinema. The playhouse had been put up in 1930, a time when Casablanca was a showcase of French modernity. My guide described it as "a brilliant-cut diamond whose radiance dazzles all North Africa." There was a photograph beside the blurb. It showed a couple posing before the bright lights of the newly opened Rialto. The man was wearing a trilby cocked back on his head, and his date was wrapped from head to toe in mink.

The guidebook gave no hint where to find the cinema, as if everyone already knew where to find it. I expected the place to be destroyed, or in a derelict state if it was still standing at all. But one morning, while strolling through the streets across from the old Marché Central, I came upon it.

To my astonishment, the Rialto had recently been reno- vated and opened once again. It was as if the launch ribbon had just been cut and the opening delegation had just departed. The place was in pristine condition.

The front doors were polished teak, glazed with beveled glass. In the foyer, the lamps were hand-cut crystal, the walls veneered in chestnut-colored wood. The floor was laid with Carrara marble, and the faces of Hollywood's idols loomed down, Rudolph Valentino and Charlie Chaplin, James Cagney, Ginger Rogers and Fred Astaire.

After the relaunch, it was fitting that the first movie show- ing was *Casablanca*. The afternoon screening was about to start. I bought a ticket and slipped inside.

In the auditorium itself the lighting was dim, the atmo- sphere one of cozy anticipation. There were no more than a handful of viewers sitting on the newly covered crimson seats. I sat at the back near another foreigner. He was wearing a baseball cap bearing the word "Casablanca." I was going to say something to him, but the houselights dimmed, and the curtains were drawn slowly back.

I had thought it would be odd to watch *Casablanca* in Casablanca, albeit dubbed into French. The guidebooks love to tell you that the movie, perhaps the most famous film ever made, was shot entirely in Hollywood. I found it strange that it should have attracted such a cult following, famous for being famous. As the first scenes came and went, I couldn't help but notice that the Casablanca depicted on-screen had very little to do with the city in which I was sitting. Indeed, I wondered if the two had ever been true reflections of each other. In the film, wartime Casablanca was a mysterious haven in which refugees heading for America would become stranded. Although the story line may have been founded on a fragment of truth, the city dreamt up on Warner Brothers' back lot was a suffocating blend of Arab styles, whereas Casablanca of the time was European from top to toe.

At the end of the film, the houselights came alive and the man with the Casablanca baseball cap began to scribble vigorously in a notebook. I leaned over and asked if he enjoyed the film. He looked at me squarely, his plump pink face confused.

"Of course I liked it," he said in an American voice. "It's the greatest film ever made."

"Do you really think so?"

The man tugged off his cap and scratched a mop of thin gray hair. "It's Hollywood perfection," he said before putting out a hand for me to shake. It was cool and clammy, like the body of a snake.

"I'm Kenny," he said. "I'm from the *Casablanca* Appreciation Group—CAG for short."

I left Kenny to scribble his notes and I went out into the bright afternoon. Leaving the movie and entering the reality was like waking from a dream, one conjured by the mind of a madman. But for the first time in a long while, I was calm. A small red taxi pulled up. I opened the door to get in, but someone grabbed my arm. I turned back. It was Kenny.

"Have time for a coffee, do you?" he said.

WE SAT IN A backstreet café a stone's throw from the Rialto. The waiter plonked a pair of ashtrays on the table, as if expecting us to smoke a pack each. Kenny asked for Dr Pepper, but had to make do with the ubiquitous café noir. It was as viscous as crude oil and coated your mouth, making it difficult to speak.

Kenny didn't wait for me to make small talk. He tapped the fingernail of his index finger on the tabletop. "I'm on a world tour," he said. "It's a kinda pilgrimage."

"Are you with a tour group?"

"No, no, I'm alone."

"Where else are you going on the tour?"

Kenny took out his notebook and flipped to the back. "After this I go to Athens," he said, "then to Cape Town, and on to Nairobi, then Kathmandu. Fifteen cities in all—five continents."

"Are you visiting holy sites?"

"Not exactly," said Kenny. "You see, I'm going everywhere *Casablanca* is showing."

It took me a moment to comprehend the scale of Kenny's journey.

"You're going all over the world to see the same movie again and again?"

"Yup."

"But . . . but . . ."

"But what?"

"But it's madness," I said.

There was an awkward pause. I hadn't meant to upset Kenny. He put away his notebook, his ready smile dissolved.

"It may be madness," I said, "but it's brilliant madness!"

"Do you really think so?"

I squinted.

Kenny's spirits perked up. The glint returned to his eye. "I want to share something with you," he said.

"Okay."

"It's my dream. You see, I've got a dream."

"Oh."

"I think about it from the minute I wake up," he said eagerly, "till the minute I go to sleep at night."

"Oh," I said again.

Kenny nodded. His glasses fell off his nose. "You'll never guess what it is," he said.

"I'm sure I won't."

"It's a theme park—right here in Casablanca."

"I see," I said.

"It's got a difference. It's gonna be the *Casablanca* Theme Park!"

Kenny outlined the details of his dream. The idea was to build a focal point for worldwide aficionados of the greatest movie ever made. There would be Rick's Café Americain complete with gaming tables, song-and-dance spectaculars, themed rides, and trivia quizzes, a museum of original props, *Casablanca* candy, and back-to-back screenings of the movie itself.

"It's going to be expensive," I said.

"Ten million bucks."

I took the last gulp of my coffee. Kenny reached over and tugged my wrist.

"I've only just met you," he said, "but you seem strong-willed, honest—like the kinda guy we could do with onboard."

"You mean . . . ?"

"Yes!" said Kenny, leaping to his feet. "Yes! I'm saying I'd like you to come in with me." He swallowed hard to clear the residue of tarlike coffee from his throat. "Give it a thought," he said. "Will you come in as my partner?"

ON THE WAY HOME I made a detour to Habous to take another look at the Spanish table. I tried to get Kenny and his dream out of my head. Previous experience had taught me you can't let an idea like that take root. Once inside you, it takes over. Before you know it, you get sucked in and you're suddenly as obsessed as the person who came up with it. There's nothing you can do.

Habous was deserted, so much so that I grew worried there had been a bomb threat. All the shops had their shutters down. There was no one on the streets and nothing for sale. I don't know why I bothered, but I went into the courtyard where the table had been on sale.

The shop's shutter was firmly closed. I peered in through the window. The mélange of Art Deco clocks and desks, paintings, lamps, and magazines was still. I turned around to leave. A man was standing in front of me. He had appeared from nowhere. He greeted me, and only then I recognized him as the shopkeeper. I asked if I might see the table.

"This is the tenth time you have come," he said.

"Looking at it makes me happy."

The shopkeeper unfastened the padlock and rolled up the steel shutter. "You know where it is," he said.

I waded back through the artifacts and gazed at the table. The rear of the shop was gloomy, but somehow a stray shaft of sunlight had broken in. It was illuminating the walnut veneer. At that moment, I understood that it was a matter of destiny. The table was meant to be mine.

The shopkeeper had gone to sit down in his wicker chair. I strode through the clutter charged with adrenaline.

"I am a writer," I said energetically. "And I am going to write books on that table, books about Morocco. They will be read all over the world, and they will inspire people to come to your country. The people who come will have money, plenty of money. They will rush here to Casablanca and will pour into your shop. Before you know it, you will be a rich man, all because you were wise enough to give me a good price for the table."

The shopkeeper's eyes sparkled as if he had seen a vision. There was a lump in his throat. He didn't say anything at first, but sat staring into space.

"My friend," he said after a long pause, "to anyone else the mirage you have painted would be worthless, but its value to me is great. Indeed, it is as great as half the value of the table. You can take it for half price."

A HERD OF BLACK rams were steered through the shanty-town by a boy of about ten. He had broken plastic sandals and was waving a pointed stick. Every so often a man would step forward and inspect one of the sheep. He would open the mouth and peer at the teeth or jab his fingers into the animal's back.

"The celebration of Eid will be here in a few weeks," said Kamal as we drove through. "People are already preparing. Every family buys a ram and slaughters it at their home."

"That boy's very young to be looking after sheep," I said.

"Hah!" said Kamal. "By his age I was working full-time."

"Weren't you at school?"

"Yes," he responded. "That's where I was working. I used to buy candy wholesale and sell them in the playground. Then I got other kids to sell my candy at other schools all around

Casablanca. By the time I was eleven, I was making a hundred bucks a week. And candy was just the start."

"What came after the candy?"

Kamal raised his eyebrows. "I hired a garage near my house," he said, "got four or five guys working for me, and started all kinds of lines. I made cheap perfume and sold it to the girls, and I bought grease from a hardware store and sold it to the boys for their hair. As long as the packaging was right, they'd buy anything. Then I bought and sold chickens and eggs, and even sheep. Eid was my busiest time," he said. "I bought two truckloads of black-market rams from Algeria and sold them to all the parents at school. Whenever I had a spare minute, I used to put up a stall during break time."

"What did it sell?"

"Advice. I used to teach guys how to pick up girls, and the girls how to pick up guys."

"How did you make time for class?"

Kamal snorted. "School was my marketplace," he said. "I only ever went there when I had something to sell."

With his natural knack for making money, I couldn't understand why Kamal was working for me. He could have been earning ten times his salary if he was in business for himself. The point only strengthened my fear that he had a secret agenda, one that involved relieving me of the Caliph's House.

Almost every week he came to me with a business proposition. First it was an apartment block in the heart of the Art Deco quarter.

"There are seventeen apartments," he said. "We buy the place, give it a coat of paint, and sell them off one by one."

"What's the catch?"

"There isn't one. The owner's an old Spanish guy with no kids," Kamal said. "He'll die soon. Maybe very soon. A little pressure and he'll give it to us cheap."

We went to look at the building. It was wonderful. The

façade was lined with rounded balconies and fine azulejo tiles from Andalucía. Inside, the ceilings were high, the floors laid with parquet, and bathrooms retained all their original fittings. The only drawback was that the entire building reeked of horse meat. The reason for this became apparent when we inspected the ground floor, where an angry-looking butcher had a shop specializing in *cheval,* horseflesh.

After the apartment block came Kamal's scheme to sell Moroccan dates to the Gulf Arabs, and then to start a private ambulance firm; after that he suggested building a blood bank for women only, and he then came up with the idea of exporting Bedouin goat-hair tents to Guatemala.

I had never come across someone so skilled at sourcing a product. He may have shunned the classroom, but in his childhood he had developed lateral thinking, an invaluable skill when you need to buy something on the cheap.

The best example was when we had to buy five thousand eggs.

WITH THE FLOORS PROGRESSING well, we started to turn our attention to the walls. I was eager to use tadelakt, the plasterwork from Marrakech made from albumen and marble dust, and polished with a flat stone taken from a riverbed. The plaster was originally developed for use in hammams, steam baths, where it could endure the blistering vapor for years on end. More recently, it has moved from the bathroom into the salon, and is a favorite with the new European gentry of Marrakech. The deep reds and blush pinks of traditional tadelakt are complemented by dozens of new colors, achieved by adding a few drops of synthetic dye.

Good tadelakt is notoriously difficult to apply, and hence, most foreigners end up with badly cracked walls and plaster that crumbles to the touch. We had sixteen thousand square feet of wall space to cover in tadelakt, most of it in the time-honored pink of Marrakech.

Kamal sent a scout to the south to search for craftsmen skilled in plastering. He bundled me into the Jeep.

"Where are we going?"

"To a little village near Rabat," he said.

"Why?"

"To buy eggs."

The walls of the Caliph's House were old, and old walls cause havoc for the tadelakt teams because of their hairline cracks. The way to prevent cracking is first to prepare the walls well, applying a coat of rough white cement, to which the plaster can take hold. Then, when the tadelakt has been applied and smoothed, it is varnished with egg white. The albumen binds the surface together, and becomes ever stronger over the months as the plaster dries out.

Kamal had calculated we needed at least five thousand eggs. If we had gone to Casablanca's Central Market, they would have cost a fortune. But through his network of cousins, uncles, and distant aunts, he had traced a long-lost member of the family who owned a battery chicken business—a million birds crammed into vast egg-laying barns.

TWO DAYS AFTER WE came home with the eggs, a tall, thin man with bright eyes and a central parting turned up at the house. I noticed his fingers were extra long, as if they had been stretched. He hardly moved, and didn't say a word until I asked him his name. He leaned forward. When his mouth was only an inch from my ear, he whispered, "Mustapha," followed by "tadelakt."

My limited experience in Moroccan house renovation had taught me to mistrust anyone who talked or smiled too much; the best people to back were the quiet types with cheerless faces. Mustapha the plasterer was the quietest, glummest craftsman I had encountered. He almost never spoke at all, and he always looked as if his world were about to collapse. He was as silent as a mime artist. When inspecting the job to be done, he didn't ask any questions, so I ranted on with all the information I thought he would need.

He started the next day with a team of five men. They all had the same extra-long fingers and the same sullen, hushed manner. I watched them through an open window as they began work in the salon. They would gesture to each other, using spoken language only when absolutely necessary. And when they walked across the room, they trod softly so as to make no sound at all.

Hamza was impressed by their quiet unhappiness.

"They are good men," he bellowed, clapping his hands together noisily. "They will bring harmony to this house."

A MOROCCAN FRIEND TOLD me that to understand his country, one had to understand the kingdom to the north. The cultures of Morocco and Spain, he had said, are linked by history, by tradition, and by blood. So in the middle of February we planned a trip to the Alhambra in southern Spain, where the great palace-fortress of Moorish kings still stands at Granada. It seemed the perfect time to visit what must be the finest Islamic palace ever constructed.

Another reason for the journey was to get away from Casablanca. I fantasized that when we came back a week later, all the work would be finished. To ensure the craftsmen would toil day and night, I asked Kamal to stay in the house until our return.

Living in Morocco, it is easy to forget that Europe is no more than a few miles to the north, albeit on another continent. We took the train up to Tangier and crossed the Straits of

Gibraltar to Algeciras. The ferry was low in the water, listing to the port side. She was called *Isabella,* the name of the queen who routed the Spanish Muslims from the Iberian Peninsula eight centuries ago. The straits may only be eight miles across at their nearest point, but they divide two continents, an ocean, and a sea.

We stood out on the deck in the breeze, watching as Africa slipped away. The minarets of Tangier grew smaller and smaller, until they were no more than specks on the horizon. Gulls swooped across the stern, where a dozen crates of fish were packed in ice. We strolled along the guardrail to the bow, where we found Europe approaching.

ANYONE WHO HAS TRAVELED in Andalucía has been touched by the spell of Morocco. The Moors retreated to African soil, but their legacy endures throughout Iberia. Their invasion of Spain took place in 711 of the Christian era, and the Islamic faith was practiced there for seven hundred years. Today you can find traces of the Moorish past in Spanish food and music, scholarship, folklore, and in the language itself.

The Alhambra palace at Granada is so exquisite that a visitor is at a loss to describe it. I was first taken there as a child. I remember walking around the gardens and through the great halls, my mouth wide open in awe. I had never imagined such beauty, such precision.

The chill winter air was perfumed with the scent of roses, lulled by the sound of water tumbling from fountains. Ambling through the courtyards again, this time with my own children, I was spellbound by the serenity, a ballet in stone. The lines and textures were easy on the eye, the sounds and smells equally pleasing. Like the ballet, there was a sense that such perfection had been effortless to create.

We stayed in a small guesthouse in the shadow of the

palace. The nights were cold, the mornings glazed with frost. I was overcome by the tranquillity. I told Rachana that I wanted to stay there forever, and to walk away from the Caliph's House. She laughed and then seemed very serious.

"You're not joking, are you?" she said.

ON THE SECOND NIGHT in Spain, I received a call. It was Hamza. He was hysterical. It sounded as if he was crying.

"Monsieur Tahir! Monsieur Tahir!"

"Hamza, what's wrong?"

"Monsieur Tahir, we are good men. We are honest," he said, taking quick, shallow breaths.

"What's the matter, Hamza? Why are you calling? Has the house burned down?"

"No, no, it's not the house."

"Then what is it?"

The guardian's voice trembled. "It's Kamal," he said. "He's a bad, bad man."

"What has he done?"

"He's . . . he's . . ."

"He's what?"

"He's filled the house with *femmes de la route,* women from the road!"

Like a teenager whose parents were out of town, Kamal had launched into a day-and-night extravaganza of wine, women, and low-grade hashish. Hamza said the workmen had been sent away through the back door. The front entrance to Dar Khalifa had then been flung open. Every hooker in the city had been invited to the party of the century.

"They are doing wicked, wicked things in every room," Hamza exclaimed. "May Allah be my witness. I have seen it with my own eyes!"

FIFTEEN

A promise is a cloud; fulfillment is rain.

KAMAL FREQUENTLY RECOUNTED TALES OF HOW he had exacted terrible revenge on anyone unwise enough to oppose him. He prided himself on meting out retribution, destroying the fortunes of those who dared to cross his path. As the months passed, he told of men he had had thrown into jail across Morocco. Two of his own cousins were languishing in Casablanca's grimmest prison. Their mistake had been to think they could get the better of Kamal Abdullah. Others had been given more original punishments. He told me of one adversary who loathed the heat. He was lured into the desert and buried up to his neck in sand. Another had been videotaped in bed with his mistress, and the footage sent to his wife.

I once asked him how he decided what form of revenge to take.

"It's not easy," he said. "You have to give it thought. You mustn't act too fast. If you hurry, you can mess up a good opportunity. There's no point in jail if it doesn't hurt someone bad."

"Jail hurts everyone," I said.

"No, no, it doesn't," he replied. "It doesn't hurt the rich."

"Then what does?"

"Tasting poverty," he said.

I feared what Kamal would do if humiliated by being thrown out of the Caliph's House. But I couldn't allow his debauchery to continue unchecked. Then again, if I rebuked him and didn't throw him out, I would appear to be as weak as I was. I contemplated rushing back from Granada to sort things out in Casablanca. I sat in front of the hotel's fireplace, staring into the flames, pondering the situation. The problem was that Kamal understood the degree to which I valued his know-how.

At last I came up with a ruse. I called him and said that a close friend was about to arrive at Dar Khalifa from England. He was traveling through Morocco, I explained, and would be staying in our absence. He was about to arrive any minute, I said. Kamal listened calmly and promised to leave at once.

Five days later we arrived home. The guardians lined up at the front door, saluted, and spat out their reports.

"He's brought shame on us all," said the first.

"He has brought shame on our families," said the second.

"And shame on our ancestors," mumbled the third.

We entered the house. I was expecting the place to be ransacked, but the opposite was true. Our bedroom had been spring-cleaned. The kitchen was gleaming as if an army of maids had scoured it from top to bottom. The rest of the house, although a building site, was scrubbed clean, too. Hamza glanced at me as we toured the rooms.

"Kamal's a magician," he said.

————

SOON AFTER MY RETURN, I called on Hicham Harass. The winter rain had caused his shack to flood. He apologized for the disorder and flapped a hand at the mess.

"None of this is precious, really precious," he said. "There are a few things I've grown fond of, but it's all rubbish. My wife likes it, but she doesn't understand what's valuable and what is not."

Hicham leaned back into his comfy chair, knocked off his shoes, and called his wife to make the mint tea.

"Women don't know, do they?" he said. "They try hard but they can't understand the things that are important to a man. Take postage stamps," Hicham continued. "Find me a woman who likes postage stamps!"

IN THE WEEK WE had been away, Mustapha the mime had begun the walls. His team applied the tadelakt with arched sweeping movements. The plaster itself was prepared in a vat they had built on the terrace. It was more than ten feet in

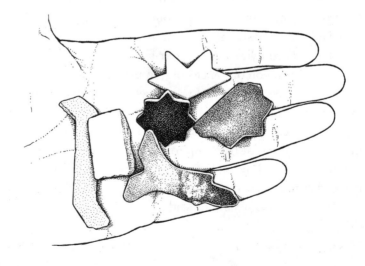

length and four feet wide. As they swished the flat trowels of plaster onto the walls and arches, the team would sing very softly—tenor voices echoing through the house. They would take it in turns to chant a verse, the others filling in with the chorus. They only sang when they were actually plastering, as if the rhythm gave consistency to their work.

They would start on walls of a room only when the floor had been tiled and sprinkled with sawdust from the cedar mills. The bejmat team spent so much time at Dar Khalifa that they moved into the house. One glance at their work and I knew that I would never have to inspect again. It was faultless, created by an ancient knowledge, a fusion of mathematics, chemistry, and fine art. The bejmat masters didn't sing. They were concentrating too hard.

The children's playroom, off the main salon, was to be the only room with glazed tiles. That way even if they covered the place in paint and glue, it could be easily wiped clean. The craftsmen spent days laying green and white tiles in a simple checkerboard design. They reached the final line, only to find the room more irregular than they had calculated. Without a word, they lifted the entire floor and laid it again, rotating the pattern by three degrees. The second time it fitted perfectly.

Every day, Aziz would accost me, and beg me over cups of mint tea to allow him to demonstrate his skill. He said he had spent his life mastering complexity and, given the chance, he could transform the Caliph's House into a labyrinth of design. Worn down after weeks of pleading, we agreed that he would lay patterned border tiles on the walls around the rooms.

Once the decision had been reached, Aziz put down his tea, got to his feet, and kissed me on both cheeks. There were tears in his eyes.

"You will weep when you see the beauty of the work," he said.

The next day a new craftsman arrived at Dar Khalifa. Aziz

had sent him to excise the pattern into the plain glazed border tiles. In one hand he carried a *manqash,* a heavy sharp-edged hammer; in the other he held a cushion. A basket of ruby red squares was brought in by an apprentice. He laid the cushion down and began to chip.

If there is any memory of the Caliph's House I shall carry to my grave, it will not be the beaming faces of the guardians, or their constant talk of Jinns. Nor will it be the din of donkeys braying in the night, or the smell of honeysuckle at dusk. It will be the *ching! ching! ching!* of the master's hammer, chipping away the cursive pattern with an accuracy only a long apprenticeship can provide.

He sat there day after day, week after week, chipping with the hammer. I would watch him, mesmerized that a man could have learned to perform such a skill with a single sharpened tool. In our world we would have dreamt up a machine to do the job. The result would be a pattern that was uniform, lifeless, devoid of any meaning. His work was fluid and animate. It had a soul.

MY CONVERSATIONS WITH HICHAM Harass calmed me down. I would arrive at his shack choking with rage at being forced to pay ten times the going rate for nails, brass hinges, or tubes of Chinese-made glue. The old stamp collector would call for tea, rub his swollen feet, and talk. Our conversations did far more than fill in the gaps of a new culture. They lowered my blood pressure and acted as a kind of therapy. After an hour of Hicham's acumen I would float back to Dar Khalifa, my mind cleansed of its troubles.

One afternoon Rachana made chicken curry with her grandmother's recipe. There was so much of it that I filled a serving dish and took it through the shantytown to Hicham Harass's shack. The old man was one of the few Moroccans I have known with a taste for extremely spicy food. Two men were standing in the narrow lane outside his home. It was obvious they were not on a social call. One was waving a notebook and shouting insults. The other was holding the stamp collector's old portable television. Hicham's wife was pleading with them, her face blushed from tears. She ushered me inside.

"Damn them," the old man said as soon as he saw me. "They will take the shirt off my back next."

I offered to lend Hicham money if he needed it. He thanked me.

"The Prophet said moneylenders were lower than thieves," he said. "They are stupid, but I am more stupid for borrowing from them."

ONE MORNING I SAW Hamza sitting alone in the garden, near the fake well he had built. His head was in his hands, as if he were in tears. I was reluctant to disturb him and decided to leave him in peace. When I met Osman in the afternoon, I asked if there was anything wrong.

"Hamza is going to die," he said.

"What's wrong with him? Is he sick?"

"It's worse than illness," he said, sliding a finger horizontally across his throat.

"Do you mean someone's going to kill him?"

"Perhaps."

It was by any standards an Oriental conversation. As an outsider, I feared I had no real hope of understanding. I asked Osman if he could elaborate.

"Hamza had a dream," he said. "He dreamt of a man riding a camel into the desert."

"And?"

Osman looked at me quizzically.

"Isn't that enough?"

"I'm not sure if it is."

"Everyone knows," said the guardian sharply, "someone who has this dream will soon breathe their last."

The next morning I saw Hamza again. He was in the garden courtyard, raking leaves somberly. I told him I had heard about his dream.

"What will my family do without me?" he moaned. "They will starve."

"I'm sure you are not going to die," I said. "It's only a dream, and most dreams don't come true."

The guardian swept back his hair with his hand. "I have had the same dream for seven nights," he replied. "There is no question about it. I will die very soon. Only Allah knows the hour."

Dar Khalifa was bathed in an air of imagined grief. It seemed ridiculous, but whenever I questioned it, the guardians waved their hands high in the air and exclaimed the dream to be an unmistakable sign. They went around the house, their heads hung low, pained expressions stretched across their faces. I asked the Bear if there was anything I could do.

"You can ask Qandisha to protect Hamza," he said.

I didn't understand. Qandisha supposedly hated me for living in her house.

"You can ask her," the Bear insisted. "She may listen to you."

I found the situation absurd, especially as it was me who didn't believe in Jinns. But how could I ask something I couldn't see to save Hamza's life?

"It's simple," said the Bear when he had heard my question. "You go to a place where bulls are being slaughtered, and you dip your finger in warm blood. Touch it to your face, just above the nose, and Jinns will become visible," he said.

Kamal agreed that the easiest way to see Jinns was to do as the Bear had described. He didn't regard it as odd at all, and drove me to an abattoir on the eastern edge of Casablanca. As anyone who knows me well can vouch, I am squeamish around the dead. It was raining hard when we arrived at the slaughter-house. The sky was so dark with storm clouds that it seemed more like night than day. We ran from the Jeep to the main entrance of the abattoir and were drenched within a second.

Inside, Kamal explained to a foreman why we had come. I found myself wondering how a British slaughterman would react if told we needed fresh blood to materialize what amounted to a ghost. The Moroccan foreman readily agreed, as if he had encountered the request often before. He led the way through the abattoir, to where the bulls were being killed.

The place stank of death and was drenched in blood. The last cries of condemned animals were drowned out by the whir of a circular blade, spinning fast, hacking through bone. In line with Islamic tradition and the belief in halal killing, the animals were bled to death. They were brought from a holding pen one at a time. Two men stepped forward and bound the creature's legs together. It took a few seconds. They held the neck rigid as the bull wrestled to get loose. A short knife slashed the jugular, and the process of dying commenced.

I tried to leave, but Kamal told me to stay. He said death was part of life, and it was good to witness where one ended and the other began.

The animal kicked in spasm for a long while, its eyes rolled up, mouth groaning, tongue at the side. A vast torrent of blood had poured from the wound. The spasms continued long after death. Once the bull was dead, the foreman motioned me to take all the blood I needed. I bent down, poked a finger into the pool, and wiped a single drop above my nose. I felt disgusted.

At the house, I shut myself in the room where I had seen the pink slime. It was there that Hamza had said Qandisha resided. The slime may have been a sign of *baraka*, but the guardians still regarded the place with fear.

I took a chair in with me and sat there for much of the afternoon. The shutters were closed. The room smelled of damp. Outside, the rain was unrelenting. I didn't try to have a conversation with Qandisha. It seemed pointless to try speaking to something I didn't believe in. The blood above my nose had been smudged. I might have cared, but my thoughts were on the abattoir. Like so many in our society, I am a hypocrite. I love to eat meat but I revile the business that provides it.

I reflected on Hamza, Osman, and the Bear, and about our own lives at Dar Khalifa. I thought about Ariane and Timur, and about the childhood they would have, and were having. They spent their days in innocence, lost in a land that looked upon them as kings. I had no idea how long we would live at the Caliph's House, but at that moment I hoped it would be forever.

A FEW DAYS LATER, word came that our furniture had arrived from India and was waiting at Casablanca's port. I had ordered it online months before. The Internet, a credit card, and a bottle of strong red wine make for a hazardous combination. One click of the mouse and you can find yourself financially destroyed. In a moment of heady enthusiasm, I had ordered six armchairs and five sofas, three king-size four-poster beds, a revolving bookcase and campaign desk, and a dining table long enough to seat a soccer team and their coach. As if this wasn't enough, I ordered an antique mahogany door from a palace in Rajasthan and a carved wooden swing taken from a harem in Mysore.

The next morning I received the firm's e-mail confirming my order and thanking me for submitting payment in advance. Payment in advance? My eyes jumped from my face. I fumbled with my wallet. My credit card wasn't there. It was on the coffee table beside the empty wine glass. I spent the morning dispatching frantic messages. But there was no hope. The furniture company in Mumbai refused to cancel the order. They advised me to take more care with my clicking finger next time.

WHEN I MET HAMZA in the afternoon, he was laughing. He said the dream of the desert rider had been replaced with another, in which he had seen a snake slithering through long grass.

"Is that good?" I asked.

"Of course," said Hamza jubilantly. "It means there is good fortune ahead."

That afternoon when I went for lunch, I found the three guardians huddled together behind a hedge. They were talking fast in whispers. When they heard me approaching, they broke off and covered their mouths. Osman pointed at me.

"There he is," he said.

The three men rushed over, followed by the gardener. Then the cook hurried out from the kitchen, and she called to the maid, who called to the nanny. After that, all the craftsmen from the house trouped out to see what was going on. They lined up respectfully as if they were in the presence of a saint.

"The Jinns listen to you," said Hamza.

"You have *baraka*," said Osman.

"You are blessed," said the maid.

I shrugged them off at first, as I hadn't even asked the Jinns to help Hamza, because I didn't believe in them. But they declared there was no doubt. Then they thanked Allah for having blessed me. I tried to explain they were mistaken, but they would hear nothing of it. They took it in turns to laud me. They said my heart was chaste, that I was like a child who had not yet been tainted by the reality of the world. The praise felt good. It was a far cry from the low status they usually afforded me. I shouted at them. Quite the opposite was true, I said, my mind was regularly filled with the most repulsive thoughts imaginable.

"Only he who is blessed would pretend he is not," said the Bear.

"He proves the *baraka* by denying it," said the cook.

"He has power because he's descended from the Prophet," said Hamza.

Osman was going to say something, but instead he hurried away into the bidonville. He returned five minutes later with his baby daughter. She was about three months old and had a high fever.

"Please touch her forehead with your hand," said Osman. "Your *baraka* will make her well."

When I was a child, my father warned me to take care not to mention our lineage when in the Arab world. I asked him why. He said that being descended from the Prophet's line was considered to be very important by very many, but it was something so gravely serious that mention of it ought never to be made.

Years later I read about the final hours of the Prophet Mohammed's life. It is said that, lying on his deathbed, he ordered his closest followers to gather around. He said he was to soon quit the mortal world but, before he departed, he was to leave them the two most precious things in his possession. The first was the Holy Qur'an, and the second was his family.

It may have seemed like a strange request, but it is a legacy that has preoccupied Muslims ever since. The immediate family of Mohammed, often known in the East as "The People of the Cloak," are revered by all followers of Islam. No other family commands such respect, nor has any other had such a dynamic bearing on Islamic society. The Prophet's direct descendants have excelled as philosophers, poets, geographers, warriors, and kings.

I was touched that Osman would consider me a healer because of the blood in my veins. At the same time I was confused and a little appalled. I gave him a bottle of medicine to bring down his daughter's fever.

"This will work better than any healing I can do," I said.

CASABLANCA'S PORT IS THE biggest in Africa. It runs for miles along the coast, a city in itself. The perimeter is lined with razor wire, sentry posts, and armed police on patrol. There are dozens of quays crowded with hulking steel gantries, ready to unload cargo ships from every corner of the world. They come from Shanghai and São Paulo, from Helsinki, Hong Kong, Yokohama, and Vladivostok. It was impossible to say what filled the uniform steel containers. The only clue was when the inspectors from the *douane,* the customs, arrived, hacked off the lead seals, and emptied the contents onto the ground.

My fear of paying Moroccan import tax was very great indeed. The port was awash with horror stories. I heard of people whose goods were impounded for years, even generations. Kamal said his own father had once become so frustrated at the tax being charged, he set fire to a container full of machinery and walked away.

We spent three afternoons in a café outside the main gate. The coffee was thicker and darker there than anywhere else in Casablanca. Like everything within a mile of the docks, it smelled of rotting fish. The room was packed with rough types, all of them dressed in tattered jelabas and worn-out barboush. There wasn't a clean-shaved jaw in the place.

Some of them played checkers with bottle caps on home-made boards. Others clustered together, swapping tall tales of their travels and misdeeds.

"They're all liars," said Kamal. "And they're thieves."

"Then what are we doing here? Why don't we go straight to the customs office?"

"Research," he said. "We're doing research."

On the fourth day, we stood outside the café at a cart that sold boiled snails by the cup. Kamal made small talk with the one-eyed vendor, and I tried to pretend I was having a good time. Everyone could tell I didn't belong there. I didn't know the rules. I feigned delight in the taste of the mollusk meal. Kamal told me to keep quiet.

"People don't eat the snails 'cause they like them," he said. "They eat them 'cause they're cheap."

The one-eyed vendor blinked slowly and refilled my cup for free. He said I appreciated his wares, that I was a good advertisement. We stood slurping snails, watching the commotion of wheeled vehicles. There were wagons laden with whole trees from Brazil, stevedores pulling carts, forklift trucks, bicycles, scooters, and rolling stock.

On the fifth day, Kamal said it was time to go into the port itself. I showed enthusiasm at the idea.

"There's a problem," he said. "We don't have passes, so we can't go in."

"How are we going to get the container if we can't enter the port?"

Kamal peered over at the main gate. Three policemen were standing guard. Anyone without a pass was turned back. We saw a man trying to offer a bribe. He was arrested, handcuffed, and taken away. A moment later a waiter from the café was ushered inside. He was taking a silver pot of mint tea to the officials in the customs office.

I looked round, but Kamal had disappeared. When I turned again, he was being waved in through the main gate. He was sporting a maroon waistcoat and was balancing a tray on his hand, and a glass on the tray.

For three hours I waited with the snail seller. We exchanged pleasantries and talked about snails. I had never imagined there was so much to learn about the tiny shelled creatures. The salesman said his family had sold snails at the port for a hundred years. They had been there, he said, before the French occupation, a time when Casablanca was little more than a village.

Then he explained how his ancestors had once been doctors. They were Berbers from the mountains, where they used to cure the sick with secret remedies.

"Did you use plants for your medicines?" I asked.

The salesman twitched. "No," he said, "we used snails. They're medicine that can heal, but there's more money in selling them as food."

I had hoped we could move the conversation forward, but the one-eyed vendor had more information to impart:

"There are so many kinds of snail," he said with relish, "and each one has a different use. You can cure typhoid with sea snails, and a cough can be relieved with tree snails, and if a woman wants to find a husband, she only has to eat boiled snails mixed with her menstrual blood."

Thankfully, at that moment Kamal arrived.

"They're playing games with us," he said.

"Can we get the furniture?"

Kamal looked me straight in the eye. "The customs want you to pay fifty thousand dollars," he said.

THE NEXT DAY, PETE called unexpectedly. I was sitting in a patch of sunshine on the lawn going through a book on Berber history. Hamza had carried my wicker chair into the sunlight, and insisted on moving it every few minutes as the sun arched overhead. I was grateful to him for attending me so well, but irritated, as it had begun to hamper my reading. The other two guardians lurked nearby. They, too, were keen to please me.

Pete's voice sounded faint, as if he was ill.

"Are you okay?"

"*Alhamdulillah,*" he said, "thanks be to God."

"But you sound weak."

"I've had typhoid," said Pete, his voice trembling.

"How's married life?"

Pete started to cough. "We're going to the U.S.," he said.

"I thought you said you'd never go back there."

"There's a reason," he replied.

"Oh?"

"I'm going to set up an Islamic mission in Austin," he said. "It's my calling. I'm going to spread the Word, gonna save Christian souls."

I would have tried to stop him, but experience has shown me that nothing can counter the zeal of a convert. Any suggestion of toning down the message only fans the flames. I wished Pete luck and said I hoped our paths would cross again before long. He knew it was a lie. He could hear it in my voice.

ONE MORNING SOON AFTER, a tall man with a trimmed black beard hurried up to me in the shantytown. He had been running and was out of breath. He handed me an envelope. I was used to being given notes as I walked through to the main road. People would often scribble down their requests and pass them to me. I helped when I could. But the man with the trimmed black beard obviously didn't live in the bidonville. He was wearing a very fine jelaba, with gold embroidery around the neck. The notes from the shantytown were usually written in pencil and were hard to decipher. They never came in an envelope, certainly not one made from imported paper.

The messenger hurried away before I could say a word. I took the letter back to the house and opened it expectantly. Inside was a single sheet of white ribbed paper, crossed with a few lines of navy blue ink. The hand that had written them was unmistakably French. No other race is capable of such refined Roman script.

Dear Monsieur Shah, the letter began, *I should like to present myself. I am Countess Madeleine de Longvic, a longtime resident of Casablanca, and a former acquaintance of a gentleman whom I believe was your grandfather. I would be honored if you could come to my home on Saturday at four, for tea.*

When I showed Rachana the letter, she held it to the light.

"Whoever she is," she said, "the lady has style. The watermark is her own monogram, and the nib looks like vintage Mont Blanc."

Rachana held the page to her nostrils and sniffed the faint hint of perfume.

"She likes beauty," she said quietly. "When you go to see her, take flowers. But don't stint. Take her orchids."

Sixteen

He who foretells the future lies, even if he tells the truth.

HOWEVER HARD I TRIED, I WAS unable to stop thinking about Pete. The rise of Al Qaeda and the bombings of 9/11 had made the American people reluctant admirers of fanatical Islam. I could imagine Pete and his Moroccan wife touching down at Dallas/Fort Worth Airport and being whisked away by police. The West's greatest fear is a convert with an Anglo-Saxon face prepared to strap explosives to his belt.

"The Feds aren't stupid," said Kamal when I told him about Pete's quest to bring Islam to the American heartland. "They'll have that guy in Guantánamo before he can sneeze." Kamal paused, took a long drag of his Marlboro, and said, "Believe me, I know what I'm talking about."

We were in the Korean Jeep, driving south down the coast road looking for a source of cut-price marble. The windows were open and the buzz of the rubber on asphalt was loud. It was on such drives that Kamal lifted the veil on his past.

"I was in New York on the morning of September 11, 2001," he said coldly. "I saw it all: the planes going into the Towers, the smoke, the dead lying around. It was fucking scary. Next thing I know, the Feds are checking on Arabs. They're looking them up and dusting them down."

"Did they interview you?"

"Sure they did," Kamal said, "they went the whole nine yards."

"Were you expecting them?"

"It was a strange time," he said, dodging my question. "The Arabs in the U.S. were as shocked as everyone else. We were against the bombings. Islam doesn't say to go fly passenger jets into skyscrapers. I suddenly found myself unable to trust any other Arab. I didn't know who was part of an Al Qaeda cell.

"Then one night I came home from work and my wife, Jen, was making dinner. I knew instantly that something was up."

"Why?"

"Because she'd never cooked anything before," he said, "not even an egg. She was terrible in the kitchen. I asked her if anyone had been to the house. She said no one had. But she didn't look me in the eye."

Kamal wiped his face with his hand.

"You can tell," he said, "you can tell when your partner's lying. It's the smell they give off."

"So what happened?"

"Next morning there was a smack at the door," he said. "I opened it and six Feds came charging in. It turned out they'd shut down the whole block. They had helicopter support, too. Jen had split. The FBI guys said they'd come the night before and told her not to let on. That was the worst humiliation. My own wife trusted them more than me."

"Is that when they interviewed you?"

Kamal smiled. "Oh, yeah," he said, "they got into every nook and cranny."

"Of the apartment?"

"Of my mind."

THE TADELAKT TEAM MADE slow progress, but it was progress nonetheless. Mustapha the mime brought a special craftsman to score a horizontal pattern high on the walls; it mirrored the design running along the terracotta skirting. Work on the floors and walls may have been moving forward, but there were no general craftsmen. We urgently needed a painter, an electrician, a plumber, a mason, and a more reliable carpenter. The problem was that no one was hired unless they had a personal link with Kamal. It was the Moroccan system in its purest form—only a member of the tribe or of a known group could ever break in. Anyone without a direct connection was lampooned as being a con man, a delinquent, or both.

The only time I wore Kamal down was with Hamza's neighbor, who claimed to be a mason. I had ordered him to take the man on as a way of pleasing the guardians. There were problems from the moment the mason's sinister shadow crossed the threshold. He took a dislike to the job and even more of a dislike to Kamal. In the week he worked with us, he managed to smash everything he touched. It ended with him chasing Kamal through the shantytown with a clawhammer.

I grew up in England and so am familiar with the great British workman and his approach to the job. He arrives late and finishes early, but only after demanding a thousand mugs of milky tea. He fills your house with cigarette smoke, stubs the butts out on the floor, and turns the place upside down, moaning and groaning like a toddler with toothache. He disappears for weeks on end, before reappearing magically at Christmas, demanding a bonus for his men.

I thought I would never meet the English workman's match. But I did at the Caliph's House. Moroccan workers surpass almost any others in the depth of their skill. They are polite and never fail to offer prolonged greetings. When they are in your house, they work hard, and never dream of asking you to make them tea. If they want it, they brew it up themselves on the brazier they always keep with their tools. They are almost perfect in every other respect, but Moroccan workmen do have one major fault. They are virtually incapable of ever finishing a job.

As I toured the great buildings of Morocco, I found myself perplexed that they had ever been completed at all. Whenever I ran through the house ranting, the master craftsmen would grin broadly and exclaim that only Allah was complete.

Then one day during the first week of February, I met a well-known Moroccan architect. I asked him how the royal family managed to get anything finished. The informant stroked his silver beard with his hand.

"It's not about money," he said pensively. "It's about domination."

I asked him what he meant.

"The royal family have patronized traditional Moroccan crafts for centuries," he said. "But don't think for a minute a craftsman will do his best work, even though it's for his king. Every man on the job has to be cajoled day and night into creating perfection."

The architect said that when King Hassan II, the father of the present monarch, was building the Great Mosque of Casablanca, he would journey to the building site as often as he could. "He would inspect the tools himself," said my informant, "and he'd choose a moualem and stand over him for hours at a time. If the work was off by the breadth of a hair, he would order the man to pack his tools and leave. He knew very well that word would spread, and that the master craftsman would never work again."

IT WAS POURING rain when Hamza took his old shovel and exhumed the ostrich egg. Osman stood over him, holding a torn umbrella and shielding him from the rain and the wind. I watched them from a distance, as ever wondering the meaning of it all.

When the egg had been retrieved, it was ushered to the stables, where the Bear rubbed it with grease. After more than a month in the ground, the once-pristine shell was a blotchy red-brown. It smelled sulfurous, like decomposing rats. The guardians were in high spirits. They wiped a chair clean and invited me to sit at their table, the spool from a giant roll of cable. I sat down and looked carefully at the egg.

"What are you going to do with it?" I asked.

"Eat it," said the Bear. "We'll eat it."

"Do you have to?"

Hamza took his masonry hammer and smashed in the top of the shell. The pungent odor increased.

"It's rotting," I said.

"It will bring *baraka* to the house."

A tablespoon was fished out from a box of tools. Osman passed it over.

"You can go first," he said.

"I can wait," I said.

"Please!" the guardians prompted. "It's your duty, your honor."

I probed the spoon into the fermenting goo and pressed it to my lips.

"How does it taste?" said the Bear, grabbing the spoon.

"It tastes like rotten eggs," I said.

ONE MORNING WHEN KAMAL was in a good mood, I asked him more about the days following the 9/11 attack. He didn't like talking about it much, as if he had been betrayed.

"The Feds were bringing in Arabs from across the nation," he said. "There were people I knew locked up without charge. The keys were chucked away. Some of them were sent down to Guantánamo. Go have a look, they're all still there."

When I asked how his wife had reacted to 9/11, the blood seemed to drain from his face.

"Her husband was an Arab," he said. "She was married to the enemy. She couldn't trust me. Trust is the basis of marriage. Without it there's nothing—just two people who used to like the same things."

"What happened to her?"

"She enlisted," he said.

"For the military?"

"Yup. She's serving at a base somewhere down in Georgia. Driving a tank or something."

However crooked I found his schemes, I would never have considered Kamal terrorist material. He liked himself too much to get blown up for someone else's cause.

"When they couldn't link you with the bombers, did the Feds leave you alone?"

"Eventually, after all the polygraphs and interviews," he said. "But the problem was that I'd met Mohammed Atta, the leader of the 9/11 strikes. We used to go to the same mosque."

"You knew Atta?"

"Yeah, I knew him."

"What was he like?"

Kamal blew his nose on his sleeve. "He was a stupid asshole," he said.

———

SATURDAY AFTERNOON WAS A long time in coming. I had
my best suit dry-cleaned, my black shoes polished until they
shone like lacquered wood, and I bought a spray of the finest
orchids I could find. They were pink with a trace of lilac around
the petals.

I took a taxi to the address printed on the letter paper and
found myself standing outside a large double-fronted villa in
the prosperous suburb of Anfa. The front door was dark brown,
and varnished in such a way that it caught the afternoon light.
Before I had even stepped onto the curb, it was opened by the
tall man with the well-groomed beard. He welcomed me and
said that Countess de Longvic was waiting in the salon.

I entered the house. The walls of the vestibule were covered with yellow silk, hung with etchings from imperial
France. The floor was rosewood parquet recently waxed and
scuffed at the edges. I followed the trimmed beard, clutching
the orchids to my chest.

There was a curious light in the salon. It was unusually yellow, as if it had been tinted by the windowpanes. The room
must have been forty feet long and almost as wide. It was dotted with European furniture: a carved sideboard and a rolltop
desk, a nursing chair, low bookshelves, three or four sofas, and
an Erard grand piano.

On one side of the room, below an oil portrait of Louis XIV,
a lady was sitting. She was about eighty years old, her face wrinkled yet childlike. Her hair was gray, pinned to the back of her
head tight in a bun. She was wearing a long lavender dress with
frills on the sleeves and a lace collar. Her dark eyes followed me
as I approached. I introduced myself, shook her hand, and presented the orchids.

"I am very pleased to have you here," she said in a soft
French voice. "I have waited a long time to meet you." Countess
de Longvic took a shallow breath and touched a finger to her
chin. "You have no idea," she said earnestly.

I smiled, muttered some apology, and asked how she came to know about me and where I was living.

"Casablanca's very small," she said. "But its grapevine has deep roots. How do you like Dar Khalifa?"

"Very much, but how do you know the house?"

The countess waved at a chair. "Please do have a seat," she said.

I sat down on a reclining oak chair and cast an eye around the room. There was none of the clutter that tends to accumulate in the homes of the elderly. Instead I noticed a refinement, a sense of precision.

"Your grandfather always sat in that chair," she said, pointing at me. "He liked the sloping back and would comment on the grain of the wood. He said a well-made chair was as beautiful to his eye as a fine piece of sculpture."

"How did you know him?" I asked.

Countess de Longvic stared into space. She picked a miniature brass bell from the table beside her and rang it twice. "We will have tea," she said.

I waited for the answer to my question, sensing that the countess preferred to reveal what she knew on her terms, a little at a time. Tea was brought by a middle-aged maid, her hair covered by a plain pink shawl. She limped, which caused the objects on the tray to rattle as she crossed the room.

"I will tell you," said the countess, pouring the tea. "I will tell you it all."

Again, there was a long pause and I began to wonder if I would ever learn anything.

"Toward the end of his life," the countess began, "your grandfather, Sirdar Ikbal Ali Shah, came to live in Tangier, as you probably know. He took a villa on rue de la Plage. He wrote books there and continued to advise two or three heads of state. His years at Villa Andalus were a period of mourning. He never recovered from your grandmother's loss in . . ."

"In 1960," I said.

"Yes, it was in January 1960," the countess said distantly. "She was so beautiful. I have never known a woman quite like her."

"You knew her?"

"Of course I knew Bobo," she said, laughing.

The countess explained how she had met my grandparents before the war in Vienna, where her husband was ambassador. They traveled together through Persia and Afghanistan, and shared a fascination for the underbelly of the lands through which they passed.

"Your grandfather taught us so many things," the countess said, "but the thing that affected me most was his advice to seek out what is not immediately seen. He said that on the surface, the carrot is a mere tuft of green, but under the ground there's a root waiting to be found."

The countess sipped her tea.

"Ikbal was a close friend and confidant to Nadir Shah of Afghanistan," she said, "and to Atatürk of Turkey, and to the Aga Khan. He moved in high circles, especially here in Morocco. But he was happiest when away from the limelight. He liked to sit with the shopkeeper opposite his house and chat about life. He always told me to meet ordinary people. 'The ordinary world,' he would say, 'is complete.' "

The maid limped in with an apricot flan.

Countess de Longvic cut me a slice.

"I used to go to Tangier every month," she said. "I stayed at the Minzeh, and would stroll down the hill to rue de la Plage. Ikbal had employed a guard, a Pashtun whom he had brought from the Hindu Kush. He wore a great white turban, Afghan clothes, and jabbed his ancient gun at anyone who passed."

She paused for a moment, narrowed her eyes, and smiled.

"Inside, the terrace was covered in nasturtiums, scented jasmine, and mimosas," she said slowly. "Ikbal would sit in the shade, writing letters or translating Sufi poetry. He always spent the mornings alone. Then, at lunch, he ate couscous with hot lime pickle. He forced any guest who joined him to smother their food in it as well."

I said that I had recently visited the Villa Andalus.

"Sometimes I pass it," the countess said gently. "I am curious, but I never ring the bell. The past is best left to itself. I find that when it touches the present, it vanishes like a forgotten dream."

"In his journals, he wrote a lot about his maid," I said.

"Afifa," the countess replied. "She was treacherous at the end, as was the Dervish."

"Dervish?"

"The old man who lived in the garden."

"Who was he?"

"He had supposedly seen your grandfather in a dream," said Countess de Longvic. "He was a Berber from the mountains. Ikbal took him in and let him live in the garden shed. He was there for years, distilling a medicine from the juice of the cactus plants. Sometimes he would come into the villa, bow down and kiss our hands. Ikbal begged him not to. He said that we were all equal before God."

I listened to the old lady's stories for two hours, but she did not mention the Caliph's House. At last, I couldn't stand it any longer.

"How do you know Dar Khalifa?" I asked.

The countess pressed her fingertips together. "I will tell you," she said, taking a deep breath, exhaling it in a sigh. "It was 1963 and the Cold War was at its height. My husband had died suddenly in Paris. He was so young. I was broken by it and needed to get away. Then in June that year an old friend in our diplomatic corps asked me to come to Casablanca. He wanted some information about a Russian company that had opened here. To the French, it sounded like a front for Russian espionage.

"I had not been to Casablanca before. The city was quite different then. Morocco had just broken free from France. The old Art Deco homes were in pristine condition, the streets bustling with people and European cars. I began to make contact with the Russian company, and to get to know the staff. They manufactured plastics. But of course that was just a façade. The firm's chief was called Sergey, and he lived in Ain Diab."

The countess stood up and walked to the window.

"He lived at Dar Khalifa," she said.

"A Russian spy lived in my house?"

"It sounds exotic," said the countess wistfully, "but it was not unusual for the time."

BACK AT THE HOUSE there was a trail of fresh blood. It led from the garden door to the main corridor, through the salon, and into the kitchen. I followed it with mounting concern. At the end of the trail was a chair, and sitting on it was the Bear. He held up a bloodied thumb.

"What happened?"

"Bad things," he said.

In the time I had spent chatting with the countess, a succession of events had filled the guardians with a new, terrible fear. The gardener had fallen from his ladder while pruning the dead fronds of the highest date palm. Miraculously, he escaped uninjured. Then the Bear had cut his thumb on a rusty spike, and a large chunk of plaster had fallen from the verandah roof, narrowly missing Hamza's head. When I met the guardians for their evening report, they were severely agitated.

"I thought there was *baraka*," I said. "I thought I had *baraka*."

"We were wrong," said Osman. "We thought you had it, but we were very wrong."

"How do you know there's no *baraka*?"

"There was a sign," said Hamza.

"It was clear as day," Osman said, wincing.

"What was it?"

The Bear lurched forward. He was holding a bucket covered by a board. He pulled the board. Inside, there was a snake. It was small, jade green, and was wriggling furiously.

"How could a snake get over the fence?" I said.

"Exactly," said Hamza. "There was no way in."

"Yes, there was no way in," confirmed the Bear.

"So?"

"So it was here all along, living here for years with its nest of snakes. Maybe they got in before the house was built."

I didn't follow. "What does the snake have to do with *baraka*?"

"If there had been *baraka*," said Osman, "the snake would have died. But you have seen it is alive, protected by the Jinns."

I felt the progress made with the pink slime and talk of

baraka had been real. We had been doing so well. But suddenly the guardians were charging off in the wrong direction. I begged them to believe in *baraka* again.

"We believe in it, of course," said Hamza. "We just do not believe it is here."

IT WAS LATE FEBRUARY and there was no sign of the decorating work ever being finished. Some days I would pace up and down, tearing out my hair, shouting at anyone who would listen. On others I would crouch in the kitchen, dreaming I was far, far away. I felt as if wolves had torn me to pieces, chewed my flesh, and sucked the marrow from my bones. There was nothing left to devour.

Kamal said that in Morocco if you pushed someone to get on with the job, they would think you were desperate.

"But I am desperate," I said.

"Well, keep it to yourself," he replied.

The Caliph's House had stalled. Any momentum we had ever earned was spent. The workers had come to understand that their employer's bark was far worse than his bite, and they were taking full advantage. They began to act like British workmen—arriving late in the morning and leaving straight after lunch. Then they asked my wife to make them tea and they stubbed their cigarettes out in the empty cups. After that they stopped coming at all. I asked Kamal to get them back.

"You've lost their respect," he said. "There's nothing you can do."

It was unlike Kamal to be defeated. I wondered if he was cashing in on my misfortune. Instead of doing anything about it, I went to the kitchen and slouched in a heap. At that moment the phone rang. It was François, the French expat. I hadn't heard from him in weeks.

"Been away in the Gulf," he said. "They're bastards out

there! Fanatics, that's what they are. You can't even get a drink. Can you believe it, a land without wine?"

In the next sentence I expected François to condemn Morocco, as he usually did. But he didn't. Instead, he lavished the kingdom with praise.

"You don't know how good we've got it here," he said. "The people are saints. Saints, I tell you!"

"But they never finish anything," I said despondently. "And now my workers are walking all over me."

François cackled. "They're good people," he said warmly.

"I thought you hated them."

"Are you mad?" he said. "I love them."

AT THE END OF the week, all the workmen arrived at Dar Khalifa. My spirits lifted. I asked Kamal if he had cajoled them to come. He replied that he had not, that they had another motive.

"It's Eid next week," he said.

"So?"

"So they want *baksheesh*."

There is no time less attractive to be an employer in Morocco than at Eid. Whether you like it or not, you are expected to dish out an entire week's pay as a bonus. In return, everyone takes an extra week off and claims their normal salary at the end of it. As well as handing out tips to the workers, I was coerced into providing an extravagant feast. The craftsmen warned there might be problems finishing the job if they failed to get enough couscous and lamb.

"They're not going to finish anyway," I said, "so why bother to give in to their demands?"

"You don't understand them," said Kamal.

EVERY SECOND DAY WE would go to the port. Kamal would slip inside and negotiate with the customs men, leaving me with the one-eyed snail seller. Over the weeks, I learned more about snails than any man should ever know. Whenever I begged him to let me slink into the port with him, Kamal refused. If the officials caught sight of me, he said, we would never get the container out. As if the situation wasn't already bad enough, word came that my second container had arrived from London, filled with books.

"Now the real problems begin," said Kamal.

"They're just old books."

"We're going to have the censorship office on our backs," he moaned.

"There's nothing to censor, believe me," I said. "No pictures of naked women, nothing sensitive."

"Try telling the censorship police that."

Kamal disappeared through the main gate in his waiter's disguise. I spent an hour or two making small talk about snails. Then Kamal reemerged. His face was drawn and ivory white, as if he had seen the specter of death.

"It's bad," he said.

"How bad?"

"Very bad."

I gritted my teeth.

"They have asked you to have all the books translated into Arabic by an official translator."

"But there are more than ten thousand books," I said. "Each one's more than two hundred pages." I did a calculation. "That's at least two million pages."

"An official translator charges ten dollars a page," said Kamal. "He can do four pages a day."

He pulled out a calculator and tapped in the figures.

"If the guy translates four pages a day," he said, "it'll take him five hundred thousand days. That's more than one thousand three hundred years."

"We can get more than one translator," I said, "to speed things up."

Kamal tapped again at the calculator.

"Either way," he said, "it's going to cost you twenty million bucks."

SEVENTEEN

*If you have much, give your wealth;
if you have little, give your heart.*

UNDETERRED BY THE OVERZEALOUS DEMANDS OF the censorship police, I decided to commission the library to be built whether I had any books to fill it or not. Having the work done would, I hoped, take our minds off the problems with the port. My attention turned to planks of wood. Time spent loitering outside the Casablanca port had taught me that Morocco imported vast quantities of timber, from the Far East and Brazil. The virgin forests in the Atlas and the Rif have long since been felled. These days Moroccans tend to plant only eucalyptus, which grows fast and provides them with valuable fuel. But there is a wood for which the kingdom has been famous since ancient times—cedar.

In Europe or the United States, I would have engaged a carpenter, described what I wanted, and let him do the rest. In

Morocco, things were characteristically more complicated. As with other building work, it was up to me to source and buy all the raw materials, and to have them transported to the Caliph's House. After that I had to find a carpenter who could design the library and turn the planks into shelves.

"I'm sure we can handle it," I said.

"You'd be surprised," Kamal replied. "Remember, in Morocco it's the easy jobs that are hardest to get done."

Now that I thought of it, he was right. Whenever I tried to get someone to change a door hinge, cut a piece of glass to size, or paint a window frame, the request was met with utter consternation. Weeks would pass, with me repeating the same pathetic demand. But if I asked someone to cut fifty thousand mosaics in dozens of intricate shapes, or to etch a pattern six hundred feet long in plaster, the job would be done without any questions at all.

"We'll need a lot of cedar," I said.

"I'll find the black market," Kamal replied.

"Can't we just go to a sawmill and buy some planks?"

"You're not in Michigan," he said. "Anyway, cedar's expensive. You can't pay the going rate. That would be ridiculous."

"Would it?"

"Of course it would," said Kamal.

EID IS A TIME for celebration, when the Arab world erupts into a festive frenzy of slaughtering rams and spending quality time with the family. Writers of travel guides like to say that the occasion is to Muslims what Christmas is to Christians. It's a nice line, but the two festivals are very different. While Christmas celebrates the birth of Jesus, Eid commemorates Abraham's sacrifice of a ram to God in place of his own son, Isaac. Abraham is a prophet of Islam, and the tale of his famous sacrifice is recounted in the Qur'an as well as the Bible.

For seven days a sense of jubilation descended over
Casablanca. The grim realities of daily life were swept aside,
replaced by a childlike hysteria. I had been irritated that the
workers were to be gone for a week, and I didn't much like
having to hand out the bundles of baksheesh. But I found myself
energized by the growing anticipation all the same.

Five days before the festival, the rams began to arrive.
Some came by truck, by bullock cart, or by train; others were
strapped to the front of scooters or simply herded down the
highways from far away. They were everywhere—huddling on
odd scraps of land, at bus stops and in supermarkets, in doorways and on traffic islands, on railway platforms and in car
showrooms, in barber's shops and at ice cream stands. A local
newspaper calculated there were more than a million rams
brought to Casablanca for slaughter at Eid.

Kamal urged me to buy a few dozen good-sized rams and
keep them to sell at the last minute.

"There's always more demand than supply," he said. "It's
simple economics."

"I find that hard to believe," I said. "The city's awash with
rams."

"You just wait," he said.

Three days before Eid arrived, a wave of terror surged
through the city—rams were running out. Rumors said that
the stream of trucks arriving from the villages had dried to a
trickle. What began as gentle panic developed into a whirlwind
of hysteria. Men and their sons formed posses and paced the
streets in search of animals. It was like the panic on Thanksgiving
morning when all the turkeys have gone. Tensions had reached
fever pitch. Grown men were brawling in the streets, playing
tug-of-war with the last pitiful rams on sale.

I might have shunned Kamal's advice to stockpile rams, but
companies across the city had done as he suggested. Two days

before Eid, the poor creatures became invaluable sales tools. Buy a new washing machine and you got a ram thrown in for free; buy a used car and you got half a dozen of them. One electronics store on Boulevard Zerktouni raffled an entire flock the night before Eid, causing absolute hysteria. So many people had bought tickets that the center of Casablanca had to be shut down.

At the same time, a whole industry sprouted up selling the accoutrements of slaughter—hatchets and short-bladed knives, skewers, and saws for hacking through bone. On every street corner touts were offering bales of straw, on which the sacrifices are made, and charcoal for roasting the meat.

Like everywhere else, the shantytown was echoing with the sound of bleating. Most of the rams had already been sold and were stashed away in the shacks, ready to have their throats slit at the appointed hour. Hamza told me that the last few animals in the bidonville were bad.

"They look healthy but they're diseased," he confided, "afflicted with illness. One mouthful of that meat and you will drop down dead."

I wondered why the guardian felt it necessary to explain the situation. Then the reason struck me. Hamza knew very well we hadn't yet bought a ram to kill.

"My cousin can get you a fine one for half the normal price," he said. "When you pick up the knife, it will bare its neck, ready for slaughter."

"We're not going to kill a ram," I said.

The guardian looked at me squarely. "No ram?"

"No, we don't want to kill an innocent animal," I said.

Hamza scratched his head. As far as he was concerned, it was a great honor to make the sacrifice at Eid, a ritual practiced by his family for centuries. To miss the occasion was unthinkable, especially as he suspected I could afford his cousin's finest ram.

ON THE MORNING OF Eid, the small whitewashed mosque in the bidonville was overflowing with worshippers. Every able-bodied man was there, prostrated on rough woven mats, praying toward the east. The donkeys had fallen silent, as had the limping dogs, and the wicked boys had been hosed down and dressed in white.

When prayers were at an end, everyone rushed home, where their rams were waiting for the knife. But no blood was spilled until news came that the king's own sacrifice had been made. Then the orgy of death commenced. Every household in the land slit a throat, except for our own. The sound of dying animals was tumultuous. Ariane was in the garden when the killing began. She asked me why the animals were crying out, why they were so sad. I kept her at Dar Khalifa. All around the house the streets were red, soaked in blood, as the head man of each house butchered an animal and skinned it. The aroma of roasting mutton began to emanate from the shacks. It hung above the shantytown in an oily cloud. While the mothers cooked the meat, their children roasted the rams' heads on homemade braziers in the alleyways. They cracked the skulls, scooped out the sizzling brains, and gobbled them up.

That night, the bidonville was ablaze with light. A crude system of streetlamps had been rigged up, a thousand wires stemming from a central cable. The lamps burned with a tremendous phosphorescent light. It made for a very beautiful sight. I couldn't understand how the electrical supply had been laid on, or who was paying for it. This became clear when, a few days later, our electricity bill arrived. It was fifty times the usual amount.

A WEEK AFTER EID, I stopped at an Internet café downtown to check e-mail. The room was windowless, fifteen feet square, with a dark patch of damp on the ceiling. Most of the computers were taken by an assortment of girls, all in their twenties or early thirties, all looking for a husband in cyberspace.

Whenever I'm in an Internet café, my eyes stray away from my screen. Everyone else's e-mail is far more interesting than my own. I try to concentrate but I can't help myself.

As usual I found my eyes veering to the side, where they locked onto the screen beside me. A woman was having a chat conversation in English with a Canadian man. She was wearing a yellow headscarf with a paisley motif. I couldn't see her face. She was oozing passion for her Internet admirer, describing how she longed to be crushed in his arms, kissed by him, married in white, and to live in a small house with flowers around the door. Eventually, she logged off and stood up to pay. It was then that I caught a glimpse of her face. It was Zohra.

I jumped up.

"Hello," she said calmly, "I was expecting to meet you."

"Really?"

"Yes, Amina said you would come."

I asked her for the money she had taken. "You owe us more than four thousand dollars," I said. "I need it back."

Zohra pushed a strand of hair under her scarf. "I'm leaving," she said. "If you come after me, you'll have a lot of trouble."

I followed, asking why she had told the police I was a terrorist, why she had run off with our money. She didn't answer. Instead, she walked faster and faster, until she had broken into a run. I ran after her down Boulevard d'Anfa. I was gaining on her, about to catch her. Then a car startled me with its horn. I turned sharply to the right, then turned back a moment later. But Zohra was gone.

THAT AFTERNOON I RECEIVED a pink slip of paper from the postman, informing me that a package had arrived for me at the central post office. I showed the docket to Kamal. He groaned.

"Your nightmare is about to begin," he said.

The central post office of Casablanca was a great white hulk of a building, constructed by the French in the days when imposing white structures were all the vogue. The moment we entered the main door, I understood what Kamal had meant. There must have been four hundred people inside, each one clutching a similar slip of pink paper. The tension was driving ordinary people to revolt. One group were waving their slips frantically, shaking their fists at the same time. Another had climbed onto the clerk's desk and were demanding to be served.

Kamal told me to relax.

"Why doesn't anyone in Morocco ever form an orderly line?" I said gruffly.

"Because that's not their way," he said.

We piled in. Kamal showed me how to get to the front by moving sideways, kicking shins with hard thrusting movements. Within minutes we were standing before the clerk. I handed him my pink slip. He glowered at me.

"Fill in this form," he said.

When I had, he handed me three more forms.

"Now these."

Forty minutes later, a slender brown cardboard tube was brought out from the storeroom. It was battered and marked along one side with a row of red crosses.

"Red crosses," said Kamal. "It means the censorship people don't like what they've found."

I recognized the cardboard roll. It contained some wall posters I had ordered for the children's bedroom. There was one of Dr. Seuss's *Cat in the Hat*, an illustrated poster of the alphabet, and a wall map of the world.

"I can't believe that the Cat in the Hat is going to offend the censorship police," I said.

"You may be surprised," said Kamal.

The cardboard roll was thrown down on a long inspection table. All around it ebbed a sea of ripped packaging and weeping Berber women with tattooed chins.

The posters were removed from the tube by the inspection officer. He was a well-built man with close-cropped hair and a week's stubble on his face. He looked like a bulldog. I smiled at him. He leered back.

"Cat in the Hat," I said. "We love him."

The officer looked at the cat and his red-and-white striped hat.

"Good, clean fun," I said.

The alphabet was the next to be inspected. The miniature illustrations were checked carefully for impropriety. The bulldog put it down and opened the world map between his outstretched hands. He regarded it meticulously, examining each continent.

He said something in Arabic.

"What's he saying?"

Kamal seemed nervous. "You can't have this one," he said. "The censorship police are taking it away. They're gonna incinerate it."

I felt my back warming with anger. "It's for my kids," I said. "How could a world map be offensive?"

"Western Sahara isn't in the same color as Morocco," said the clerk.

"So what?"

Kamal slipped me a pained glance. "Keep quiet," he said. "This is serious."

I didn't understand what he was talking about. It was like a sketch from Monty Python.

"They're not going to take it!" I said.

My eyes scanned the inspection desk. There was a roll of packing tape, a couple of pens, and a modeling knife. Without a thought, I grabbed the knife, pushed out the blade, and excised the affected region. The clerk blinked, the map still grasped tight between his outstretched hands. I kissed the kingdom of Morocco and Western Sahara and handed them to the clerk.

"Do-it-yourself censorship," I said.

AFTER WEEKS OF BEING becalmed with no work done at all, the wind lifted and the workers returned. Mustapha the mime's tadelakt team found new energy and even learned to smile. They mixed up a new vat of plaster and thrust trowels of it at the walls, swishing it smooth. Before the tadelakt was dry, the second team would score a pattern into the plaster. Within days they had finished the dining room and the salons, the children's playroom, and the bedrooms above. The plumber turned up in overalls instead of the gray suit he usually preferred. He took out his biggest hammer and started smashing one of the floors. I would have questioned what he was doing, but I was so delighted that I ran up and shook him by the hand. A new mason started work, too. He finished off the staircase and fitted the balustrades. Then a sculptor arrived with a fountain I had ordered five months before. The house echoed with the sound of hammers, saws, and singing.

We even managed to get the tiles on the verandah clean. When I told Kamal I needed an army of people to scour them with acid, he sent five men to our house. They proved to be expert scrubbers, despite the fact that they refused to wear goggles and kept getting acid in their eyes. I asked Kamal how he had ever found a team of men so skilled in scrubbing.

"They better be good at it," he said. "They work in our hammam as masseurs."

I was so overcome that the work was on the move again that I asked the bejmat craftsman, Aziz, to build a mosaic fountain for the wall in the children's courtyard. Kamal would have vetoed the idea if he had got wind of it, so I waited until he was out of the house.

Moroccan mosaic work, known as zelij, is the pinnacle of the kingdom's traditional design. Unlike mosaics in the West, which tend to be square, zelij come in hundreds of shapes and colors. It takes years to learn to cut them, and as a result, the craft comes at a price.

I took Aziz aside. He spoke no French, and I no Arabic, and so I mimed the idea with my hands. I wanted a classical Moorish arch with a waterspout, sending water tumbling into a lower trough, which would, in turn, feed a large basin in the middle of the green tiled courtyard. The children could play in the water, I hoped, paddling in the long, hot summer afternoons.

Aziz said he could prepare the fountain, *Inshallah,* if God willed it, in a month. He scribbled a price on a scrap of paper—seven thousand dirhams, about seven hundred dollars. For once, it sounded reasonable, considering the fountain would feature five thousand mosaics, each one cut by hand.

A little later Kamal turned up. I didn't tell him about the fountain. He disapproved when I communicated directly with the craftsmen, as it endangered his own position. Instead, I asked why the workers were striving so feverishly to get all the work done. Kamal smiled wryly.

"I passed a rumor in the shantytown," he said. "I whispered it to the vegetable seller. It looks as if word got around."

"What did you tell him?"

"That the king's coming to visit you," he said.

WE PLANNED TO TRAVEL to Azrou in search of black-market wood. The town, south of Meknes, is set against a backdrop of cedar forest. Low-level contacts had hinted of a thriving black market. It was just a matter of finding it. Kamal liked nothing more than ferreting out the black market. He shunned established shops. Whenever I went toward one, he caught my collar and led me away. "You can't go in there," he would say, "that's a rip-off joint." I couldn't remember the last time I had bought anything from a shop. If we needed anything for the house, we would go to Derb Ghalef, the sprawling shantytown of stalls on the southwestern edge of Casablanca. It sold everything, from endangered reptiles in cages to antiquities from France, from red balls of Dutch edam to children's clothes, satellite receivers, and giant-screen TVs. Much of it was contraband, smuggled in from Spain or across the border from Algeria.

"Why don't the police raid the stalls?" I asked.

"Are you crazy?" Kamal replied. "They own most of them."

The trip to buy a black-market cedar tree was put back because of problems with our Jeep. The engine had developed an alarming rattle. A mechanic was called. He looked under the hood and gasped.

"It's a very big engine," he said.

I nudged Kamal. "Are you sure this guy's up to the job?"

"We can trust him," he said. "He's the second cousin of my aunt's husband. He's practically family."

While the Jeep was being fixed, I suggested we line up a new carpenter.

Kamal repeated his caution that Casablanca's carpenters were the last men on Earth you could trust.

"There must be one trustworthy carpenter in the city."

Kamal looked at his watch. "There is one," he said pensively. "He should be up and running by now."

We took a small red taxi to the nearby suburb of Hay Hassani. The cab veered off the main street and trundled down a succession of smaller and smaller alleyways, until it reached a dead end. The lane was only a few inches wider than the car. We had to get out through the windows.

Kamal tapped on a rusting blue steel door. A bolt inside slid back and a frightening figure stepped out. He was about six foot five, as round as a barrel, and had no neck at all. He looked like Bluto from *Popeye*. I swallowed hard. The taxi driver gulped. Kamal strode up and kissed the man's cheeks. They hugged, then kissed cheeks again.

"This is Rachid," he said. "He was my bodyguard in the old days when I used to get into fights."

Rachid the bodyguard was the kind of man you wouldn't want to meet in an alleyway on a dark night. But, as I soon discovered, his looks were deceiving. He was gentle as a kitten. He said he had never liked fighting, that it was bad for his nerves. That's why he had taken up carpentry instead.

He led us into his workshop. There were two cumbersome cutting machines; both bore the word "Leipzig" in ivory-white lettering. They looked about a hundred years old. They were made back in the days when corners weren't cut and everything from toasters to teapots was made from cast iron.

On the workbench was an unfinished coffee table. Its edges had been expertly tooled, its uppermost surface detailed with a pattern of concentric octagons. The craftsmanship was very fine indeed.

Rachid tapped the dust off a half-finished chair and invited me to sit. Then he served us mint tea, and cracked his knuckles until Kamal told him to stop. In the silence that followed, I explained about the library. I said it was to fill a room eighty feet by seventeen, that it was to have shelves rising from the floor to the ceiling.

"I want cedar," I said.

Rachid the bodyguard bit his upper lip anxiously. "That's expensive."

"Black market," I whispered, tapping my nose. "We're going to get it on the black market."

"You will have to line the walls in cork," he said, "otherwise moisture will come through and damage the books."

I smiled at Rachid. He glanced at the floor meekly. I liked his attention to detail.

"You can have the job," I said.

IN THE FOURTH WEEK of February, Countess Madeleine de Longvic dropped in. Dar Khalifa wasn't ready for visitors, and I encouraged people ferociously to stay away. Most of them took my advice, warded off by the shantytown, the mud, and the sea of evil boys who threw stones at anyone they did not recognize. But the countess, who had no fear of the shacks, the dirt, or the boys, was lured by her curiosity of the past.

I was standing on the upper terrace when I heard the sound of a car approaching, splashing through the puddles. It was so rare for a vehicle to penetrate the bidonville that we always rushed to see who it was. The countess's royal blue Jaguar was purring down our lane. It came to a halt at the garden door. A liveried chauffeur stepped out and pulled the passenger door back with a gloved hand. From above, I saw the hat first. It was turtle-green velvet, as wide as the wheel of a men's racing bike, and crowned with a single ostrich feather.

The countess rang the bell. Hamza lunged for the door. A moment later I was in full apology mode. I apologized for the state of the house, for the noise and the cold. When Rachana had been introduced, I apologized for the way her hair was tied. Countess de Longvic stooped down and kissed Ariane on the cheek.

"You do not see the perfection around you," she said.

It was a chill bright day. The garden was a thousand shades of green, cheered by the winter rain. We sat on the lawn and drank darjeeling tea. Ariane laid her dolls out on the grass and pulled off their heads.

"I remember the house as being darker inside," the countess said at length. "I seem to recall several more walls."

I explained about the army of hammer-wielding masons.

"They were very enthusiastic," I said. "In fact, they were unstoppable."

"It's much improved," said the countess, "you can see all the way through to the garden. I think the masons did you a service."

I steered the conversation to where our last one had closed—to Sergey, the Russian spy.

"Ah, yes," she said in an unhurried tone, "I seem to recall he rented the house from a Frenchman. It flowed with Stolichnaya. All the rooms stank of it. Sergey had it shipped in every month, crates and crates, brought through the diplomatic pouch. There was caviar, too, and Russian pickles. That was all Sergey ever served—caviar and pickles, washed down with neat vodka."

"What happened to him?"

"As the British say so diplomatically," she said, "he was found to be engaged in activities incompatible with his status."

"Spying?"

"Of course."

We stopped talking, and watched Ariane struggle to do cartwheels on the grass. Hamza and the other guardians crouched nearby, watching us through a hedge.

"This is an oasis," said the countess. "There's no other villa like it in Casablanca."

"Someone told me it belonged to the Caliph of Casablanca," I said. "But I can't find out anything about such a man."

Countess de Longvic held out her glass as I poured more tea. She sat in silence, staring at the first spring flowers.

"The Caliph owned all the land around here a century ago," she said, after a long while. "It was a sizeable estate. There were rolling fields all the way down to the sea and out toward Tamaris. His family lived on these lands for three hundred years. They were powerful, rich beyond imagination, and had great influence."

"Who was the Caliph of Casablanca?"

"He was a member of your family," said the countess airily. "He was a Sharif, one of the Prophet's descendants."

"Why did he leave Dar Khalifa?"

"The Caliph died in the 1920s," said the countess, "and the estate was inherited by his oldest son. He gambled the family fortune away and was left with nothing. I heard that he shot himself when his debtors took the house."

"Do you think he killed himself here at Dar Khalifa?"

The countess sipped her tea.

"I suspect that he did," she said.

THE NEXT NIGHT, THE clatter of a machine woke me. I checked the clock. It was three forty-five. The engine's growl was deep and irregular, unlike a passenger car. I assumed it was the bulldozer returning to the shantytown. But the sound grumbled through the bidonville all the way up to the house.

I went down expecting trouble. Kamal was at the door.

"I've got the container," he said.

In a way known only to himself, Kamal had managed to get the paperwork cleared and the Indian furniture released from the port. We had escaped without paying anything at all. The container was unloaded by a dozen burly men. They were nightclub bouncers whom Kamal had picked up en route. Their shift had just finished and they were willing to work for a tip.

The container doors were pulled back and the furniture was hauled into the salon. It was elaborately packed, each piece wrapped in twenty layers of cardboard, then packed into crates.

"Why do we have to unload it now, in the middle of the night?"

"Because you don't want people to see!" Kamal hissed.

He said he had learned the habit of secrecy from his father.

"But I've got no secrets."

"Everyone has secrets," he said.

EIGHTEEN

Every beetle is a gazelle in the eye of its mother.

IN EARLY MARCH, SICKNESS struck the Caliph's House. We all went down with it, the children first. Vomiting was followed by diarrhea so severe that there were moments I feared for our lives. Not since taking a shaman's brew of ayahuasca in the Upper Amazon had my digestive tract been thrown into such disarray. When the doctor arrived at Dar Khalifa, he found us crouching around toilet bowls.

"You have been poisoned," he said darkly.

It was no great feat of detection.

"I've worked that out already," I said.

Between the fierce waves of retching, we tried to under-stand what had poisoned us. We hadn't eaten in a restaurant for days, and our own kitchen was kept meticulously clean. The doctor inquired where our water came from.

"From the well," I said. "We've had it cleaned. The water's pure."

Hamza was called, and gave his own opinion, that the illness was caused by bad spirits, by the Jinns. I assured him that, as a medical man, the doctor didn't believe in Jinns.

"Of course I do," the physician corrected sharply.

"There must be a scientific explanation," I said.

"We will see," he replied.

Hamza led him away to inspect the kitchen, leaving us huddled around the toilet bowls. I wondered how a doctor with a belief in the underworld could reach an accurate conclusion. A few minutes later, Hamza brought him back to the bathroom.

"The well is poisoned," he said resolutely.

"But we had it cleaned by a professional," I said.

"Someone has deliberately infected it," the doctor said suspiciously.

"Who would have done such a thing?"

"Perhaps it was the shantytown's Godfather," said Rachana.

I cross-questioned Hamza. "Has anyone put anything in the well?"

He looked at the ground. He didn't answer.

"Hamza!" I growled, giving in to a new wave of retching. "What's going on?"

The guardian washed his hands together nervously. I could tell he was holding something back.

"Tell me!" I shouted.

"The Jinns," he said. "Qandisha."

Had I the strength, I would have leapt up and throttled Hamza then and there. I was sick of the talk of Jinns. To hell with cultural sensitivity. We were all violently ill, and as usual, the Jinns were being blamed.

"Forget the bloody Jinns!" I shouted. "I never want you to speak of them again."

The doctor asked Hamza something in Arabic. They chatted calmly for a moment or two.

"Now I understand," said the doctor, breaking into a smile.

"What is there to understand?" I said. "Whenever something goes wrong, the guardians blame it on the damn Jinns."

"Of course they do," said the physician. "And the Jinns are to blame for the poison, indirectly."

"What do you mean, indirectly?"

The doctor put away his stethoscope. "Hamza tells me that a female Jinn lives in your house."

"Qandisha," I said.

"Yes, that's her name, or what they call her. No one would dare use her real name. She doesn't want you to live here. She said she'll kill you all if you don't leave. The guardians are very frightened, so they are trying to keep this Qandisha happy. They don't want her to hurt you or the children. But they're very worried."

"What about the poison?"

The doctor smiled again. "To keep Qandisha happy," he said, "Hamza has been putting half a chicken into the well for her every night."

"Damn it, Hamza!"

"He's just doing what he thought was right," said the physician. "He wants to solve the problem, to get Qandisha out."

I wished I were back in Britain, a land industrially cleansed of superstition.

"If we wanted to get Qandisha to leave and never come back," I said, "how would we do it?"

"It's easy," said the doctor. "You would hold an exorcism, of course."

COUNTESS DE LONGVIC HAD said that my grandfather would travel to Casablanca once a month to buy coffee from a shop near the Central Market. I checked his diaries, but there was no mention of the city. When I told the countess this, she laughed.

"Of course not," she said. "He never called it Casablanca. He always referred to it as W.H., for 'White House.'"

My grandfather had been brought up in a time when confidentiality was king. Like Kamal's father, he was infatuated with secrecy. His diaries were full of anagrams, acronyms, and his own code words, often translations from Dari, the language of Afghanistan. I scanned the diaries again. The countess was right. There were regular monthly entries for W.H., the code for Casablanca. The note against it usually included the initials H.B. For example, he wrote "Checked on H.B.," or "H.B. doing well," or "Gave fifty dirhams to H.B."

I telephoned the countess and asked if she knew about the mysterious initials.

"He used to say he came to Casa for the coffee beans," she said. "That it reminded him of the coffee he had in Kabul."

"But what about H.B.?"

"Is it a kind of coffee?" she asked.

"No, that wouldn't make sense," I said. "He may have been eccentric, but an obsession with coffee beans doesn't sound right."

I would have asked Kamal for his opinion, as he was good at crosswords. But he didn't turn up for an entire week. I called his long-suffering girlfriend and asked if she knew where he was.

"Probably run off with another girl," she said. "I wish her luck."

Rachana told me to check with the police. I didn't because Kamal himself had once warned me about contacting the police.

"Ask them for directions," he had said, "and you'll find yourself behind bars."

IF I NEEDED AN exorcist in Britain, I wouldn't know whom to ask. The English yellow pages certainly don't have a listing, and if I stopped someone in the street and asked them, I'd probably be dragged away to an asylum. There were many things that were hard to find in Morocco, but an exorcist was not one of them. The guardians beamed with delight when I lined them up and asked for their advice on exorcists.

"In the mountains," said the Bear.

"Yes, at the top of the mountains," said Hamza.

"But how do I make contact with them?"

"Go and ask at Sidi Abdur Rahman," Osman suggested.

Until then I had only heard gossip about the tomb of the saint Sidi Abdur Rahman. It lay on an outcrop of rocks two hundred yards into the Atlantic, a mile from the Caliph's House. I would often pass it and found my eyes drawn to the cluster of whitewashed buildings propped up on a plinth of jagged rocks. It looked like something out of a science fiction film. When the tide was in, it became an island, and when the tide was out, you could walk across to it if you dared.

Morocco has hundreds of such tombs. They are a focal point for anyone hoping to be healed or to attain *baraka*. Ordinary people flock to them in times of need. If their mother is sick, or they can't get pregnant or find a wife, they go to the tombs and pray, make a sacrifice, or beseech the resident sorceress to cast a spell. A wizened old woman in the bidonville once told me that the tomb of Sidi Abdur Rahman was the most blessed place in all Casablanca. She said that you could be touched by its power simply by looking at it.

In most Arab countries, people revere the tombs of the good, especially those of Sufi mystics. But I had not come across a Muslim country in which such strength was drawn from the burial grounds of saints. For me, the deep unwavering belief in them hinted of Morocco's pre-Islamic past.

Osman explained that I should go to the tomb before dawn on Friday. He said he would take me. Thankfully, the tide was out when we got there. The sky was lightless but not dark, the air very cold, a breeze sweeping in over the surf. The waves were far out, black crests breaking into white. It was hard to believe we were on the edge of a great city. The tomb itself had an outlandish presence. It seemed to glow. The only sounds were of the waves in the distance and the faint hum of a voice in prayer.

Osman led me over the jagged rocks, toward the island. It was comforting to have him there. I have never been unnerved in Morocco, but if there was a place to be afraid of, it was surely the tomb of Sidi Abdur Rahman. Where the rocks ended, a crude stairway began. We ascended it and found ourselves on the islet.

A group of four women were crouched on the path praying, faces veiled, bodies rocking gently back and forth. Beside them was a cluster of knapsacks.

"They have come from far away," Osman said. "Their need must be very great."

We walked up the path toward the tomb. Coarse one-room buildings lay on either side, the homes of pilgrims who had come and never left. Spend time in Morocco and you hear tales of people so fearful of Jinns that they move into a mosque or a shrine and refuse to go home. Kamal had told me that his own father was once so frightened of bad spirits that he slept in a mosque for an entire year.

To the left of the path was a patch of bare rock, a place of sacrifice. It was early but the specter of death had already visited. We stood there as dawn broke, the first rays of pallid pink light reflecting off the rock pools of fresh blood. Osman motioned to a door.

"That's where the sorceress lives," he said.

"Shall we go there?"

"First we must buy some lead," he said.

I didn't understand why the metal was needed. But I handed ten dirhams to a man with a pile of the silver strips.

Osman strode up and tapped at the sorceress's door. A woman appeared. She was short and broad shouldered and had a cocked eye. Osman greeted her with respect, and I held up the lead foil. The woman fluttered a hand at the door in invitation. We slipped inside.

The room was extremely small, damp, and cold, its ceiling hung with bunches of dried leaves. There was a pile of white seashells heaped in one corner, and a Qur'an on a stand in the middle. We sat on our haunches.

"Tell her we need an exorcist," I said.

Osman took a breath, smiled nervously, and explained. The sorceress frowned, sneezed, then talked about Jinns.

"What's she saying?"

"She says she can see it in your face," he said.

"See what?"

"That there is a Jinn inside you."

"It's not in me, it's in the house," I whispered gruffly.

"It's the same thing. She says she has seen the Jinn."

"What's he like?"

More chatter, then nodding.

"It's not a male Jinn. It's female," he said. "She's strong, powerful, and very angry."

"What about the exorcist?" I said.

Osman put the question to the sorceress. She took the lead and melted it in a saucepan over a gas burner. When it was liquid, she poured it into a steel bucket half filled with water. There was a crackle and a muffled fizz of something very hot becoming cold. The woman pushed up her sleeves, delved for the lead, and inspected what she found. She said something to Osman. His face paled with fear.

"The Jinn is *b'saf,* very great," he said. "She wants to kill you. There's danger. One exorcist won't be enough. You will need twenty of them."

"But where do we find so many exorcists?"

Osman translated the question. The sorceress inspected the silvery metal again.

"In Meknes," she said.

ON THE SEVENTH NIGHT after his disappearance, Kamal rang the bell. He was wearing a white blindfold and had been led to Dar Khalifa by a small boy. I welcomed him, but didn't comment on his apparent loss of sight. I knew an explanation would be forthcoming. We sat down and Rachana brought in a tray of coffee. Kamal fumbled for the cup. I remarked how nice the garden was looking.

"I can't see it," he said.

"What happened this time?"

"Emergency laser eye surgery," he said.

The thing about Kamal was that he told the truth as if it were a lie. I would always assume he was lying, only to find out later it had been the truth. He had taken time off only days before, claiming to have diabetes. I had telephoned the hospital. To my surprise, his explanation had borne out.

He fumbled for a crumpled scrap of paper in his pocket and held it in my direction. It was a prescription for glasses.

"There's no time for you to go blind," I said frostily. "We've got to get twenty exorcists. We've got to go to Meknes."

Kamal lifted the corner of his bandage and peeked over at me, blinking. "I know just who to ask," he said.

WORK AT THE HOUSE continued. On some days there were more than sixty craftsmen bustling away at the floors and walls, the masonry and woodwork. At least half of them had moved into the salon, where they slept in rows like conscripts heading off to war. By the middle of March the winter blues were behind us. We were on a fresh course, sailing toward stifling heat. The garden was alive with bees, tempted by the scent of honeysuckle, jasmine, and the fire red hibiscus flowers. And birds of every shape and size flapped around the trees—storks and woods pigeons, ibis and turtledoves.

The artisans remained unable to complete any job they had begun. The painter would pause before making the final sweep of his brush, and the mason would leave the last nail sticking out. The curse of unfinished work caused me to drown in frustration, but there was nothing I could do. We would have been able to move into our bedrooms months before we did if a simple band of tiles had been finished around the bathroom walls. Without them, the tadelakt team couldn't do their plasterwork, and without that, the plumber couldn't do the bathroom fittings, and the electrician had to hold back, too. It was the same downstairs. The sitting rooms were waiting for a few stray panes of glass. Until they were glazed, the painters refused to start, and the floors could not be oiled until the ceilings had been done. Everything at Dar Khalifa was inextricably linked, in a great twisted mess of interconnecting lines.

Part of the problem was communication, not verbal but cultural. It was true I could hardly have a conversation with any of the craftsmen, but I got the feeling that even if I had spoken fluent Arabic, we would still have been unable to understand each other.

I reminded myself not to be deceived by Casablanca. It was an enormous thriving city, with the latest European fashions, fast cars, and chic restaurants. But all that was froth on the surface. The real Casablanca was a place of die-hard tradition, in which ancient Moroccan customs endured. The artisans had learned their skills as apprentices and were part of the rock-solid underside that kept the kingdom on course.

The inability to finish work brought out the worst in me. I

found myself taking it out on Kamal, who took to wearing glasses with lenses as thick as milk-bottle glass. He was the only person who could understand my tirades.

"Why the hell can't they finish one damn thing before they move on?" I complained again and again.

Kamal would creep behind me, his head low. "It's the Moroccan way," he would reply. "We may not finish things, but we start them so well!"

One morning Rachana found me cringing in the bathroom, unable to come out and face the world. I felt as if a nervous breakdown was coming on.

"You can't go on like this," she whispered gently.

"I know," I said, my mouth foaming at the side. "But they're driving me mad. They can't finish anything."

"There's only one way to get the house done," she said.

"What's that?"

Rachana smiled. "You have to be like a Moroccan," she said.

TOWARD THE END OF March, I was walking down Boulevard Mohammed V, the main avenue through the old town, when I spotted a coffee seller. The shop was old-fashioned, very plain, and right in front of the French-built Marché Central. It was the kind of establishment that survives because of the quality of the product it purveys, and not because of newfangled marketing techniques. I went inside.

A woman in her thirties stiffened on her chair and welcomed me. She said she had not seen me before.

"We don't have many new customers," she said.

"It's my first time here," I replied.

"We sell coffee from Brazil," she said. "Have you had it before?"

I said that I had, that I liked it very much.

The woman seemed overcome with delight. "Some people

prefer coffee from Asia," she said, "but my grandfather says you must concentrate on one product if you want to sell it well. He must be right, because he has been selling coffee here for sixty years."

Along the wall behind the cash register was a picture of the king and a series of polished copper urns. They bore the names of fine Brazilian beans—*Yellow Bourbon, Fazenda Jacaranda,* and *Carioca*. I asked which was the darkest roast. The saleswoman tapped a thumbnail on the last urn, marked *Boléro*.

"You must take this one," she said.

I asked about her grandfather. "Is he still alive?"

"Of course," she replied. "He's old, very old, but he sits there every afternoon."

She pointed to an armchair in the window. Its stuffing was coming out at the sides, and the cushion was compressed as if it had been well loved. I paid for my coffee and took the brown paper bag. Then I hesitated. The woman breathed in.

"Is there anything else?" she asked.

"Um, er . . ."

"Yes?"

"This may sound stupid," I said, "but my own grandfather used to come to Casablanca every month from Tangier. He came to buy coffee. It is very, very unlikely," I went on, "but perhaps he used to come to this shop."

The saleswoman straightened her back and smoothed a hand down her dark mane of hair. "Did he like Brazilian coffee?" she asked.

RACHANA WAS RIGHT. THE only way to get the house completed was to head full force into the storm. I don't know why I hadn't thought of it before. It was as if blinders had been wrenched from my eyes. I ran up onto the upper terrace and surveyed the Caliph's House. Normally, I would have looked down, cursing at all the unfinished projects. But instead, I jotted down all the other things we could start doing.

First, I wanted to convert an old stone workshop at the side of the house into a hammam, and then to renovate the dilapidated guesthouse at the end of the vegetable garden. After that, I had plans to build another fountain and decorate the room across from my library with a fabulous mosaic floor. Until then I had held back in the name of moderation. I jotted down eight new projects and handed the list to Kamal.

"Which one do you want to do first?" he asked.

I looked at him squarely, my eyes glowing red. "We'll do them all at once!" I said.

THE ROAD TO MEKNES sweeps down across the farmlands of the Saïss Plateau and rolls up to the walls of the imperial city itself. The furrowed fields are the color of bitter chocolate and are so fertile that the people who live there walk tall with pride. Meknes and its sister city, Fès, form the cultural heartland of Morocco. The sorceress at the tomb of Sidi Abdur Rahman had been economical with her information. When asked for a source of exorcists, she had given me no more than the name "Meknes."

Kamal waved aside all questions when I asked how we might pick up the trail once we arrived. He claimed to know a man with the contacts to unlock the door. It was only a matter of finding him. I pestered Kamal for details, but as usual his lips were sealed.

On the journey to Meknes, we stopped en route at the small town of Khemisset and ate *merguez,* piquant mutton sausages, at a roadside café. When the call to prayer sounded in the early afternoon, the owner of the place unfurled his rug and bent down in prayer. While he prayed, his son guarded the cash box that held their takings. The boy rapped his hands together in a slow clap throughout the time his father was praying toward Mecca. When the man had finished, he went back to the counter, and his son put his hands in his pockets again.

Kamal noticed me wondering why the child was clapping while his father prayed. I had assumed it was an act of piety.

"Can you understand it?" he said.

"Understand what?"

"The father needs his son to guard the money," he said, "but he doesn't trust him. He thinks the boy will grab some cash when his back is turned."

"So?"

"So he tells the boy to clap," Kamal said. "If the clapping stops, it means the boy's hands are stealing the cash."

ONCE AT MEKNES, WE parked the Jeep near the magnificent Bab Mansour gate. Kamal opened the back door and ferreted about in a cardboard box he kept in the car. It contained an assortment of filthy mildewed clothes stinking of stale cigarettes and discotheques. I had asked him frequently to chuck the box out. But to Kamal its contents were far more than grubby old clothes. They were indispensable disguises. He threw me a crumpled jacket and pair of slacks.

"Put those on," he said.

Ten minutes later we were sitting at a café inside the medina, stinking like drunks after a night out, waiting for the low-level contact to arrive. Kamal wouldn't reveal the reason for disguises. It was his way of controlling the information. But when I asked about the exorcists, he was abnormally forthcoming.

"They're a brotherhood," he said, "called Aissawa. They come from Meknes and can suck Jinns from the walls."

"Will they travel to Casablanca?"

"If you pay them enough, they'll go anywhere," he said.

An hour later, the contact arrived. I thought it was going to be him as he approached from across the square. He was talking on two cellular phones at once, in a crude display of elevated status. I hoped desperately that he would walk past. But he reeled over and kissed Kamal's cheeks. He looked like a pimp. His face was confident and brash, with a flat nose and small devious eyes. I disliked him the moment he slapped his moist, spongy palm onto mine.

"This is Abdullah," Kamal said. "He knows all the exorcists in town."

"I don't like the look of him," I whispered.

"Looks aren't important," Kamal snapped in reply.

Abdullah the pimp swiveled a chair around and sat on it

back-to-front. I am not certain, but I think it was his way of showing he was top dog, at ease with himself. He took out a pea-sized fragment of kif resin and conjured it into a joint. Kamal ran through the formalities of greeting, talk of old times and shared memories. Then he cleared his throat and I heard the word "Jnun."

The pimp's beady eyes seemed to shrink in size, until they were no larger than marbles. He jabbed the end of the joint into his clenched teeth and sucked very slowly and very hard.

Kamal told him about the Caliph's House and its resident Jinns. The pimp slid his slippery palm down his nose. He said something in Arabic. I couldn't understand the words, but I knew what he meant.

"He's talking about money, isn't he?" I said.

Kamal didn't reply.

Abdullah took another drag and blurted out a line of numbers.

"What's he saying? How much?"

We sat there, dressed down in our grubby clothes, the air heavy with marijuana smoke.

I asked about the exorcists. Kamal and the pimp were too busy to reply. They stared at each other, each waiting for the other to break. To anyone passing, they would have looked like two men sitting in mellow contemplation. But there was nothing mellow about it. They were doing battle.

I excused myself and crossed the square to buy nougat from a makeshift stall. When I got back, Abdullah was gone.

"What happened?"

"He's going to line the exorcists up," Kamal said.

"How many?"

"The group's fifteen, but he's throwing in an extra ten for free."

NINETEEN

The answer to a fool is silence.

MOVE TO MOROCCO AND IT'S IMPOSSIBLE not to give in
to delusion. However hard I tried, I couldn't help but think on
a grand scale. In London, we had lived in a microscopic apartment, and as a result, everything I thought about was small in
scale. But living at the Caliph's House changed the way I perceived the world. I began to plan enormous expeditions, to
dream up subjects for obscure encyclopedias to write, and I
became obsessed with using every inch of available space.

   Part of it was being in Africa. The sky was vast, the landscape severe and unrelenting. There was a sense that anything
was possible, that I was no longer held back by the telescoped
outlook of Europe. The danger was a motivator, too. One of the
reasons to break free from Britain had been to shed the cozy

sense of security, the safety net that trapped us and held us back. In Morocco, the lack of safety was an energizing force, but at the same time it was a constant concern. I had seen more accidents than I could count: car wrecks with people half dead lying on the ground, building sites where workmen had tumbled from scaffolding, children maimed by fireworks on a Sunday afternoon. For the first time in my life I became completely alert. In the West, you can drift from day to day in the knowledge that the society will protect you and your children. Any problems, and someone will pick you up and dust you off. But after five minutes on North African soil, I knew it was up to me to guard my family. No one else was watching them.

KAMAL AND I DROVE south from Meknes to Azrou on the trail of black-market cedarwood for my library shelves. Everyone had warned me to take care. The cedar business, they said, was a trade abundant with thieves. Then there were the rumors to contend with. One informer had told me that all the cedar on sale in Morocco was afflicted by an invisible blight. It looked good on the surface, he assured me, but get it home and a plague of maggots would swarm out and eat their way through your home. The vegetable seller in the shantytown had said cedar was beset not by worms, but by spirits. Bring the ill-fated planks into the house and the Jinn inside them would slink into the walls. I reminded him we already had a profusion of Jinns. He looked very perturbed.

"Then there will be a war," he said anxiously. "Your house will be destroyed!"

The small town of Azrou was perched on the brink of the Middle Atlas, at four thousand feet. It had the mood of a colonial hill station. The buildings were low, unmistakably French, their European roofs glistening against the cobalt sky. I suggested we start right away looking for dodgy characters who could lead us to the black market in cedarwood.

"It's not the time," Kamal said.

"When is the time?"

"Midnight."

So we spent the afternoon sleeping in the Jeep. Every so often someone would tap on the window with a coin and hold up a bundle of feather dusters, smuggled cigarettes, chewing gum, or ballpoint pens. Evening came and turned into night. I kept looking at my watch, counting the minutes.

At ten-thirty I shook Kamal by the arm and made him wake up. We clambered out of the car, took refuge in a café, and ordered café noir. There was the usual crowd of long-faced men in jelabas and the clouds of black tobacco smoke. The waiter brought us a pair of clean ashtrays, served the coffee, and coughed into his hand. He asked for payment.

"We will pay you when we are ready," said Kamal.

The waiter put out his palm and mumbled a price. "I can see you are from Casablanca," he said. "And I don't trust city men."

On the stroke of eleven Kamal got up, crossed the street, and ambled over to a boy who was selling Marlboros one by one. But he wasn't buying cigarettes. He was searching for the key to unlock the black market. After a few minutes of conversation, the boy hurried away and Kamal slipped back into the café.

An hour passed.

Kamal was lighting a cigarette when a man sailed up through the smoke and paused at our table. He was short and nervous, with a shiny rust-colored face. He reached over, shook my hand gently, and sat down. There was something not quite right about the handshake. I glanced at his right hand. He was missing three fingers and a thumb. Kamal later told me that in Morocco a carpenter without fingers was respected as a man with experience. He said the best carpenters had no fingers at all.

A whispered conversation in Arabic followed. There was talk of qualities and quantities, and of the police. The contact grinned a great deal and helped himself to Kamal's Marlboros. Whenever the police were mentioned, he would scratch his chin with the lone finger of his right hand and crow with nervous laughter. Eventually, he led us out of the café and into the street. We met up with another man, also missing fingers, and ended up at a shop that sold used toilets. Despite the late hour, all the lights were on. I didn't have a clear idea why we were there or what was going on. But as usual, I held back while Kamal made the arrangements.

The nervous man pulled the lid off one of the toilets and fished out half a dozen samples of cedar. He slapped them on the table and drew our attention to the various qualities. They were graded, he said, by the amount of knots and by the dryness of the wood. The driest wood with no knots at all was *première qualité*. It came at a price—double that of second quality.

I examined the samples and asked if the agent had enough of the first quality to make eight hundred feet of shelving. My question was greeted with much grinning. The contact strode over to the shop's far wall and pulled back a stand featuring a display of pink imported toilets from France. A low entrance was revealed. Kamal and I were ushered through.

We found ourselves in a warehouse filled with the pungent aroma of fresh-cut cedar. As my eyes grew accustomed to the dim light, I made out the stock—thousands of thick planks piled up to the roof, the size and shape of railway sleepers. In one corner stood a circular saw. It was stripped of any safety features, the butcher of countless careless hands.

Three hours of negotiations followed. At the end of it, I was far poorer, but had secured enough first-grade cedar to build the library. The agent promised to have the wood delivered to

Dar Khalifa as soon as he could. He pressed the remains of his right hand into mine, grinned broadly, and sloped off into the night.

ON THE JOURNEY BACK to Meknes the next day, we passed rows of stalls at the side of the road, manned by an army of teenage boys. They sold avocados and chameleons, bouquets of roses and red ceramic pots. There were no villages or houses for miles around. I wondered how the boys got there and why they had selected such a remote setting for their trade. We had not planned to stop, but when I saw the chameleons being held up cruelly by their tails, I ordered Kamal to hit the brakes. I sent him to buy up their entire lizard stock—twenty chameleons in a range of sizes. They cost me five hundred dirhams, about fifty dollars. It was daylight robbery.

Five miles after the stalls, the road was empty again, lined with eucalyptus trees and scrub. The sunlight was so bright that Kamal shielded his eyes with his hand as he drove. He said he couldn't remember a brighter afternoon. The road curved to the left, then the right, and evened as it rolled on toward the north. For the first time in a long while we had a good view ahead.

A man was waiting in the shadow of a fir tree before the horizon. He was bent over with age, his body shrouded in a hooded jelaba. I saw him first.

"Let's give him a ride," I said, "and we can set the lizards free at the same time."

"Those people are nothing but trouble," said Kamal.

"What about charity? Please stop. You must stop," I said.

Kamal eased down on the brake and we slid to a slow, awkward stop. The man limped over with his knapsack. I called out to him in greeting and told him to climb aboard. He grunted thanks. While he staggered over, we got out and liberated the chameleons. A second later, we heard the sound of the engine starting. I swiveled round to see the Jeep driving off. It is a moment I will not forget. We dropped the lizards and ran up the road, shouting insults.

It was no use. The car was long gone.

"Bastard," I said.

"May Allah steer him into a tall tree," Kamal quipped.

"Don't say that. I don't want the car damaged."

"You're not going to get it back," said Kamal. "By nightfall it'll be cut up in Meknes and sold for scrap."

We sat at the side of the road in disbelief, waiting for something to happen. He didn't say it, but I sensed Kamal blaming me for buying the lizards. They had led to our downfall.

"Poor lizards. Poor old man," I said defensively.

"Damn the lizards, screw the old man. He wasn't even old. He was just pretending to be old," said Kamal. "He was a thief."

After fifteen minutes of waiting, we heard a car approaching from the direction of Meknes. It was the first vehicle we had seen. The road was so straight that we caught sight of it long before it reached us. The car was moving very fast, sunlight reflecting off the roof. I screened my eyes with my hands.

"It looks like the Jeep."

Kamal peered out to the distance. "It is the Jeep," he said.

"Is he coming back for the shirts off our backs?"

"Let me handle this," said Kamal.

He picked up a sharp-edged stone and ran toward the car as the thief skidded to a halt.

"Don't hit him!"

"Of course I'm gonna hit him!"

The thief opened the driver's door a moment before Kamal reached him with the rock. He was shouting something in Arabic. It sounded as if he was begging for mercy. Kamal's expression was one of passionate anger. I had seen his wrath before. He was quite capable of killing if he wanted to. The thief shouted again, clambered out, and lay spread-eagled on the ground. I didn't understand what was happening. He was pleading, repeating the same words over and over.

"What's he saying?"

Kamal didn't answer. He tossed away the stone, visibly moved. His fury melted away.

"What's he saying? Why did he come back?"

The man begged for mercy.

"*Allahu akbar!* God is great!" said Kamal.

"What?"

"I can't believe it."

"*What?*"

"He says that he brought the car back to us because . . ."

"Because?"

"Because if he did not, no one would ever stop to help an old man again."

AT DAR KHALIFA WORK had begun on the fountain. A truck had arrived from Fès laden with baskets of square ceramic tiles. They were blue, white, red and green, yellow and turquoise, orange and black. A pair of *zelijis,* tile cutters, sat in the courtyard on wads of cotton padding. They were calm, circumspect, the kind of men who could spend an eternity in reflection. An apprentice heaved the first basket of tiles into the courtyard and began marking out the mosaic shapes. Tracing with a bamboo stick dipped in white homemade ink, he sketched around a sample. On a single ceramic square, he would mark a number of shapes, and pass the tile to the zeliji to cut out the shapes.

Two thousand mosaics were needed to make up the central medallion alone, and the entire fountain required more than twice that, each chip of ceramic cut at the house. Aziz had said that it would take a month to prepare all the mosaics. At first I

thought it would take far longer. But as I watched the craftsmen's hammers chipping, I saw there was hope. They worked
at a furious pace, tapping the angles of each zelij with their
sharp-sided hammers. The individual mosaics they created
ranged from simple squares and chevrons to S-shaped curves,
rhombuses, trapezoids, and eight-pointed stars. Each mosaic
shape had a name. There were spire-shaped points called
quandil, and gentle curved shapes known as *darj,* a triangle
called *taliya,* and an octagonal shape that the zeliji said was
known as *kura.*

Moroccan mosaics differ greatly from their Western cousins, which tend to be made from vitreous glass. The fragments
of glass are the same color throughout, whereas Moroccan
mosaics are ceramic and are merely glazed with color on the
upper surface. Cutting ceramic is far harder than cutting glass,
which breaks in straight lines. When placed edge to edge, the
ceramic zelij fit so snugly together that there is no space for
grouting between them. Instead, the mosaics are set in plaster,
with the underside edges cut at an angle so as to hold better in
place.

A FEW DAYS AFTER our return from Meknes, I walked past
the Brazilian coffee shop across from the derelict Bessonneau
building. It was a Friday morning, and the streets were unusually busy, the spring sunlight showering down. I noticed an old
man sitting in the window. He was bundled up in a polyester
blanket. His eyes were shut. I opened the door, went inside, and
greeted the saleswoman. She asked how I had liked the coffee.
When I praised it, she thanked me.

"You are a man who likes good things," she said, "I can see
by your shoes."

I glanced down. I was wearing an old pair of black brogues.

"They shine like mirrors," said the woman. "The mouth and the feet are far apart, but they both have good taste."

I pointed to the old man asleep. "Is that your grandfather?" I asked in a whisper.

"Yes, that's him."

"It's a pity he's sleeping," I said.

The saleswoman pulled out the drawer of the cash register and slammed it shut. The old man opened his eyes.

"Nadia," he croaked. "How much?"

"Sit down beside him," said the woman. "I will serve you a cup of Bourbon Santos."

I sat down and a silvery-gray cat leapt up onto my lap. The old man peered out at the street.

"Do you like Brazilian coffee?" he asked.

"It's the very best," I said.

The man smiled, nodded, and rubbed his glasses with the corner of his shirt.

"My grandfather used to like it, too," I said. "He came to Casablanca to buy it once a month."

"Was he from Fès?" asked the man.

"No, he was an Afghan."

The man pushed his glasses up his nose and leaned forward. "I knew an Afghan once," he said faintly. "He lived in Tangier."

I breathed in sharply. "That may have been him," I said.

"He was a Sufi. He was a wise man."

"Was he called Ikbal?"

The man's tongue ran over his cracked lips. "Yes, that was his name," he said.

I didn't say anything or show emotion, but inside I was dancing.

"He used to come every few weeks," the man said slowly. "Then he stopped coming."

"He was knocked down by a Coca-Cola truck," I said.

The elderly coffee seller seemed disheartened. He removed his glasses and wiped his forehead.

"Hussein was lonely without him," he said.

"Who's Hussein?"

"He was the reason your grandfather used to come to Casablanca," he said.

THE GUARDIANS WERE NOT pleased when the cedarwood arrived. They stood in the lane and told the truck driver to go back to Azrou. He would have done as they ordered had I not been walking in from the shantytown.

"What's going on?"

"This man has brought cedar from Azrou," said the Bear angrily.

"Excellent, let's get it into the house."

"You can't do that," said Hamza.

"Why?"

"Because cedar is a cursed wood. It is favored by Jinns!"

"It can't all be favored by Jinns," I said.

Osman pointed at the sky. "Yes, it can, and it is," he said knowingly.

I am more sensitive to local folklore than almost anyone I know, but there comes a point when you have to draw the line. The guardians had long since passed that line. They ruled the house by a regime of invented fear. I was sick of them dictating what was cursed and what was not, how to do something and whom to trust. I pushed them away and signaled the timber truck to unload.

"You will regret it," Hamza said menacingly.

FOR THREE WEEKS HICHAM the stamp collector was con- fined to bed. I called our doctor to attend to him. He tramped through the shantytown's knee-deep mud, listened to the old man's heart, peered down his throat, and announced he had life-threatening flu. He was ordered to stay at home in a blanket, to rest, and to receive no visitors at all.

Our conversations had become the cornerstone of my week. I looked forward to them, as I did to hearing Hicham's straightforward take on the world. During his illness, I kept away from the old man's home on doctor's orders. I would often see his wife buying vegetables opposite the mosque. She would give me a report on her husband's health.

On the Monday of the third week, she waved to me as I walked through the bidonville.

"He wants to see you," she said.

Hicham was sitting in bed when I found him, in the middle of the one-room shack. He was wearing his old tweed coat, flat cap, and socks on his hands. I asked how he was feeling.

"Like a prisoner," he said. "Like a cold prisoner."

"I've brought you some stamps. There's one from Mongolia, and a few new ones from Afghanistan."

The stamp collector tugged the socks off his hands, thanked me, and snatched the postage stamps. He arranged them in lines and inspected each one with his magnifying glass. He nodded to himself, muttering in Arabic as he squinted through the lens. When he had examined the last stamp, he put the magnifying lens down and peered over at me.

"You have made an old man very happy," he said.

MY FANTASY OF TRANSFORMING the guesthouse into a pleasure pavilion was inspired by the Moroccan tradition of building *menzeh*. Devoted to occasional moments of leisure, they are in their own way a Moroccan version of the European folly. Many of the kingdom's royal palaces have such pleasure pavilions hidden in a garden, veiled from the main building by a screen of trees. They are decorated with samples of the very best bejmat, roofed in green tiles called *qermud,* and furnished with simple chairs, cushions, and rugs.

Turning the guesthouse from a derelict ruin into a Moroccan pleasure pavilion was remarkably easy to do. The place needed to be gutted first, the rusting iron roof removed, and electricity and water plumbed in. Then the walls would have to be replastered, the floors surfaced with bejmat, and the crown of green tiles laid on the roof.

Work was due to start in the middle of April. I had sketched out the general idea on the back of an envelope and given it to a builder from Ouarzazate. He gave a quote that was so low no one believed it, least of all me. I hired him all the same.

There were problems from the start. Osman caught wind of the project and declared it would end in failure. He said the outbuilding had been abandoned for a reason. When I asked him what the reason was, he walked off in a huff. Hamza was equally disapproving. He pulled me aside.

"Do not make this mistake," he said.

"Can't you tell me why the guesthouse was abandoned?"

"It is not your business," he replied.

"If it's a matter of the Jinns," I said, "you don't have to worry anymore. The exorcists are coming to Dar Khalifa."

The guardian's face froze. "When? When are they coming?"

"When they are ready," I said.

LATE SPRING EBBED INTO early summer, and the smell of the air changed. It was more fragrant, balmy, as if good things were on their way. With the winter far behind us and long, hot days ahead, my spirits were lifted a little more. I would roam around the empty rooms looking forward to the time when we might occupy them. The bulk of the decoration had been done, although enough details remained missing to prevent full-scale habitation of anywhere but the temporary bedroom we all shared on the long corridor.

One morning I was writing letters at my Indian-made campaign desk when the telephone rang. It was before eight. I wondered who would call so early. The voice on the line was deep, loud, and spoke excellent English. It asked if I was related to Sirdar Ikbal Ali Shah. I said that I was his grandson.

"We must meet," said the voice.

"Can you tell me who you are?"

"I will explain when we are face-to-face."

That afternoon I was twenty minutes early at the agreed meeting place, a café off Boulevard Hassan II. I supposed the Countess de Longvic had passed on my number to the mystery caller. I had tried telephoning her, but the maid said that she had left for the West Indies.

I ordered an espresso and pulled out my notebook. On the surface, Moroccan cafés are all the same—a blur of cigarette smoke and elderly men dressed in long jelabas and yellow leather slippers creased at the toes. But peer a little deeper and a world of unexpected interest is revealed. At the table beside me, a man in thick glasses and a Fès hat was carving matchsticks with a razor blade. Next to him, a tall suave figure was leaning back on his chair, drawing deep on a water pipe. The waiter swaggered over and slipped him a wad of banknotes from under his tray. The customer stuffed the money under his jelaba and glanced to the left and right.

My mystery caller was fifteen minutes late. I ordered a second espresso and filled a few pages of my notebook. A cold black shadow fell across the lines. I glanced up. A bearded man was standing over me. He was slim, in his mid-fifties, and was dressed in a gray linen suit. He stretched out a hand.

"I am Hussein Benbrahim," he said.

I didn't know what to say. I fumbled to put the notebook away, and motioned to the seat beside me. The man sat down. He had a dark face, much of it masked by the graying beard. His shoulders were broad, his posture unnaturally good.

"The coffee merchant told me about you," he said.

"And me about you," I replied.

"So you know already about our connection?"

"No, no," I said, "I don't. All I know is that you exist . . . that my grandfather came to Casablanca because of you."

Hussein asked the waiter for a café crème. He nodded.

"Yes, he used to come here because of me."

"Why?"

"Ikbal was a friend to my grandfather," he said, leaning toward me. "He was more than a friend. He was a brother."

"A brother?" I didn't understand.

"Not a brother as you understand it," he said. "A Masonic brother. You see, my grandfather and your grandfather were Freemasons."

"I knew my grandfather had belonged to a lodge in Edinburgh," I said.

Hussein leaned a little more forward, rested his elbows on the table, and pressed his hands together.

"Exactly," he said. "They met at Edinburgh Medical Infirmary during the First World War. Ikbal was an Afghan and my grandfather was a Moroccan, and so they were natural friends. They became Masons together and stayed in contact throughout their lives."

"When did your grandfather die?"

"In 1963," Hussein replied, "three years after Ikbal moved to Tangier. My parents died when I was a small child, and my grandfather brought me up. With his death I had no one to take care of me. We have no close relatives, and so I would have been sent to an orphanage. But Ikbal rescued me. He had promised to see to my welfare if something happened to my grandfather."

"A Masonic duty?" I said.

"A duty between brothers."

"But you didn't go and live with him in Tangier?"

"No, I stayed at a boarding school in Casablanca," Hussein explained. "Ikbal came to see me every month. He would bring me books and food. It was only later I learned that he was paying my school fees. He left a bank account for my further study. It's because of him that I became a surgeon." Hussein paused for a moment. "He always told me I had steady hands," he said.

"But why didn't he mention you? He didn't even talk of you to his close friends here in Casablanca."

Hussein stared over at me very hard. "Real charity is given anonymously," he said. "Speak about it and the meaning is lost."

FOUR WEEKS AFTER THE first mosaic was cut, the job of laying out the fountain's pattern began. A new moualem arrived at Dar Khalifa. He was fine-boned and fragile, like a figure crafted from Meissen porcelain. Hamza led him into the house and through to the courtyard where the zelij cutters were sitting. The master craftsman unfurled a sheet of sackcloth on the green tiled floor and set to work.

The central medallion was sketched out first. Then the sixteen outer rosettes were drawn and, after that, the background. The moualem used tweezers to position the smallest hand-cut mosaics for the central medallion. So adept was his skill that he laid out all five thousand mosaics upside down, without any need to see the actual pattern on the reverse. His hands moved at the speed of light, plucking individual mosaics from the assorted piles and dropping them into place. I asked how he could do the job without seeing the colors.

"Only a blind man knows the weakness of the eyes," he said.

While work on the fountain continued, in the library, the cedar was prepared into eight hundred feet of shelves. The wood was fabulously aromatic. Its scent filled the entire room. Rachid and his team of four helpers stripped down to their underwear and tied cloths round their mouths. There was so much sawdust that anyone enticed by the smell of cedar was blinded by the blizzard. The guardians paced up and down outside. They were still agitated that I was using cursed cedarwood and furious that I had overruled them. The wood may have been jam-packed with Jinns, but there was no sign of them. The house was still standing.

THE ONLY WAY TO deal with the rising tension was to escape from Dar Khalifa. I spent more and more time downtown, working in cafés, watching the bustle. Kamal would know to find me at the Café Rialto, opposite the cinema. I acquired a fondness for its tarlike coffee, which tasted of almonds.

One afternoon, he parked the Jeep outside the café and marched up to the table where I was sitting. He had the latest news about the gangster's plan to rob us of the Caliph's House. He sat down and started spreading a dossier of papers out on the table. We were discussing the boundary line when a uniformed policeman strode up. He flicked his hand at the Jeep.

"What's this doing here?" he said.

I berated Kamal for parking illegally.

"We're about to move it," I said.

"I don't mean the car," responded the officer heatedly. "I mean the badge. How did you get it?" The policeman jabbed a thumb at an official-looking sticker on the driver's side of the windscreen. It had the green five-pointed star of Morocco on a background of red.

"How did you get that, the Chief of Police badge?" the officer demanded again.

Kamal leapt up. He stepped over to the car. "If you want to know how I got the badge," he said arrogantly, "then give me a ticket."

The policeman chewed the end of his pen.

"Come on, give me a ticket!" Kamal shouted.

"Take this car away or I will take you to the station," said the officer.

"Give me a ticket, you coward! You'll be posted to the Sahara before you know it!"

I bent down to pay the bill. When I looked up, the policeman was gone.

"Where did he go?"

"He ran away."

"Have you got a relative on the force?"

"No," said Kamal. "I bought the badge in the bazaar for a buck."

COUNTESS DE LONGVIC TELEPHONED on her return from the Caribbean. She said that her daughter's mansion on the island of Martinique was very lovely but extremely damp. The greatest moment of a long journey, she declared, is the one when you arrive home.

I said that I had discovered the real reason my grandfather came to Casablanca every month.

"For the coffee?" said the countess.

"No," I replied. "To keep a promise he had made to a fellow Freemason."

I heard the rattle of pearls on the other end of the line.

"You know about Hussein Benbrahim?"

"I do now," I said. "But if you knew, why didn't you tell me?"

"I may not be a Mason," said Countess de Longvic, "but when I make a promise to keep a secret, my lips are sealed."

ONE MORNING A FEW days later, I found Rachana slumped at the kitchen table. Timur was nearby on the floor, screaming.

"I was mad to listen to your promises," Rachana said softly without looking up. "I am a prisoner here in this madhouse, in your madhouse, in your fantasy!"

"It'll get better," I said. "It must get better."

Rachana raised her head and looked through me. "You escape it—you spend the afternoons in your smoky, macho-man cafés."

"That's research," I said defensively.

"Well, I want to do research, too!"

I had no choice but to promise Rachana I would find her an assistant of her own. She was sick of all the squabbling between the legions of staff I had hired to make life easier. Almost all her time was taken up with settling the minor disputes and the bickering between the cook, the nanny, the maid, the gardener, and the guardians. Now she was calling for someone to stand at her right hand, to keep all the others at bay. I hoped Rachana's attention would be diverted as it usually was, and that we could continue on our rocky course. Days passed. I did my best to distract her, but she did not forget. In one outburst after the next, she called for liberty, to be unshackled from the Caliph's House.

ON MOST AFTERNOONS, ARIANE would toss the remains of her favorite dismembered doll into a wicker basket and go and sit with the guardians while they worked. She would play for hours and listen to their repertoire of stories—tales of honor, courage, and revenge from the Arabian epics. Within weeks of her arrival in Morocco, she had picked up French and some Arabic. Despite her young age, she became an invaluable translator. Sometimes she would push little Timur into the garden, where the two of them would prevent the guardians from doing any work at all. One afternoon I found the Bear rocking Timur in his arms while he recounted a folktale to Ariane. I apologized to him.

"They are wasting your time," I said.

The Bear looked deep into Timur's eyes. He breathed in, then out, and sighed very hard.

"Children are life," he said.

RACHANA'S LIBERTY ARRIVED AT the house early one evening in the form of a fleshy, well-built woman called Rabia. She regarded the world through a pair of large gogglelike glasses strapped on with elastic round the back of her head. In sign language, she made it known that word had reached her ears that a job was up for grabs. On the face of it, Rabia lacked the qualifications needed. She spoke no English and no French and had only arrived in Casablanca the previous week, from a remote village in the desert. There was, however, something that did make her appealing—the fact she instilled terror in everyone she met. Had I been braver, I might have opened the door at that first meeting and pointed to the street. But neither Rachana nor I had the guts. Two days into her reign at Dar Khalifa, Rabia had subdued everyone, including Rachana, the children, and me. We tiptoed around hoping not to fall into her magnified range of vision. The cook, the nanny, and the maid went about with glazed eyes, as if they had been whipped. As for the guardians, they locked themselves in the stables and refused to come out.

RABIA'S REIGN OF TERROR continued. She singled out the maid, Malika, for special treatment. The poor woman had lived through great hardship, which is why we had employed her in the first place. Scandalizing for Morocco, she had been married twice, divorced, and then had given birth to a daughter out of wedlock. The child, aged three, was living with Malika's mother nearby. Malika was very religious, but she had two shortcomings. The first was drink. She preferred rum, but would gulp down anything she could get her hands on, before refilling the bottle at the kitchen tap. She treated Dar Khalifa as a kind of social club—turning up in the morning, getting sloshed, before staggering away into the afternoon heat. Her second weakness was lying. She couldn't help it, but she lied about everything. It was her way of hiding a dependence on alcohol. Rachana and I had grown fond of Malika. Like everyone else, we liked her so much that we put up with her errant ways.

One afternoon, Rabia was on patrol as usual. She strode about the sitting rooms sliding a fingertip over the tabletops before inspecting it very closely.

"Malika!" she bellowed.

After a long delay the inebriated maid appeared, straining to remain upright. Rabia moved in close and sniffed Malika's breath.

"You are drunk."

"*Lah, lah!* Rabia, no, no! I am not. I promise. I am not!"

Rabia stormed into the kitchen and reappeared a moment later holding a shoebox.

"Hold this box in your hands," she said to the maid.

Malika fumbled to take the box.

"I will ask you again," said Rabia. "Did you drink alcohol?"

"No!" shouted Malika, swaying. "Of course I did not!"

"You promise on all that is sacred?"

The maid nodded. "Yes, I promise!"

Rabia pulled the elastic strap tight on her head. "Then open the box."

I heard Malika screaming before I could see what was inside the shoebox. It was a copy of the Qur'an.

"You have lied on the Holy Qur'an!" Rabia hissed.

Malika emitted an agonizing wail. Fearful at receiving eternal damnation, she turned toward Mecca and fell to her knees in prayer.

Within a week, she and Rabia had left our payroll. Neither one explained why she had decided to leave. When I asked for the reason, both women told me that God had made the decision for them.

ARIANE HAD SPENT THE day on a field trip to study pollution at the beach. She had learned that tossing empty bleach bottles into the ocean was bad, and that collecting other people's garbage and bringing it home was good. She and Timur were now fast asleep, dreaming against the echo of dark-backed toads. Rachana and I were watching *The Sound of Music* on my laptop. The Von Trapp family had sung "So Long, Farewell" and were now hiking over the mountains to Switzerland. I was about to switch off the light when I heard Osman shrieking. It was clear there was something serious going on. I ran outside in my pajamas.

"Osman, Osman, where are you?"

"Here, Monsieur Tahir!"

The guardian was on the ground near the pool. He was not alone. Pinned out under him on the grass was the shape of a man.

"I've caught a thief!" he cried jubilantly, as if he had just brought down a tiger. "Get a rope, and call the police! Quickly!"

Osman, Hamza, and the Bear spent every waking moment fantasizing about catching an intruder. It was all they ever spoke about.

I ran up and down panicking for a while, wondering what to use as a rope. Then I remembered an episode of *Hawaii Five-O* in which a drug dealer had been trussed up with a light cord. So I ran into the kitchen, found a new lamp Rachana had just bought, ripped off the cord, and rushed back to Osman.

"Have you called the police?" he said, struggling to keep the thief down.

"Not yet. I don't know the number."

"Go to the station and bring them! Quick!"

I ran to the Jeep, got it fired up, and sped through the bidonville. The sergeant at the local station was asleep outside. I woke him.

"We've caught a thief!"

"Oh."

"Can you send a police truck?"

The idea of a criminal seemed to worry the officer. "Is he dangerous?" he asked.

"Yes, I expect he is."

He scribbled down an address. "Take him to this other station," he said.

I rushed back to the house. Osman had tied the man so tightly that his arms had gone blue.

"I'll break his feet," he said. "Then he won't be able to run away!"

"Don't be so cruel!"

"Let's keep him in the boiler room for a few days," he said. "We can starve him and poke him with sticks."

"That would be torture," I said.

Osman grinned wider than I had ever seen him grin. "Yes," he gasped. "Torture."

I instructed him to drag the intruder to the car. He gave him a couple of sharp kicks to the stomach, then slung him over his shoulder. Five minutes later we were on our way to the police station. Once there, the thief was unloaded and hurled on the ground. He groaned miserably. A sergeant took his name, kicked him in the belly and then in the head, found me a chair, and kicked the man again.

Osman acted out how he had caught the thief, grappled him to the ground, trussed up his arms, and taped his mouth. Ten sheets of pink paper were interleaved with carbon and loaded into an ancient Arabic typewriter. A detective in civilian dress took down all the details, while the criminal was kicked into the cell.

There were half a dozen other offenders already locked inside. They were a fearful-looking bunch. One was covered in blood as if he had been stabbed; another had a shaved head and a six-inch scar down his cheek; a third was clutching the bars, leering at the officers.

When the report had been completed and the thief was locked up, the detective asked if I wanted to press charges.

"I just don't want him to come back to the house," I said. "He'll be very angry now."

I turned to glance at the cage and caught my first good look at the man's face. He was in his early twenties, with bulbous eyes, a bald head, and a mouth filled with very sharp teeth. We had eye contact. His look was so cold that I feared for my life. The detective seemed to read my mind.

"Yes," he said slowly, "yes, he'll probably come for re-venge."

"But I have two little children."

"Then we must send him to prison," said the officer grandly.

I nodded, signed the report, and asked what else I could do to oil the wheels of justice.

"One last requirement," the detective explained.

"Yes, anything," I said.

"You must go into the cage and have a discussion with the intruder."

I looked the policeman in the eye, then turned to take in the cage. The prisoners were lined up at the bars. It was as if they were waiting for me, smiling meekly, on their best behavior.

"No, sir," I said politely. "That is not going to happen."

THREE WEEKS AFTER OUR meeting with the pimp, there was still no sign of the exorcists. I cursed myself for having been cajoled into paying a deposit. But it was the first time I had hired a troupe of exorcists, and I didn't know the protocol. Kamal listened to my outburst when it came. I condemned him for introducing me to the repellent pimp in the first place.

"Get in the car," he said.

"Are we going to drive back to Meknes and get our hands on him?"

"Forget about the pimp," he said. "We're going to the dogs."

Casablanca is a city that never ceases to surprise. When you first arrive, you assume it's a modern metropolis. But then you begin to glimpse the many layers and conclude that the newfangled buildings and nouveau riche are no more than a façade laid atop a bedrock of raw tradition. After that, you begin to see the mixture of new and old, and your doubts begin all over again.

The night I went to the dog races with Kamal was one of the strangest of my life. Nothing particularly interesting happened. We watched half a dozen tired old greyhounds stagger around the old Art Deco velodrome, and a crowd of beefy men waving their betting slips. There was the interminable smog of cigarette smoke and the banter of gamblers boasting of their hope. But I left with something far more valuable—a sense that Casablanca had transgressed the boundaries originally set out for it by the French. It was a rare hybrid of a place, a hotchpotch of people from different corners of the same kingdom, thrown together in a great human stew. You never heard a word of praise for Casablanca. It was the butt of every joke, the place people came to but never admitted coming from. No one belonged there. But at the same time, we all belonged.

TWENTY

Live together like brothers and do business like strangers.

THE EXORCISTS COULD BE HEARD FROM a mile away. They came rolling through the bidonville on the back of a cement truck, blowing homemade trumpets and whooping like madmen recently escaped from a sanatorium. Rachana heard them first. She rolled her eyes and asked if the troupe was really necessary.

"You told me to act like a Moroccan," I said, "and exorcisms are what Moroccans do."

Ten seconds later, the truck screeched to a halt outside the house, and the pimp leapt down. I didn't recognize him at first. He was wearing a gold lamé turban and was carrying a cane. He bowed subserviently when he saw me, lit a pipe stuffed with marijuana, and whistled to the exorcists to follow him into the house.

The guardians were excited by the visitors. They said the team had *baraka*.

"You can see it in their eyes," Hamza said, wincing.

"They have power," said Osman admiringly.

"Power to cast the Jinns out," I declared.

"Hush," said the Bear. "They will hear!"

The exorcists were bundled into the library, where they crouched on the planks of cedarwood, smoking hashish. I counted them as they went in. There were twenty-three men and one woman. You could tell from a glance that they weren't from Casablanca. There was a rawness about them, a candor, a sense that they lived without secrets. Some of them were tall, others short or stout, but their faces were all cut from the same sheet of dark, wind-chapped leather. The pimp tweaked the joint from the corner of his mouth.

"They are from the mountains," he said.

"Can they dispel the Jinns?"

The pimp looked at them and then at me. "They will suck them from the walls and swallow them whole."

"How long will it take?"

"Maybe a day, maybe a week."

Our conversation was interrupted by the sound of a visitor at the garden door. Hamza slipped out, then reappeared, leading the gangster's wife into the salon. She was wearing high heels, tight floral leggings, and a tweed coat. Her hair was tied up in a pink bow, her face made up in greasepaint.

"I smell hashish," she jeered.

"It's the exorcists," I said politely. "They're going to suck the Jinns from the walls and swallow them whole."

Madame Nafisa grimaced. "Do you have permission?" she asked.

"Permission from whom?"

"From the City Hall."

The pimp sidled up like a pye-dog in pursuit of a poodle. I

left him to flirt with the gangster's wife, and went with Kamal to buy a goat. The exorcists had asked for a herd of them. Less than that, they hinted, and they could not be certain if the Jinns would get swallowed at all.

"We will need to kill a large goat in every room," one of them crowed.

Hamza nodded vigorously. "I told you," he said, "you need to kill a goat in every room."

Such slaughter was unworkable if only because of financial constraints. An adult goat was at least three hundred dollars. An entire herd would cost many thousands. In any case, I suspected that the meat would be dragged back to the mountains, as an exorcist perk.

"You'll have to make do with one goat," I declared. "Say what you want, and you'll still get only one. It's all I can afford."

The pimp narrowed his eyes. "Make sure it's a big one," he said bitterly.

IN THE WEST, BUYING fresh meat usually means trawling the chilled display cabinets in a supermarket, in search of a polystyrene pack that looks okay. In Morocco, "fresh meat" referred to an animal that was still alive. It was quite normal to choose your chicken from a cage before its head was whacked off in front of you. The same went for sheep. Part of the buying process was to watch its throat being slit. Back in London we tended to buy lamb in modest quantities, a pound or two at the most. The idea of purchasing an entire animal was unknown.

As someone who had grown accustomed to selecting meat shrink-wrapped in polystyrene, I had a hard time dealing with the execution process and the reality of the system. I like the hooves, the feathers, and the stray tufts of fur to be clinically removed. I like my meat to be anonymous, severed from its connection to life.

Kamal said he knew where to get goats on the cheap. He drove down to the docks, then turned right onto the road that led to the industrial zone of Ain Seba. We passed rundown stone factories and warehouses dating to the time of the French occupation. Every so often we would see an old villa, roofless and forlorn, cupped in a copse of mature date palms.

"The French thought they had found paradise," said Kamal, "but look what became of it."

He pulled up to a derelict warehouse a stone's throw from the ocean. Two men were sitting at a café next door, pushing bottle caps over a checkerboard with their thumbs. They looked up, surprised to see a car.

"This is where the goats are brought when they come from the countryside," Kamal said. He led me up a concrete stairway. It opened out into a long corridor, strewn with straw and blood, echoing with the sound of animals in distress.

"They're in here," said Kamal.

He pushed a door and we were suddenly afloat on a sea of goats. There were hundreds of them, white, brown, and black, all squirming to avoid our legs. A fierce-looking man with oversized hands waded over and hugged Kamal. He grabbed a hefty goat by the horns, threw it on the scale, and barked out a price. Kamal shook his head. The terrified creature was tossed back into the waves, saved from the guillotine because he was too fat.

The process continued until an animal of the right weight was found. Kamal peered into its mouth and jabbed its back with his hands.

"Are you checking if it's tender?" I asked.

"No," he said. "I'm seeing if it has *baraka*."

A goat slaughtered for a ritual has to be selected very carefully. For an exorcism, the taste of the meat is less important than the spirit of the animal. Kill a goat with bad karma and bad luck can slide toward disaster. I handed over a wad of hundred-

dirham bills and the goat's legs were trussed up. Kamal and I
staggered with it to the car.

BACK AT DAR KHALIFA, we found the exorcists passed out in
the library. My initial reaction was one of anger. They were
flouting their duty to rid the house of its Jinns. The only person
who was awake was the pimp. He was nestled in a corner
rolling a joint.

"They're asleep," I yelled.

"They're preparing," he said.

"Get them up!"

He licked his lips and struck a match on the floor. "That's
impossible."

"Are they that badly stoned?"

"It's not kif they've taken," he said. "They made tea from the
yellow flowers in your garden."

I might not have understood the comment, but my time in
the Upper Amazon had introduced me to the noxious effects of
the flowers of the datura plant. Sometimes called "the trumpet
of the Devil," they lure the foolish to touch them or to taste
them. Of all the flora in the jungles of Peru, there is none so
intoxicating. I had taken it myself unwittingly while staying
with the Shuar tribe. They said the plant gave them second
sight, the ability to peer into the real world.

Datura's qualities have been known since the times of the
Spanish conquest of the Americas. The plant was first brought
back to Europe by the conquistadores, along with tomatoes,
potatoes, chilies, and tobacco. It did not find a culinary use, but
it was favored by witches, who used it in their spells. They created an ointment from the flowers and applied it to their fore-
heads and to the skin of the inner thigh. To help aid in
absorption, the concoction was massaged into the skin with the
shaft of a besom, a twig broom. The witch would get a sensa-

tion of flying, before passing out. When she awoke, many hours later, she was certain that she had flown on her broom.

I had warned Ariane never to touch the plants, which were dotted about all over the garden and the courtyards. They thrived in the rich red African soil. One look at the exorcists proved datura's potency. I walked through the library, prodding them.

"They're not here with us," said the pimp.

"Datura's very strong," I mumbled.

"They know that," he replied. "They have taken it to enter the world of the Jinns."

In the evening, the exorcists came back to life and asked for a feast. They said that they required feeding if they were to do their work. I began to sense they were nothing but frauds, random people rounded up by the pimp, ready to make some extra cash. The cook prepared two platters of couscous and meat and told Hamza to take them into the library. She wouldn't go near the exorcists, claiming they could stop your heart merely by looking at you.

When Kamal arrived at the house that night, I told him of my suspicions.

"I think they're con men," I said. "Shall we kick them out?"

He looked horrified. "Don't talk like that," he said.

After the feast, the exorcists smoked themselves into a delirium, drank several gallons of mint tea, and fell fast asleep again.

I asked the pimp when they would start with the exorcism.

"They've already begun," he said distantly.

"No, they haven't! They've been lying about, doing nothing."

Kamal pulled me away.

"Don't talk like that," he said again. "Show them respect."

So I backed away and left the troupe to sleep. Meanwhile, Ariane had made friends with the goat. It was a friendship that was unlikely to be long. She fed him carrots, caressed his soft black hair, and refused to go to bed unless he could sleep beside her.

"We'd better let him sleep," I said. "He's got a big day ahead of him tomorrow."

"I love my goat," she whispered.

THE NEXT MORNING, I was up at dawn, woken by a commotion in the shantytown. Hamza knocked at the door and urged me to come right away. I pulled on my clothes and went out to the main track. The bulldozer had returned. Nearby to it, a man with a clipboard and wire-rimmed glasses had been surrounded by an angry mob. He was signaling to the machine's operator to start destroying the shacks.

The situation was getting out of control. Our house was full of exorcists, and the bidonville was on the verge of a riot. And at that moment, the fanatics rumbled back with their trailer. They got out, marched up to the whitewashed mosque, and pushed the wizened imam out the door. It was an attempted coup d'état. A wave of anger surged through the crowd as the shantytown's residents realized what was happening. They ran into the mosque, chased out the young bearded men, and reinstated their old imam. The driver of the bulldozer took advantage of the scurry and fired up his engine. Hamza tapped me on the shoulder.

"Quick, tell the official not to break down our homes!" he shouted. "He'll listen to you."

"I'm sure he won't."

"Please, Monsieur Tahir."

The official appeared surprised when I strode up and told him that I lived in the middle of the shantytown.

"You can't knock these houses down," I said.

"We have to," he replied, tapping his clipboard with a pen.

"If you do, there will be a lot of angry people," I said. "They might do anything. They might beat you up."

A vexed expression slipped over the official's face. He seemed like a good, honest man with no experience.

"It's an explosive situation," I said.

"Is it?"

I pointed at the crowd. They whinnied with anger as if cued to do so. The official shoved his clipboard into his bag and waved the bulldozer to retreat.

THE EXORCISTS LOUNGED AROUND all morning and into the afternoon. They pestered the cook for more platters of food, sent the guardians to go and buy them cigarettes, and told Kamal to find them a bottle of vodka. I couldn't believe everyone was putting up with it.

At sunset, I marched up to the pimp, who hadn't moved in almost a day, and instructed him to get on with the exorcism.

"It cannot be hurried," he said.

I took out a hundred-dirham bill and rustled it in my hand like a dry leaf. He snatched the note and clapped his hands. The exorcists staggered to their feet. The pimp shouted some words in Arabic.

Then the exorcism began.

THE PIMP ADJUSTED HIS gold lamé turban and ordered Hamza to open every door and window in the house as wide as he could. Hamza called Osman and told him to get on with it. Osman called the Bear and passed the command on. He ordered the gardener to do the job. As lowest in the pecking order, he had no choice. The gardener sauntered away while the guardians clustered around the exorcists.

"It's going to start," said Osman very softly.

Before the exorcism could get under way, the Aissawa pulled on their white cotton jelabas and crept around the house. They spread out into groups of three or four, wandering through the rooms on tiptoes. They took a moment to stand in every corner, before moving on diagonally to the next.

"What are they doing?"

"They're searching for the heart of the house," said Kamal.

"How do you know that?"

Kamal glanced away. "Everyone knows," he said.

It took more than an hour to locate the heart of the Caliph's House. I would have thought it was in the garden courtyard, near the room the guardians had always kept locked. But I would have been wrong. The exorcists agreed unanimously that Dar Khalifa's heart was in the middle of another courtyard, the one outside the kitchen.

The pimp rummaged in his sack and fished out a handful of cheap tallow candles. He passed them to the oldest exorcist, a man who looked as if he was about to drop dead. He kissed them before handing them out to his brothers. The candles were lit and placed in the corners of the yard. Their long wicks flickered in the darkness. A rough square stone was carried in and positioned at the center of the courtyard beside a drain hole. The yard had become a temple, and the stone its altar.

One of the exorcists murmured something to the others. A few minutes passed, and I heard Ariane screaming hysterically on the lawn. I rushed out. Her fingers were knitted together around the neck of the goat. A pair of the Aissawa were trying to wrestle the animal away.

"You have to let them take it," I said to her.

Ariane was in tears. "Where are they taking my goat?" she cried.

It was a difficult moment, one we never would have shared had we remained at the apartment in London. We were taking part in a ceremony, the kind that our ancient ancestors would have known well. But how could a small child understand it? How could any of us understand it? A perfectly healthy animal slaughtered to please an invisible force that probably didn't exist. I wanted to try to explain it all to Ariane. I wanted to tell her that the sacrifice said much about ourselves, and what we felt we must do to believe. But I could not explain.

"Where are they taking my goat?" she said again.

I wiped away her tears.

"To a better place," I said.

IN THE COURTYARD A cooking pot had been filled with milk. One of the Aissawa was stirring it. His eyes were closed, as if he was in a trance. He was moaning incantations. The reluctant goat was dragged into the house by the horns. It took three of the exorcists to get it to the makeshift altar. The creature bleated furiously at first, but then fear took over and it fell very silent. It seemed to know that something of great consequence was about to take place.

A spoon was dipped into the milk and held to my lips. I slurped it down. It tasted of stale tobacco. The same spoon was offered to everyone—to the two dozen Aissawa, to the guardians and the gardener, to the maid, the nanny, and the cook. Then came the turn of my wife and the children. Rachana refused to let Timur drink from the spoon.

"He's too young," she said. "He could catch a disease."

I opened his mouth and dripped a few drops of the white liquid into it.

"A ceremony's no time to think about cleanliness," I said.

"You're beginning to believe in all this, aren't you?" Rachana said sullenly.

I was about to deny it. But something held me back. She was quite right. I was being drawn in. There was something powerful, something irresistible about it. Ceremonies appeal to our primitive mind. I didn't know why, but I couldn't help becoming involved. I found myself believing there was a real purpose to the ritual, that I was helping in some way.

When the milk had been consumed, a tambour was struck hard and slow, like a death knell. Its rhythm gave a framework to what was about to take place. *Boom, boom, boom.* The goat's legs were trussed up. *Boom, boom, boom.* The knives were taken out. *Boom, boom, boom.* They were scraped against each other. *Boom, boom, boom.* The chief exorcist stepped up to the altar. *Boom, boom, boom.* He rolled up his sleeves.

"*Bismillah ar-rahman ar-rahim,*" he declared. "In the name of God, almighty, the merciful."

Boom, boom, boom. There was a glint of steel in the moonlight. *Boom, boom, boom.* Then silence. The animal kicked, and a pool of dark, oily blood seeped out over the terracotta tiles. *Boom, boom, boom,* went the tambour.

"Now it has begun," said Kamal.

The shrill scream of a *nafir,* a seven-foot horn, rang through

the house. The oldest exorcist hacked off the goat's head, bent
down, and sucked the wound with his mouth. Then three others stepped forward, touched the fresh blood to their lips,
savoring it, before hanging the carcass in the middle of the
yard. Blood rained down, and was collected in a used paint can.
The old exorcist took the long knives and skinned the animal.

He slashed the abdomen open first and inspected the
entrails with his hands. They glistened like jewels in candlelight. It was an appalling yet very beautiful sight. Then the exorcist chopped out what looked like a kidney and swallowed it
whole. After that, he excised a much smaller morsel and passed
it to one of his fraternity, who nailed it up on the far wall of the
yard.

"What's that?"

"The gallbladder," said Kamal.

"Why?"

"It will protect the house."

The trumpets resounded, echoing through the salons like
harbingers of death. And the exorcists disappeared. I wondered
if they had already finished their work. The pimp slunk over and
slapped me on the back. I was going to ask if he was finished.
But before I could, they reappeared, one at a time.

They were dressed in robes the color of wheat, over which
they wore the traditional red cloaks of the Atlas, interwoven
with zigzag lines. Their heads were crowned with gold and
orange turbans, and their feet were bare. Each one carried an
instrument—goatskin tambourines called *bendir,* clay drums
known as *tbilat,* piercing woodwind pipes called *ghaytah,* and
garagab, outsized iron castanets. They filed back into the courtyard, where they paid homage to the dismembered goat. It was
impossible not to be affected by the noise. Just as sacrifice
appeals to something primitive inside us all, so did the noise of
their instruments. The music, if you could call it that, created a

deafening wall of sound. Kamal, the guardians, and I watched as the Aissawa set fire to a bunch of poplar leaves, blew out the flames, and toured the house with the smoke.

In each room, they performed the same ritual, spraying the corners with milk, salt, and blood. They danced back and forth, rustling the bouquet of smoking leaves as they chanted a solemn mantra.

The pimp collapsed into a wicker chair on the verandah and rolled a hashish cigarette. I went up to ask him what it all meant. He waved me away.

"Sometimes it is better not to speak," he said, taking a long, satisfying drag on the joint.

I went to check on Ariane. She had been distraught at being parted from her pet goat. In the bedroom, Timur was asleep in his cot, but there was no sign of Ariane. A wave of parental panic ripped through me. I ran out of the bedroom and down the long corridor.

Kamal was sitting with the guardians on the lawn.

"Have you seen Ariane?"

They shook their heads. I rushed up onto the verandah and into the main salon. She wasn't there. As I approached the courtyard where the goat was hanging, I could hear the echo of the exorcists in the distance. I glanced at the goat's carcass, still dripping with blood. The skin was lying on the ground below it, and beside that was the head. Next to the head was Ariane. She was crouching there in her pajamas.

"Baba," she said gently, "what happened to my goat?"

This time it was my eyes that welled with tears. Hers were dry. She was not so sad as confused. An animal she had played with, and considered a pet, had been taken away by strange men, killed, skinned, and decapitated. It hadn't happened on television, or in a market, but in the middle of our home.

"Baba, why is my goat's head on the ground?" she said. "I don't understand."

I picked her up and smoothed back her hair.

"I don't understand either," I said.

ALL THROUGH THE NIGHT, the exorcists roamed the Caliph's House. I cuddled up in bed, Ariane in my arms, the vibration of the drums trembling through our dreams. The guardians stayed awake all night. I found them at sunrise, sitting together on the stone steps that led up to the verandah.

"Is it over?"

Osman held up his hand. "Not yet."

I walked through the salon, then the library, and the bedrooms upstairs, but the exorcists were not there. The house was very quiet, like the silence after an earthquake. There had been noise and terror, but now there was peace. All the rooms were splattered with blood and stank of smoke. They smelled as if something had happened, something grotesque. I couldn't pinpoint the change, but there had been change all the same.

I wandered into the garden courtyard. There, in the room at the far end, I found the exorcists. They were sitting on the floor in a circle, with candles all around. Some of them were chanting. I couldn't understand why I hadn't heard them outside. The air was pungent with waxy smoke and the same asphyxiating stench of burnt poplar leaves. Kamal was sitting against the back wall. He had dark circles around his eyes.

"Is it over?" I asked.

"No."

"Are the Jinns gone?"

"Almost."

The oldest exorcist rummaged in the sack, pulled out a cockerel, and stood to his feet. The bird flapped once, then again. A sharp twist of the fingers and its neck was snapped. More flapping, and the head was pulled clean off. The old Aissawa let the blood drip onto the floor as the chanting rose to a crescendo. The candles flickered, as if a breeze had swept through. The blood dripped, and the drumming began. It was cold, haunting, like the sound of a funeral march. But there was something compelling about it. It drew you in. You couldn't help yourself.

One of the younger men stood up and fell to the floor. His body was gyrating, shaking, his eyes rolled upward. The drumbeat grew stronger and faster like a whirlwind gathering speed. Another of the Aissawa got up and fell down, then a third. The drumbeat grew faster still, faster, and faster. I felt myself pulled in. All the air in the room seemed to be sucked away. The candles went out.

The female Aissawa stood up and began tearing at her hair. Her eyes were closed tight, her costume sprayed with wax and blood. The drums didn't cease for a moment. Their sound formed a backdrop, a stage, an ambience. The woman pushed up the loose sleeves of her jelaba. She sank her front teeth into her arm.

The drums continued.

They died away only when the sun had risen above the date palms at the end of the garden. The exorcists lay down in the salon and fell asleep again. They were exhausted. There was silence, a sense that a great upheaval had taken place but had now ended. It was like the last scene of a Hollywood movie, in which the stars hug each other, their faces blackened with dirt, their clothes shredded. But unlike the movie ending, there were no credits to roll.

The guardians strolled up and fell into line. They saluted, then held out their hands for me to shake.

"Qandisha has gone," said Hamza.

"Gone far away," Osman chipped in.

"Is Dar Khalifa our house?" I said.

"Yes," said the Bear, very softly. "It now belongs to you."

As dusk descended I thanked the pimp and his Aissawa exorcists. They piled onto the cement truck and drove slowly out through the shantytown, back to the hills. When they were gone, I closed the front door and breathed in deep. It was all over and, at the same time, it had just begun.

TWENTY-ONE

Never give advice in a crowd.

COUNTESS DE LONGVIC TELEPHONED THE next day. She had heard that the demons had been cast out from the Caliph's House, she said.

"Maybe they were never here at all," I replied.

The countess emitted a shrill gasp. "Don't say that," she warned, "or they'll be back in a flash."

"Do you believe in the Jinns?"

"*Mais oui,* but of course," she said.

I was thinking of how to reply. The countess cut in:

"Live here in Morocco long enough and they creep into your blood," she said. "It may sound strange to your ears, but it's they who decide."

"Decide what?"

"They decide whether to allow you to believe in them," she said.

THE MONTH OF MAY reintroduced the fierce heat that October had stolen from us. The days were long and scorching, filled with the sound of bees in the hibiscus flowers and of feral dogs fighting in the bidonville. Rachana and the children were happier than I could have dreamed. Unlike me, they seemed to have forgotten about the days of the exorcism. The guardians were content, too. They went about their duties of endless raking, patrolling, and skimming drowned butterflies from the pool. An entire month slipped by and I never heard a word about the Jinns.

The main work began to come to an end. The floors were complete, as was the tadelakt on the walls, and the magnificent mosaic fountain. The woodwork was stripped and painted, the glass in the windows replaced, and all the work that you never think of was done—the roofs were sealed and new hot water boilers installed, the plaster moldings touched up, wrought-iron railings fitted, and trellises laid. A team of twelve men hauled the great Indian doorway into place. Then the Rajasthani swing was suspended on the verandah before it, beneath a trellis crowned in passion vines.

At long last we could concentrate on the finishing details. There can be no country on Earth better suited to buying decorations than Morocco. Every corner of the kingdom has its own unique styles, each one perfected through centuries of craftsmanship. In the medina of Fès, we bought brass candlesticks, appliqué lamps, and miles of brightly colored sabra silk, woven from the fiber of the agaz cactus. In Essaouira, we found a coffee table veneered with the scented thuya wood, inlaid with mother-of-pearl. And from a merchant in the High Atlas

Mountains, we bought a dozen Berber tribal rugs, fabulous concoctions of color and design.

But it was in Marrakech that we gave in to all temptation. The medina there is an emporium of art and craft like none other; the narrow streets are packed through the long dusty days with a frenzied tangle of life. There are donkey carts piled high with pots, armies of vendors laden with silver lamps, and an ocean of small boys touting rough wooden toys. There are blind men soliciting alms, sunburned tourists with cameras in hand, pickpockets and undercover cops, bicycles and scooters, fortune-tellers and snake charmers, madmen and hustlers. We pushed forward into the fray, wondering how we would ever escape.

Every inch of space was taken up with goods for sale—trays of fresh nougat glimmering in the afternoon light, heaps of pistachios and dried apricots, roasted almonds and shelled pecans. There was saffron, too, mountains of it, and pickled lemons, figs, and slabs of beef carved from the bone.

The moment before we were all sucked down and suffocated, a finger beckoned us into a shop. Inside, it was cool, calm, and filled with an alluring blend of wares. The owner slammed the door shut behind us, bolted it, and served mint tea.

"Welcome to my oasis," he said.

Half joking, I asked if we were being kept prisoner. The shopkeeper, a skeleton of a man, passed me a glass of tea.

"I am not keeping you in," he said, "I am keeping them out."

We drank our tea and explored the treasures stacked on open shelves. There were terracotta pots adorned with zigzag motifs, camel headdresses from the Sahara, and mats made from the fibers of esperto grass. There were kelim rugs, too, woven in vibrant reds, yellows, and greens; silver brooches, calligraphic pendants, and ancient Berber marriage contracts inscribed on cylinders of wood. On the back wall was a bronze fountainhead in the form of a gazelle and, beside it, a clutch of brass divination bowls etched with cryptograms.

My eye was caught by a fabulous cedar door propped up in the window. It was adorned with the Star of David and with lines of Hebrew script. The shopkeeper noticed me inspecting it.

"You are surprised, are you not? Surprised at seeing a Jewish door."

I said that I was. The merchant straightened his back.

"There may be tension between Arabs and Jews," he said, "but without the Jews, Morocco would be a far poorer place."

I said I had heard that the king retained more than one key Jewish adviser, and that I had read about the country's Jewish heritage.

"My ancestors were Jews," the lean merchant said. "We came here from Andalucía seven centuries ago and we are proud of our traditions. For generations we practiced our Jewish faith and lived alongside the Muslim Arabs. But then, two hundred years ago, the Sultan of Morocco charged terrible taxes on Jewish families. There was no choice but to convert to Islam."

Before leaving the sanctuary of the shop, we bought a divination bowl, a kelim, and a small silver box. The merchant eased the bolt back in the lock, wished us well, and slipped me his business card. I glanced at his name. It was Abdul-Rafiq Cohen.

BACK AT CASABLANCA, A black-and-white postcard was waiting for me. The picture showed a group of camels and Saharan women huddled in a stark caravanserai. It was from Pamela, the well-read American woman who was living at my grandfather's villa on Tangier's rue de la Plage. She wrote: *I am traveling in the south of Morocco. The meals have been wonderful, all except for one, at Sidi Ifni. We were served a very suspect steak. God knows what kind of meat it was. It was inedible. It was even rejected by my traveling cat.*

AT THE END OF May, I flew to London for three days, for the launch of a film I had made. It was one of those dull trips filled with forced conversation and solitude. Every moment I was there, I missed the children, Rachana, and the Caliph's House. I met an old school pal who was still trapped in the cycle of zombie commuting and pseudo-friends. We laughed about English life, the terrible blight of flat-packed furniture and of information overload. He seemed impressed that I had moved to Casablanca. We had always conspired to break free together, but something had held him back. As I left I joked that he would put up with the chicken tikka sandwiches and the dreary weather until the end. His expression faltered.

"It's all I know," he said.

An hour after I arrived back at Dar Khalifa, there was a knock at the door. I told Rachana it would no doubt be Hicham in search of some postage stamps. But it wasn't him. It was his wife. The whites of her eyes were the color of beets, as if she had been weeping. I asked her to come inside, but she said she could not stay.

"My husband died two days ago," she said. "His heart stopped."

I expressed my great sadness.

"He said if something happened, I should give you this."

The stamp collector's wife, Khadija, held up a box. I took it into my study, switched on the desk lamp, and opened it. Inside was a stack of stamp albums. Hicham had taught me a great deal about Morocco, and about life. I sat down, depressed by the loss of a wise friend. At the same time, I was happy, happy that our paths had crossed at all, and that we had shared so many fine conversations, paid for in postage stamps.

THIRTY DAYS AFTER THE exorcism, Osman said he had
something to show me. He led me down to the stables, where
he and the other guardians tended to lurk, drinking mint tea. I
asked him what it was. He told me to wait and to follow him.
There are four stables at Dar Khalifa, arranged in an L shape.
One was the guardians' room; the others were full of old ladders and rope, gardening tools, barbed wire, and broken chairs.

Osman pushed the door of the stable on the left. There was
so much clutter inside that it hardly opened at all. Again,
Osman pushed.

"Can you see that?" he said.

"What?"

"The doorway? The old doorway," he said.

I peered in. All I could see was a tangle of ladders and
chairs, fence posts and pots. I couldn't see a doorway, I told
him. The other guardians appeared, and after an hour of struggling, they managed to haul the doorway from the stable. They
laid it out on the lawn.

It was crafted from cedar and was the shape of a keyhole,
the front side painted with geometric designs.

"It's wonderful and so old," I said. "Why didn't you tell me
about it before?"

"We didn't know it was there," said the Bear.

"Don't you know what's in the stables?"

"Of course," Hamza exclaimed, "but it wasn't there before."

"It was hidden," said Osman, under his breath.

"Hidden by the Jinns," said the Bear.

The doorway was restored by Rachid the bodyguard and
was put as the entrance to our bedroom. I was thrilled. It was
like getting something for nothing, like finding money on the
street. Hamza took every opportunity to describe the advantage of living in a house newly recovered from the Jinns.

"Things become visible," he said, "things that were hidden
for years."

"What sort of things?"

"Treasure," he said. "All old houses like Dar Khalifa have treasure."

I said I didn't believe him.

"The old door proves it," he replied. "It was not there and then it was there."

"Do you really think a treasure is going to materialize?"

"Of course it will," Hamza explained. "You can sit back and wait."

A FEW DAYS LATER, I took a stroll down to the ocean before breakfast. It was a clear day. The beach was deserted, except for a man riding his Arab stallion through the waves as they broke on the shore. I took off my shoes and walked into the water, staring out at the horizon. I remember thinking it odd that my bare feet were on the same latitude as Atlanta.

On the way back, I walked very slowly through the bidonville, taking in the usual morning bustle. There was a man calling out for knives to sharpen, a vegetable seller arranging his wares, and a woman winnowing her family's grain. Children were hurrying to the school at the whitewashed mosque, where the stern mistress awaited them with her flexed orange hose. I was going to poke my head in the door and greet the teacher, when the imam came up. I expected him to ask for money.

"Thank you for your generous donations," he said.

I didn't know what he meant. I had given nothing except for the school supplies.

"The things for the school?" I said.

"No, no," the old imam replied, "thank you for all the money you have given."

"Money?"

"Yes, Hamza has brought us the donations," he said. "We have used it to repair the roof and to install electricity."

I didn't know what to say. I hadn't given Hamza any money to give to the mosque.

"It wasn't from me," I said awkwardly.

"You are as modest as Hamza said you are," the imam mumbled. "He told me the money was from you, but that you would deny it if I ever mentioned it."

The imam ducked his head and kissed my hand. I strode back into Dar Khalifa, washed over in shame. I later realized that every Friday after they had been paid, Hamza, Osman, and the Bear would visit the mosque and hand the imam a third of their wages in a donation on my behalf.

I WAS OVERCOME WITH guilt at benefiting from the death of Hicham Harass. His widow was left with almost nothing, while I had inherited a lifetime of valuable stamp albums. She was too proud to take handouts, and whenever I called on her, she insisted that God was taking care of her. Each time I visited the shack behind the mosque, another precious possession was gone—the carriage clock, then the radio, after that the prized Qur'an. Rachana came up with the solution—to take the stamp albums to Europe and sell them to a collector there. I sent them with a friend who was going to London. He brokered a deal and wired back a considerable sum of money in return. As soon as it arrived, I hurried over to give it to Hicham's widow. I passed her the envelope of banknotes and explained that the albums were a kind of insurance policy, the kind that could be cashed in. She straightened her headscarf, wiped a tear from her eye, and said:

"Up in heaven there is an old man cursing you for what you have done. But down here on Earth there is an old woman who is very thankful."

AS OUR FIRST YEAR in Morocco drew to a close, I found myself thinking a great deal about the move. The learning curve had been severe. I concluded that a life not filled with severe learning curves was no life at all.

Live in a new country and you find yourself making compromises. Make them, and you are rewarded many times over. Morocco has an antique culture, one that's still intact, with the family at the core. For me, the greatest thing about living here has been that Ariane and Timur can play against an inspiring backdrop, teeming with a full spectrum of life. As a parent, I have escaped the sense of guilt that drowns all parents in Britain, where the Victorian conviction persists that children should be seen and not heard. I encourage Ariane and Timur to be loud, to shout, to dance in the streets, to be themselves.

Renovating Dar Khalifa has been a rich, vivid expedition. At times I have shouted, ranted, or fallen on the ground in defeat. But the secret was to get up and carry on, however harsh the situation. I have gained so much from escaping England, but most of all I feel proud to be myself again.

A FEW DAYS AFTER the death of Hicham Harass, the guardians crept into my study while I was writing at the Spanish table. I had stressed again and again that when I was sitting there, no one was to disturb me. The only exceptions were if the children were in trouble or if the house was on fire. From the guardians' faces, I could see there was no emergency. I looked up and waited for their excuse.

"We need to speak to you, Monsieur Tahir," said Hamza, pushing ahead of the others.

"Is it important?" I asked.

The three men nodded. "Yes," they said together. "Yes, it is important."

I put down my fountain pen. "What is it?"

"The Jinns have gone," said Osman.

"It's good, isn't it?" I said. "Now we can live in peace."

The guardians edged closer.

"We have better news for you," said Hamza.

"What could be better than having a house without Jinns?"

The Bear stepped forward. He was holding a tatty dossier.

"The Jinns were hiding this," Osman added.

"What is it?"

"The treasure," he said.

Hamza took the dossier from the Bear and placed it on the table. I untied the ribbon and pulled the folder open. Inside there were a number of browned pages and a scale plan of our land.

I asked what it meant.

Osman pointed to the plan. "You own the gangster's house," he said.

HICHAM HARASS WAS BURIED on a hillside shaded by poplar trees on the southern edge of Casablanca. His grave was marked by a stick in a mound of freshly dug earth. All around there were other graves, a great rolling quilt of them, white stones glinting in the evening light. I would go there and sit at Hicham's mound and watch the shadow thrown by his stick inch to the east. There was a silence in the cemetery, the kind I had rarely encountered in Casablanca, the silence of peace.

The guardians begged me not to visit the old man's grave. They said there was no place in Morocco more perilous to be than a cemetery, especially at dusk.

"When the sun goes down," said the Bear, "the Jinns rise up from the graves and search for fresh-faced men."

ON THE FIRST DAY of July, Kamal arrived from the port with the container full of my books. By some amazing sleight of hand, he had humored the censorship police and had side-stepped the charges. As ever, I had no idea what lies he had told, if he had told any at all.

That night Rachana and I moved upstairs into our new bedroom, and the children into theirs across the hall. We had spent almost an entire year squashed up in a small room downstairs. Living in the main house was like reaching adulthood—a little daunting, yet so full of possibility. Words couldn't describe the joy of lying in bed, knowing that the building work was over.

My head was heavy on the pillow that first night we spent upstairs. Rachana and I lay down on the bed and both burst into laughter. It seemed too good to be true, to be in our own bedroom. Rachana put her hands behind her head and stared up at the ceiling.

"We could sell this house and do it all again," she said.

I didn't answer at first. I was in shock. I thought of all the trouble we had had with the architect, the workmen, and the Jinns.

"Are you absolutely out of your mind?"

"It's been hard," she replied. "But we've lived."

It seemed as if a great burden had been lifted from my shoulders. Of course there would be problems ahead. We were adrift on an ocean of problems. But there was a feeling of genuine achievement, that by embracing the challenge we were stronger, and in some way more complete. Most satisfying of all was the sense that we had at last been accepted by Morocco, by our guardians, and by the Caliph's House.

GLOSSARY

Agaz: a cactus found in Morocco, the fiber of which is used to make sabra silk cloth.

Aissawa: a brotherhood of exorcists originally formed in the sixteenth century, hailing from Meknes, famed for their spiritual music.

Arabesque: the style of intricate patterns of interlaced lines used in Arab art.

Arabian Nights: a large collection of stories of unknown authorship originating in what is now Iraq and beyond. Famously translated by Sir Richard Burton in the nineteenth century; also known as *A Thousand and One Nights.* Used to refer to the style or atmosphere of the medieval Middle East.

Baba: literally "father," used as a term of endearment by children in place of "Daddy." Also used as a term of respect for an old man.

Baksheesh: money given as a bribe or as a reward.

Baraka: literally "blessing" or "blessed."

Barboush: popular sharp-toed goatskin slippers worn by men and women in Morocco, in yellow or other colors.

Bejmat: handmade terracotta tiles, glazed or unglazed, used for the floors of houses and verandahs.

Bendir: traditional goatskin tambourines of Morocco.

Berber: one of several original non-Arab tribes.

Bidonville: French word for shantytown.

Bismillah: Arabic, literally "in the name of God"; said by Muslims before starting or finishing many actions, such as eating, driving, and so on.

Bistiya: Moroccan dish made with sweet pastry, beneath which lie wafer-thin layers of pigeon (or chicken), almonds, and egg.

B'saf: Moroccan Arabic, literally "a lot" or "much."

Café noir: literally "black coffee" in French, referring to the extremely strong coffee served without milk in most Moroccan cafés.

Caftan: a loose-fitting garment for women, often embroidered.

Caliph: the successor of the Prophet Mohammed; used also to refer to a governor or man with considerable political power.

Couscous: a dish of steamed semolina, extremely popular in Morocco, usually served with stewed vegetables, meat, or both.

Dar: Moroccan Arabic word for house.

Dari: one of the languages of Afghanistan.

Darj: a shape of hand-cut zelij mosaic.

Datura: a plant of the potato family with long, trumpet-like flowers, brought from the New World by the Spanish conquistadores, used as a hallucinogen by European medieval witches and others.

Dirham: the currency of Morocco; there are about 8 dirhams to the U.S. dollar and 16 dirhams to the pound sterling.

Douane: French word for customs.

Eid: Eid al-Fitr, the "small" Eid, marks the end of Ramadan. Eid al-Kabeer arrives about a month later, and that larger one marks the sacrifice of Abraham, who killed a ram in place of his son Isaac.

Esperato: a rough natural grass woven into floor matting and so on.

Fantasia: a display of horsemanship popular in rural areas, in which participants charge and fire their antique weapons as they ride.

Fasi: someone from Fès, or the style of that city.

F'lous: Moroccan Arabic word for money.

Garagab: large iron castanets, played by Moroccan musicians.

Genie: see *Jinn*.

Ghaytah: piercing woodwind pipes popular in the Atlas Mountains and other regions of Morocco.

Hajj: the Islamic pilgrimage to Mecca; one of the life duties of all Muslims.

Hammam: literally "bath," but often used to refer to a Turkish-style steam bath.

Harem: a section of a traditional house, reserved for the womenfolk.

Hejab: the act of covering the hair with a scarf or veil used traditionally by Moroccan women.

Imam: the leader of prayers in a mosque, who also usually recites the call to prayer (see *Muezzin*).

Inshallah: Arabic, literally "If God wills it."

Jelaba: long, flowing hooded robe worn by both men and women in Morocco.

Jinn: a fraternity of spirits created by God from fire and mentioned in the Qur'an; Muslims believe they inhabit the world along with humans.

Jnun: Moroccan Arabic term for a Jinn.

Kasbah: a fortified castle or citadel, particularly one situated in rural desert areas.

Kelim: a brightly colored woven carpet.

Khalifa: Arabic word for Caliph.

Khobz: literally "bread," often referring to hard round loaves of home-baked bread.

Kif: hashish resin.

Kura: a shape of hand-cut zelij mosaic.

Magic square: a mathematical arrangement of numbers, in which the lines add up to the same total in whatever direction they are read.

Manqash: a heavy, sharp-edged hammer used for cutting zelij mosaics and for excising a pattern on glazed tiles.

Marrachi: someone from Marrakech, or the style of that city.

Medina: an older walled city, with narrow streets and tight mass of houses and markets.

Menzeh: a pavilion for relaxation, typically set in the gardens of a palace or large house.

Merguez: spiced mutton or lamb sausages.

Minaret: the tower attached to a mosque from which the prayer is called.

Moualem: literally "master," referring to a craftsman in a traditional Moroccan form of art.

Muezzin: the call to prayer or, more correctly, the person who calls the prayer.

Nafir: a long brass trumpet or horn, up to seven feet in length.

Qermud: the curved green or blue glazed titles used in roofing traditional Moroccan buildings.

Quandil: a shape of hand-cut zelij mosaic.

Qur'an: the holy book of Islam, revealed over a number of years to the Prophet Mohammed in Arabic.

Ramadan: the holiest month in Islam, in which Muslims are required to fast between dawn and dusk.

Riad: a traditional courtyard garden of Morocco; also used to describe a house with a central courtyard of this type.

Sabra: form of natural silk, woven from the fibers of the agaz cactus.

Salon Moroccain: a formal reception area common in Moroccan homes, reserved for the receiving of guests.

Sehura: a sorceress.

Sharif: literally "noble," a title reserved for a descendant of the Prophet, but also used in Morocco as a term of respect.

Souq: a market, often a particular specialty market within a medina.

Sufi: an adherent of an Islamic mystical fraternity.

Tadelakt: traditional Moroccan plasterwork, said to have originated in Marrakech, created with lime, marble dust, and egg white. Similar to Venetian plaster.

Tagine: popular Moroccan stew, named after the round conical pot in which it is cooked.

Taliya: a shape of hand-cut zelij mosaic.

Tarboosh: the proper term for a round velvet-covered or felt hat, commonly known in the West as a fez.

Tbilat: traditional Moroccan clay drums, often arranged in pairs, with a larger and smaller drum attached.

A Thousand and One Nights: see *Arabian Nights*.

Thuya: a scented gnarled wood from the region near Essaouira.

Zelij: traditional Moroccan crafts of geometrical mosaics, hand-cut from glazed tiles.

Zeliji: a person skilled in cutting zelij mosaics.